The Early Modern Englishwoman:
A Facsimile Library of Essential Works

Series II

Printed Writings 1641–1700: Part 4

Volume 5

Eleanor Davies, Writings 1641–1646

The Early Modern Englishwoman: A Facsimile Library of Essential Works

Series II

Printed Writings 1641–1700: Part 4

Volume 5

Eleanor Davies, Writings 1641–1646

Selected and Introduced by

Teresa Feroli

General Editors

Betty S. Travitsky and Anne Lake Prescott

Routledge
Taylor & Francis Group
LONDON AND NEW YORK

The image reproduced on the title page and on the cover is from the frontispiece portrait in *Poems. By the Most Deservedly Admired Mrs. Katherine Philips* (1667). Reproduced by permission of the Folger Shakespeare Library, Washington DC.

First published in paperback 2024

First published 2011 by Ashgate Publishing

Published 2016 by Routledge
4 Park Square, Milton Park, Abingdon, Oxon OX14 4RN

and by Routledge
605 Third Avenue, New York, NY 10158

Routledge is an imprint of the Taylor & Francis Group, an informa business

Publisher's Note
The publisher has gone to great lengths to ensure the quality of this reprint but points out that some imperfections in the original copies may be apparent.

British Library Cataloguing-in-Publication Data
Douglas, Eleanor, Lady, d. 1652.
Eleanor Davis, writings 1641–1646. — (The early modern Englishwoman. Series II, Printed writings, 1641–1700, part 4 ; v. 5)
1. Prophecies.
I. Title II. Series III. Feroli, Teresa.
828.4'09–dc22

Library of Congress Control Number: 2010938058

ISBN: 978-0-7546-6218-1 (hbk)
ISBN: 978-1-03-291878-5 (pbk)
ISBN: 978-1-315-25685-6 (ebk)

DOI: 10.4324/9781315256856

CONTENTS

PREFACE
BY THE GENERAL EDITORS

Until very recently, scholars of the early modern period have assumed that there were no Judith Shakespeares in early modern England. Much of the energy of the current generation of scholars has been devoted to constructing a history of early modern England that takes into account what women actually wrote, what women actually read, and what women actually did. In so doing, contemporary scholars have revised the traditional representation of early modern women as constructed both in their own time and in ours. The study of early modern women has thus become one of the most important – indeed perhaps the most important – means for the rewriting of early modern history.

The Early Modern Englishwoman: A Facsimile Library of Essential Works is one of the developments of this energetic reappraisal of the period. As the names on our advisory board and our list of editors testify, it has been the beneficiary of scholarship in the field, and we hope it will also be an essential part of that scholarship's continuing momentum.

The Early Modern Englishwoman is designed to make available a comprehensive and focused collection of writings in English from 1500 to 1750, both by women and for and about them. The three series of *Printed Writings* (*1500–1640*, *1641–1700*, and *1701–1750*) provide a comprehensive if not entirely complete collection of the separately published writings by women. In reprinting these writings we intend to remedy one of the major obstacles to the advancement of feminist criticism of the early modern period, namely the limited availability of the very texts upon which the field is based. The volumes in the facsimile library reproduce carefully chosen copies of these texts, incorporating significant variants (usually in the appendices). Each text is preceded by a short introduction providing an overview of the life and work of a writer along with a survey of important scholarship. These works, we strongly believe, deserve a large readership – of historians, literary critics, feminist critics, and non-specialist readers.

The Early Modern Englishwoman also includes separate facsimile series of *Essential Works for the Study of Early Modern Women* and of *Manuscript Writings*. These facsimile series are complemented by *The Early Modern Englishwoman 1500–1750: Contemporary Editions*. Also under our general editorship, this series includes both old-spelling and modernized editions of works by and about women and gender in early modern England.

New York City
2011

INTRODUCTORY NOTE

[A complement to Teresa Feroli's facsimile edition of Eleanor Davies' pre-1640 texts (Ashgate, 2000), this pair of volumes contains 60 texts by Lady Eleanor, selected from the corpus of 66 printed between 1641 and 1652 because they are highly representative and in reproducible condition. Because many of these texts are heavily annotated, Dr Feroli has provided copious transcriptions of the annotations, as well as helpful transcriptions of hard-to-read and occasionally crossed-out passages, to assist her readers. This high number of texts has led us to three departures from our usual practice, each made to assist readers in using the volumes. First, we have included modern page numbers at the foot of each page. Second, we have numbered the texts in the Table of Contents, and each reference in this Introductory Note to a text included in the volume is followed ***[in square brackets and in bold font]*** *by the number of that text as designated in the Table of Contents. Extracts are identified by the page number of the original. Finally, Wing numbers, where they exist, have been supplied in the Textual Notes, rather than as a block at the head of the References. Following Lady Eleanor's biographer Esther Cope, Dr. Feroli refers to Eleanor Davies as 'Lady Eleanor' throughout. The decision to use 'Davies' as Lady Eleanor's surname follows recent scholarship. Readers should note, however, that Wing lists her surname as 'Douglas', as do many libraries, archives and earlier scholarly articles. – The General Editors]*

Eleanor Davies: (1590–1652)

A daughter of George Touchet, Baron Audeley, and his wife Lucy, Lady Eleanor Davies spent her early years in an aristocratic family with dwindling economic resources. In 1609 her father arranged her marriage to the poet and prominent barrister Sir John Davies in an exchange of aristocratic ties for money. She bore three children, only one of whom, Lucy, survived into adulthood. John Davies died in 1626, and in 1627 Lady Eleanor married the professional soldier Sir Archibald Douglas. Douglas died in 1644.

In 1625, Lady Eleanor's life took a dramatic turn when, by her account in 1641, a 'Heavenly voice' told her: 'There is Ninteene yeares and a halfe to the day of Judgement, and you as the meek Virgin' (**[1]** p. 14). That same year, 1625, she published her first treatise, *A Warning to the Dragon*, initiating her controversial career as a writer of prophetic tracts. Between 1641 and 1652 she produced some 66 of them out of a corpus of 69 treatises. As a group, these tracts focus on a complex of personal and political events that Lady Eleanor thought indicated the fast approach of the 'last days' foretold by the biblical prophets Daniel and John of Patmos. Three key personal events informed her writings during this period: her tribulations as a prophet, her struggles to regain inherited properties after being widowed, and her outrage over the execution in 1631 of her brother Mervin, Earl of Castlehaven, on charges of rape and sodomy. Believing that the course of the English Civil Wars showed that the world was nearing its last days, she emphasized three political developments in particular: the rise of Parliament and the New Model Army, the execution of the powerful William Laud, Archbishop of Canterbury (one of her brother's judges), and the defeat and execution of Charles I.

A striking feature of Lady Eleanor's writing is her use of the Bible to gauge the cosmic significance of events, great and small, taking place in her nation and in her personal life. While to modern readers her claims for the apocalyptic significance of her own sufferings may seem outlandish, her approach to Scripture and to the apocalyptic books in particular is in harmony with that of many religious radicals in her age who used typological interpretations of Scripture to verify their calculations concerning the imminent arrival of the last days. Such claims on Lady Eleanor's part, in my opinion, attest not to a narcissistic desire for self-promotion but to her fervent belief that she was called by God directly to warn the people of her nation of the impending Day of Judgement.

The years between 1625 and 1641 were difficult for Lady Eleanor. Neither her two husbands nor the king received her prophecies well. Soon after she first published in 1625, John Davies burned her prophetic writings. Lady Eleanor told him 'within three years to expect the mortal blow' (**[20]** p.15), and he died shortly afterwards, in 1626. Her second husband, Douglas, likewise burned her books, and Lady Eleanor cryptically predicted that 'worse then death should befal' (**[20]** p. 23) him – he apparently lost his wits in 1631, and until he died in 1644 lived apart from his wife under the care of family members. In 1633, after Lady Eleanor travelled to Amsterdam to publish three treatises for English distribution, the Commission for Ecclesiastical Causes, at the prompting of Charles, sanctioned her. The Commission found her guilty 'of unlawful printing & publishing of books' (**[36]** p. 11), for which she spent two years in the Gatehouse prison. In late 1636 or early 1637, she was jailed again – this time in Bedlam – for literally occupying the bishop's throne at the Cathedral of Litchfield, declaring herself 'primate and metropolitan', and defacing the Cathedral's tapestries.

Writings 1641–46: The End of the Old Order and the Advent of New Jerusalem

In terms of Lady Eleanor's prophetic career, the years between 1641 and 1646 were productive and triumphant. She published with greater ease, thanks to the Long Parliament's suspension of censorship regulations in 1641, and spent no time in jail for her activities as a prophet, although she was imprisoned in July of 1646 for unpaid debts. She witnessed the execution in January of 1645 of a personal enemy, Archbishop Laud, asserting that the timing fit her prediction of the last days' approach, a prediction strengthened, in her view, by the New Model Army's defeat of Charles later that year.

The Lady Eleanor, Her Appeale To The High Covrt of Parliament **[1]** appeared at a turning point in England's political situation and marked a shift in the author's prophetic career. Lady Eleanor directed the *Appeale* to Parliament, rather than to members of the royal family, calling attention to its increased power. Her text also shows that she had codified her prophetic identity, for the first time claiming her prophetic mission as originating in a call from a 'Heavenly voice' (p. 14) telling her to expect the last days in the aforementioned nineteen and a half years. She would reproduce this vocation narrative in exactly this form in eleven later treatises.

In her next four treatises, Lady Eleanor meditated on Charles's waning fortunes, comparing him to Samson betrayed by a wily woman (in his case his French Catholic wife, Henrietta Maria) and to the doomed king Belshazzar in the Book of Daniel. Her *Samsons Fall* **[2]**, presented to Parliament and published in January of 1643, thus describes Charles as a new Samson. Appended to this is *To ... Parliament* **[2** and **3]** in which she offers to restore Charles to himself, in the sense of his true nature as one who is 'fearefull of the Lords coming' (**[3]** p. 3), and to the service of Parliament. Her *Samsons Legacie* **[3]**, prefaced by *To the Most Honorable*, expands on the comparison of Charles to Samson and offers more commentary on life in England during the first Civil War (1642–46); in particular she upbraids Laud, here likened to the Beast prophesied in Revelation, for destroying her tracts in 1633. *Amend, Amend; Gods Kingdome Is At Hand* **[4]** is a reissue of *Given to the Elector*, originally directed to Charles's nephew, the Elector Palatine, first printed in Amsterdam in 1633, and reprinted in 1648 and 1651 **[34, 57]**. The body of the text is a verse rendering of the story in Daniel 5 of the ill-fated king Belshazzar and of God's monitory handwriting on the wall, but Lady Eleanor opens the 1643 version with an anagram explicitly warning the king that: '*Belchazer*, Be-*Charles*' (p. A2).

Lady Eleanor's last tract of 1643, *The Star to the Wise* **[5]**, integrates the topical references of her earlier treatises, particularly those regarding Charles, into a more comprehensive vision of England as the direct addressee of Revelation and of herself as the prophet chosen to communicate this fact to her nation. She directs the text to Parliament and promises that peace, in the form of the second coming of Christ as portrayed in Revelation, is on the horizon. God conveys this message of hope and redemption, she says, just as he did at the time of Christ's birth: through a woman. She compares her imprisonment in Bethlehem Hospital or 'Bedlam' to Mary's journey to bear Christ in a Bethlehem 'Barn' (p. 11).

Lady Eleanor's tracts of 1644 continued to alert her readers to the imminent end of time, but now in a more considered and scholarly way. This is most evident in her Latin tract *Prophetia de die* (late 1644; not reproduced here because of the poor quality of the unique copy in Trinity College, Dublin). But it is also the case in *The Restitvtion Of Reprobates* **[6]**, in which she cites the early Christian but heterodox theologian Origen to buttress her belief in an infinitely merciful God who does not damn sinners forever. She supports her case with a catalogue of related scriptural passages, and closes with the hope that her 'WORDES' (p. 30) will bring comfort to those in Hell. *Apocalypsis Jesu Christi* **[7]** addresses the religious leaders gathered at Westminster to work out a new religious settlement. This tract predicts that Laud, who had been imprisoned since 1640 in the Tower of London, will ultimately be 'cast out of heaven' (p. 32) and reminds the Westminster Assembly that the author has delivered many accurate prognostications. *Her Blessing To Her Beloved Daughter* **[8]** is a meditation on motherhood in the life of her nation that pits Charles's French Queen, Henrietta Maria, the 'occasion of this LANDS *deep* CONSVMPTION' (p. 17), against Lady Eleanor, a type of the woman clothed with the sun in Revelation 12 who reveals 'the truth of the Resurrection time' (p. 35). She tells the tract's addressee, her daughter Lucy, that because she has been her 'mothers Copartner' and 'sole support', she can look forward to '*endlesse Joy, life eternall*' (p. 38).

In January of 1645, Archbishop Laud was executed on charges of treason (at the prompting of the Scots who sought to advance a Presbyterian model of church government). Lady Eleanor's response was both personal and political: she saw Laud's death as God's justice for his role in her brother's 1631 execution and in her own 1633 trial and imprisonment. More broadly, she saw Laud's death as coinciding with the Day of Judgement that she had predicted after her call in 1625. *The Word Of God, To The Citie of London* **[9]** focuses primarily on the death of her brother, linking it to those of Laud in 1645 and of Thomas Wentworth, Earl of Strafford – one of Charles's principal advisers – in 1641, so as to assert that time's end approaches. Her broadside *As not unknowne* **[10]** again pronounces on Laud's death, claiming that it is the fruition of her prophecy, and that he is justly punished for having suppressed her writings in 1633. To drive this point home, she attaches some legal documents from the proceedings against her. In *The Brides Preparation* **[11]** Lady Eleanor uses some imagery from Revelation that she correlates with current events. She continues in *Great Brittains Visitation* **[12]** to emphasize the imminence of the last days: Revelation 7 indicates that when 1644 is complete, 'disolution comes quickly' (p. 26). Laud's political stances, she continues, had engendered the chaos that made this imminent. She takes a similarly assertive stand on this matter in *For Whitsontyds Last Feast* **[13]**. As her title suggests, she believes that the Whitsunday (Pentecost) of 1645 is the last, and that this is fitting because 'the second *Comming* of the *holy Ghost*' (p. 5) will arrive, as Peter (by way of Joel) proclaims at the first Pentecost, just before the Last Judgement (Acts 2: 17–21, 33; Joel 2: 28–32). *The* [*Second*] *Co*[*ming*] **[14]** again projects the end of 1645 as the time of the Last Judgement, but her emphasis shifts to a denunciation of those 'witts or Scoffers' who make 'sport' of 'those tydings of the great Day' (p. 17).

A tonal shift from urgent insistence on the approaching end of time to more reflective theological statements is apparent with the publication of *Of Errors Ioyned with Gods Word* **[15]**. This tract, addressed to Parliament, attempts to correct some errors Lady Eleanor has detected in King James's interpretation of Revelation. (Here, she may be referring to his *A Paraphrase Upon the Revelation of the Apostle S. John* that appears in his *Workes* of 1616.) In November of 1645, Lady Eleanor reissued her *Prayer* **[16]** of 1644. There is no extant copy of the original 1644 tract, published after a significant Royalist military victory. This event appears to have prompted Lady Eleanor to drop her usual mode of mapping the predictions in Daniel and Revelation onto England's political situation and instead to implore God's 'pardon and forgiveness' (p. 4) for her unworthy people. She also published in 1645 a translation of her 1644 *Prophetia de die*, *Prophesie of the Last Day* **[17]**. In this text, of which only a fragment remains, she proclaims that the last days are coming soon, as can be seen in such signs as the 'raging & roaring' of Satan evident in '*the madnesse of the World*' (p. 8). (She also published *I am the first and the last* in 1645; extant copies are in poor condition and so are not included here.)

Lady Eleanor's first published tract of 1646, *For the blessed Feast Of Easter* **[18]**, celebrates the 1645 defeat of the Royalist army by the, in her view, blessed New Model Army. In a text published less than two months later, *The Day of Ivdgements Modell* **[19]**, she returns to the imminence of the Last Judgement. In a series of typological interpretations of Revelation 7 and 14, she is excited even further by the parallels to her own times. Her last three treatises of 1646 represent the full array of her self-reflexive, theological, and topical modes of discourse. *The Lady Eleanor Her Appeal* **[20]** (distinct from *Her Appeale* of 1641), directs its remarks to Thomas May, Secretary of the Parliament, and recounts her experiences as a prophet as well as her relationship with George Carr, a boy she encountered and housed just prior to her own calling, who possessed uncanny powers of prediction. Her *Je Le Tien* **[21]** is her second work on the general redemption of the damned at the Second Coming. In it she rehearses many of the arguments from *The Restitvtion of Reprobates* **[6]** but inserts a criticism of contemporary Anglicanism's relative neglect of the Book of Revelation. Lady Eleanor's final tract of 1646, *The Revelation Interpreted* **[22]**, portrays Buckingham, Laud and Charles as figures straight out of Revelation whose existence points to 'the Last day at hand' (p. 12). Earlier in her career, Lady Eleanor had gained notoriety for predicting the 1628 assassination of Charles's most trusted advisor, Buckingham, and in this tract she continues to denounce the now deceased former Admiral of the Navy as the beast that emerges from the sea.

Writings 1647–52: Political Upheaval and Personal Reflection

In July of 1646, Lady Eleanor was imprisoned for debts related to printers' fees, and she appears to have remained in the Gatehouse through the spring of 1647. Undeterred, she published several treatises in 1647. The first, her aptly titled *The Gatehouse Salutation* **[23]**, written in verse, promises that at the Second Coming there will be 'no more pain, prison, strife' (p. 6). She tacitly refers to her imprisonment again in her third treatise on Christ's salvation of the damned, *The Mystery of General Redemption* **[24]**, when she mentions the 'worlds general pardon' (p. 4) and when she denounces the 'illegal constructions' (p. 28) that have kept people from belief in God's infinite mercy. When she produced her *Ezekiel the Prophet* **[25]**, in April of 1647, she appears still to have been in prison, and in this text she meditates on a visionary experience she had in 1634 while in the Gatehouse. At that time, she insists, 'the Holy Ghost' (p. 4) visited her in her cell for an hour, leaving behind the scent of ambergris. It is not clear whether she was still in prison when she took up her meditation on Ezekiel for the second time in 1647, in *Ezekiel, Cap.2.* **[26]**. As Esther Cope observes, this tract emphasizes the prophet's encounter with a 'rebellious nation' (*Handmaid*, p. 133).

Whether Lady Eleanor was in prison in August of 1647 when she produced *The Excommunication out of Paradice* **[27]** is also unclear, but this is the first in a series of tracts addressing the situation of Charles, now held captive by the Army. Directing her treatise to Cromwell, she claims that Charles will soon be '*brought to judgement*' (p. 16). When she took up her pen again to write in early spring of 1648, she found herself once more in prison, this time at the King's Bench. Her *Reader, The heavy hour at hand* **[28]** proclaims, as the title suggests, the approaching end of the world. In *Wherefore to prove the thing* **[29]** (also issued in 1648 under the title *And without proving what we say*), Lady Eleanor meditates on her legal struggles to retain her rights to the manor at Pirton (bought for her by Davies as her jointure) and on the hapless king. When she regains her property, she says, Charles's plight may improve. Her *Writ of Restitution* **[30]** again laments her legal struggles, extending her discourse about property so as to assert the redemption of the damned. Those who fail to recognize Christ's sacrifice as 'Restitution' seek, in her view, to disinherit the Son of God.

With the start of the second Civil War in the spring of 1648, Lady Eleanor turned from her property to her role as a prophet. In *Apocalyps, Chap. 11* **[31]** she announces that the ill treatment of her books since 1633 is a sure sign of the Apocalypse. Once more, in *The Lady Eleanor Her Remonstrance* **[33]**, she notes England's failure to heed her warnings and warns of the approaching Last Judgement. *Of the generall Great Days Approach* **[32]** addresses Sir Thomas Fairfax, the commander-in-chief of the New Model Army, informing him that biblical evidence and contemporary events point to Great Britain as the addressee of John's message in Revelation. In the same month, September, Lady Eleanor reissued her 1633 tract *Given to the Elector Prince Charles of the Rhyne* **[34]**. The later edition includes a brief address to the reader, printed comments in the margin, and two closing stanzas dated September 1648. These last remind Charles that the tract's addressee, his nephew the German Prince Charles, has been imprisoned and so too, since 1645, has he.

Charles and his execution on 30 January 1649 are the focus of Lady Eleanor's first four treatises of that year. The first, *Her Appeal from the Court to the Camp* **[35]**, appears to have been written during Charles's trial. She directs it to Fairfax and advises him of both the legitimacy of her prophetic career and the illegitimacy of Charles's reign. *The Blasphemous Charge Against Her* **[36]** uses the occasion of Charles's trial to revisit her own trial of 1633. The text consists of a letter to the imprisoned king, urging him to seek her forgiveness, and a set of documents related to her trial. (The Folger Library's copy omits the prefatory letter to Charles and instead indicates that he has been executed.) Her next tract, *The Crying Charge* **[37]**, is a companion piece to *The Blasphemous Charge*. Directed to the court presiding over Charles's trial, it accuses the king of sanctioning her brother's execution and includes a copy of Castlehaven's declaration of fealty to the Church of England on the scaffold. In *The New Jerusalem At Hand* **[38]**, Lady Eleanor extends her preoccupation with questions of inheritance to the situation of Charles's children, disinherited by his death, and to the claim to the throne of Lady Eleanor's now deceased second husband Douglas who, she insists, was in fact King James's first son, a claim she deems further legitimated by his possession of the prophetic gifts that he demonstrated in a letter to the London clergyman, Dr James Sibbald; she reproduces a copy of this letter as evidence. (Douglas had made an apparently specious assertion that he was the son of James and the daughter of James's tutor, Sir Peter Young.)

By the second half of 1649, the execution of Charles appears to have lost its immediacy for Lady Eleanor, as she incorporates this event into a broader vision of an England nearing the end of time. In June, she reissued her *Prayer* of 1644 with *A Prayer or Letter for the Peoples Conversion* **[39]**. This latter tract reviews the events since the publication of her 1644 *Prayer* and argues that the English people have committed real 'Treason' by '*Shuting*' (p. 10) out God. With *Sions Lamentation* **[40]**, written to mourn the loss of her oldest grandson, Henry Hastings, Lady Eleanor returns to her career-long interest in explicating the cosmological significance of events in her personal life. She sees the death of this young man, only nineteen and about to marry, as a 'warning piece of those very perilous dayes stoln upon us' (p. 2). (An identical version of this tract held at the University of Illinois and lacking the title page is sometimes referred to as *Zach. 12.* because it begins with an epigraph from Zechariah 12:10.) In August, the Commonwealth printer Robert Ibbitson published yet another version of her 1633 *Given to the Elector* under the title *Strange and Wonderfull Prophecies* **[41]**. As Esther Cope observes, this tract testifies to the increased public interest in Lady Eleanor's predictions in the aftermath of Charles's execution. It contains a series of non-authorial printed glosses that link points in her prophecy to specific events associated with Charles's death. *Strange and Wonderfull* is unique in Lady Eleanor's canon for containing the editorial hand of a person other than herself. (In addition to Ibbitson, the only other printer known to have been involved with the production of her tracts is Thomas Paine.) Lady Eleanor subsidized the printing of all of her tracts; Cope surmises that as a result many are of poor quality.

The importance of prophecy itself is the subject of her tract on education, *For the Right Noble Sir Balthazar Gerbier* **[42]**. Gerbier had proposed to open an academy for the sons of noble families, and Lady Eleanor urges him to include the Bible in the curriculum so that his students, like Lady Eleanor herself, can promulgate the typological readings of Scripture that draw connections between contemporary events and those in the Bible which herald the arrival of the last days. In October 1649, in *For the Most Honorable States* **[43]**, she again published advice, this time to the Council of State, which had taken the reins of government. Reviewing episodes in Amos, Mark and Luke that describe the casting out of devils from those they had possessed, she comments on the need to cast out such devils as Laud and Charles from the nation. She continues to reflect on the reign of Charles in a new edition of a tract first published in 1644, *A Sign* **[44]**. (No copies of the 1644 version survive.) Here she compares King James with Hezekiah and Charles with Manasseh, faulting Charles for adopting idolatrous religious practices. She also proposes a new projected date for the end of time – 1655 – although she would not refer to this date in subsequent treatises. Historical reflection again takes centre stage in *The Everlasting Gospel* **[45]** of December 1649. Here, Lady Eleanor recounts her prophetic career, comparing, in one notable instance, her flight to Holland to publish her 1633 tracts to the Virgin Mary's flight to Egypt to escape Herod's massacre of newborn children. Embracing her literal role as mother, rather than her metaphorical one, she closed out 1649 by publishing her daughter Lucy's answer to a theological question about the Trinity, *The New Proclamation in Answer* **[46]**.

In her six treatises of 1650, Lady Eleanor continues in the more reflective vein she espoused in the second half of 1649, but with diminished emphasis on Charles. She meditates on some key concerns that characterized her career up to this point – prophecy as not limited to biblical times but continuing in her own age, the imminence of the last days, and her struggles to regain her inherited property – while introducing the claim that her authority as a prophet transcends that of Parliament. In addition, her criticism of England's politics now focuses on general trends – frequently, her times' 'backslidden' condition – rather than on specific events or individuals. In *The Bill of Excommunication* **[48]**, she attempts to re-establish the sanctity of religious life in England by proposing that the Sabbath move from Sunday – a day she now associates with desecrations such as sports – to Monday. As a prophet, she argues, she is more qualified than church or state officials to make this decision. She uses the death of Fairfax's father from a festered toe to assert in her *Arraignment* **[47]** that God's power is greater than that of the Army. In *The Appearance or Presence of the Son of Man* **[49]**, she adopts an air of resignation about her travails over her property – Heaven is, after all, her true jointure – and then remarks that, coincidentally, a fire broke out in London in 1650 just when she was cast out of her estate at Englesfield.

She found herself in prison in September of 1650, in her words, at Queen's Bench (which probably means Upper Bench) when she produced *Before the Lords Second Coming* **[50]**, a text that invokes the rhetoric of 'Freedoms and Liberties' (p. 5) and 'Tolleration or Liberty of Conscience' (p. 13) to underscore the failure of those in power to recognize theirs as an age of prophecy. Her *Elijah the Tishbite's Supplication* **[51]** of October calls upon God to make his presence known and insists that the number 50, as in 1650, points to a 'Blow' (p. 7). The significance of the number 50 reappears in *Her Jubilees Appeal* **[52]**, a tract noting that a bad end had come in 1650 to one John Stawell who, like James, had set aside his 'first wife' for a second. Lady Eleanor, of course, had maintained for some time that her deceased second husband Douglas was the son of James's 'first wife' and thus the true heir to the throne.

In the penultimate year of Lady Eleanor's career, 1651, she produced seven texts that embrace her standard autobiographical and theological concerns and that demonstrate an increased emphasis on historical reflection and on the superiority of heavenly to earthly authority. Throughout her career Lady Eleanor had attributed great significance to anagrams; like other radical visionaries of her age, she saw them, in Clement Hawes's words, as articulating a 'sense of the total immanence of God in language' (Hawes, p. 60). Toward this end, she frequently used her maiden name, Eleanor Audeley, to create the anagram: 'Reveale O Daniel' as testimony to the legitimacy of her prophetic vocation. In *Hells Destruction* **[53]**, her meditation on the circumstances of her 1646 imprisonment in Woodstreet Compter on charges of failing to pay her printer Thomas Paine, she illustrates another perspective on the supreme significance of language. She finds fault with the arrest warrant that identified her as '*Eleanor* Lady *Davers*' (p. 6) and turns to the Bible to demonstrate the importance of accurate naming. Another earlier imprisonment, this time that of 1633, played a role in her next treatise, *Of Times and Seasons* **[54]**, helping to establish her main point: heavenly power surpasses earthly. In sending her to prison in the Gatehouse, Laud did not exercise control but merely enacted the prophecy in Revelation 12 regarding the Serpent and the Woman clothed with the sun (of whom Lady Eleanor is a type).

The Woman's triumph over the Serpent is the theme of *The Serpents Excommunication* **[55]**. The title page shows what is apparently a strangely shaped Ash branch, and the tract, written in verse, refers repeatedly to imagery associated with trees including, notably, Eden's Tree of Life. Picking up on the arboreal theme, one 'M: Tuke', whose praise of Lady Eleanor is appended to the tract, describes her prophecies as a '*Rod*' (p. 7). [Tuke identifies himself as her kinsman, and stylistic markers suggest that he was the minister Edward Tuke who wrote *Jehovah Jireh Merito Audiens, praeco Evangelicus, An Angell from Heaven, OR An Ambassadour for Christ* (1642) and *The Souls Turnkey, OR, A Spiritual File For Any Prisoner lockt up in the Dungeon and Chains of Sinne and Satan* (1656). Tuke may well have been the only male to commend Lady Eleanor's prophetic writings in print.] At the end of October, Lady Eleanor returned to the topical concerns characteristic of her tracts of the 1640s when in her *Benediction* **[56]** she praises Oliver Cromwell for his defeat of Charles II and the Scots at the Battle of Worcester in September of 1651. By substituting an 'h' for the 'c' in his surname, she transforms O CROMWELL into the anagram: HOWL ROME. In 1651 she also reissued new editions of earlier tracts; her *Given to the Elector* **[34]** and her *Blasphemous Charge* **[36]**. She reissued these bound together as *Given to the Elector* appended by T*he Dragons Blasphemous Charge against Her* **[57]**. The 1651 version of *Given to the Elector* contains new marginal comments, including a reference to another female prophet of the day, Grace Carey, and closes with a synopsis of events between 1633, when Lady Eleanor issued the first version of her text, and the 1649 execution of the King. Likewise, the 1651 *Dragons Blasphemous Charge* presents a set of printed comments in the margins, some of which duplicate Lady Eleanor's handwritten comments in the margins of the Folger Library's copy of her 1649 *Blasphemous Charge*.

In December of 1651, Lady Eleanor found herself in jail yet again, this time in the Fleet and for reasons she does not specify in her writings, and it was there that she produced what she regarded as her magnum opus, *The Restitution of Prophecy* **[58]**. Its interest derives not from its chief purpose – to urge watchfulness in the face of Christ's imminent return – but rather from its encyclopaedic compendium of cosmic and mundane as well as public and private concerns, including Henrietta-Maria's Catholicism; Queen Mary's bloody and Queen Elizabeth's glorious reigns; the trial and execution of her brother; Sir Kenelm Digby's poisoning of his wife Venetia Stanley; General Fairfax's response to one of Lady Eleanor's tracts; the crimes and executions of Laud and Charles I; and wool as a good defence against cold weather. She organizes this jumble of topics according to the three apocalyptic parables in Matthew 25, and so her text falls into three sections under the rubrics the ten wise and foolish virgins; the talents; and the separation of sheep from goats. Despite her efforts to structure her tract, *Restitution* remains a text teeming with images that Lady Eleanor does not fully explain. In many ways, her text embodies the chaos of an age that is, in Lady Eleanor's view, dissolute and thus ready for the Second Coming.

Lady Eleanor died in July of 1652 (of unknown causes), her two treatises published in the spring of that year having summarized the theological and autobiographical reflections that had characterized her prophetic career. Her *Tobits Book* **[59]**, published as a 'Lesson … for Lent' (title page), examines the apocryphal Book of Tobit to encourage readers to recognize that suffering is always followed by redemption. She effectively combines her belief in the redemption of the damned with her belief in the impending Second Coming so as to assert that although hers is a condemned generation, God will afford it the magnificence of the New Jerusalem. Attesting to Lady Eleanor's independence from both the established Church and the radical sects, hers is the only extended commentary on Tobit printed in those years, perhaps because more militant Protestants opposed its publication in the canonical Bible. Her final tract, *Bethlehem Signifying The House of Bread: or War* **[60]**, passionately defends Lady Eleanor's destruction of some of the tapestries at Litchfield Cathedral in 1636, one of the acts that had led to her imprisonment in Bedlam. The tract presents a rather melancholy reflection on her strenuous efforts to reveal the truth to a generation determined to bury it. Her daughter Lucy captured Lady Eleanor's extraordinary devotion to her prophetic vocation in the epitaph she prepared for her mother: 'In a woman's body a man's spirit, In most adverse circumstances a serene mind, In a wicked age unshaken piety and uprightness … Nay she was full of God to which fulness Neither a smiling world could have added, Nor from it a frowning world have taken away' (Quoted in *Handmaid*, p. 162).

References

Cope, Esther S. (1992), *Handmaid of the Holy Spirit: Dame Eleanor Davies, Never So Mad a Ladie*, Ann Arbor: University of Michigan Press

_____, ed. (1995), *Prophetic Writings of Lady Eleanor Davies*, New York: Oxford University Press

Feroli, Teresa (2006), *Political Speaking Justified: Women Prophets of the English Revolution*, Newark: University of Delaware Press

_____ (1994), 'The Sexual Politics of Mourning in the Prophecies of Eleanor Davies', *Criticism* 36: 359–82

_____ (1994), 'Sodomy and Female Authority: The Castlehaven Scandal and Lady Eleanor's *The Restitution of Prophecy* (1651)', *Women's Studies* 24: 31–49

Hawes, Clement (1997), *Mania and Literary Style: The Rhetoric of Enthusiasm from the Ranters to Christopher Smart*, Cambridge: Cambridge University Press

Hindle, C.J. (1936), 'A Bibliography of the Printed Pamphlets and Broadsides of Lady Eleanor Douglas the Seventeenth-Century Prophetess', *Edinburgh Bibliographical Society Transactions* 1.1: 65–98

Mack, Phyllis (1992), *Visionary Women: Ecstatic Prophecy in Seventeenth-Century England*, Berkeley: University of California Press

Matchinske, Megan (1993), 'Holy Hatred: Formations of the Gendered Subject in English Apocalyptic Writing, 1625–51', *English Literary History* 60: 349–77

_____ (1998), *Writing, Gender and State in Early Modern England: Identity Formation and the English Subject*, Cambridge: Cambridge University Press

Nelson, Beth (1985), 'Lady Elinor Davies: The Prophet as Publisher', *Women's Studies International Forum* 8: 403–9

Pickard, Richard (1996), 'Anagrams *etc.* The Interpretive Dilemmas of Lady Eleanor Douglas', *Renaissance and Reformation* 20 (3): 5–22

Porter, Roy (1994), 'The Prophetic Body: Lady Eleanor Davies and the meanings of madness', *Women's Writing* 1.1: 51–63

Smith, Nigel (1989), *Perfection Proclaimed: Language and Literature in English Radical Religion, 1640–1660*, Oxford: Clarendon Press

Spencer, Theodore (1938), 'The History of an Unfortunate Lady', *Harvard Studies and Notes in Philology and Literature* 20: 43–59

Watt, Diane (1997), 'Alpha and Omega: Eleanor Davies, Civil War Prophet', *Secretaries of God: Women Prophets in Late Medieval and Early Modern England*, Cambridge: D.S. Brewer, 118–54

TERESA FEROLI

1. *The Lady Eleanor, Her Appeale To The High Covrt of Parliament* (1641; Wing D1971) is reprinted, by permission of The British Library, from the clear copy found in the Thomason Tracts Collection (shelfmark E.172.[33]). The text block of the original measures 150 × 85 mm. Pages 14 and 15 are misnumbered.

Hard-to-read words:

8.18	invincible
8.19	workemanship
8.20	heavie

THE LADY ELEANOR, HER APPEALE TO THE HIGH COVRT OF PARLIAMENT.

PSAL. 123.

Behold, even as the eyes of Servants looke to the hand of their Masters, &c.

Printed in the yeere, 1641.

MAT. 8.4.

See thou tell no man, but goe thy way, shew, &c.

[illegible] to the hands of the [illegible], &c.

MAT. 8. 4.

TO THE HONORABLE ASSEMBLY OF THE High Court of *Parliament*.

MOst Honorable *Lords*, Noble *Knights*, and *Gentle-men*: This *JOSEPH*, and about to take his flight, hated hetherto, for the *Evill-report* brought of his *Brethren* : Also a Striplin grown up of 17. yeares; many collours or peeces whose Coat too, craves Your patience, to heare him a few words here.

A 2 The

TO THE

HONORABLE ASSEMBLY OF THE *High Court of Parliament.*

MOST Honorable *Lords*, Noble *Knights*, and *Gentlemen*: This *JOSEPH*, and about to take his flight, hated heretofore, for the *Euill-report* brought of his *Brethren*: Also a Stripling grown up of 17. yeares; many colours or peeces whole Coat too, craves Your patience, to heare him a few words here.

A2 The

The Preface.

THe roade way not to baulke, a preface omitted neither to the reader:*complement, although layd aside, soft lineing of that sort, these therwith prefaced not; rather preferred for all weather serviceable, a peece of plaine Leather. In Paradice our livery made up without hands, that of Skinnes: And for that precious Stone, without hands cut out; this peece or appollogie serving, set here without coullours or flowers, as for enammeling such, having none Artificiall.*

And heretofore a shew, having bin of these handled: Though the substance

A3 *unma-*

unmanifested or maine summe ; Times mistery unknown that treasure, till the Evening and fullnesse of time, as those Trenches filled even with Water before the fire fell, and purifying-pots, those first with Water filled : likewise the mistery of times and seasons so late revealed, made knowne for the fayling of the future. This good Wine kept till now.

And this thing now, who knowes not too well ; tedious to touch and fowle : but Blaines and Running-Soares nothing else all over, from the Elbow unto the feete : so this annoynting commended to all, for the blessed Readers *and* Hearers *both :*

Farwell.

From ***Kensington,***
the ***Angell signe.***
Whitsontyde, **1641.**

THE

LADY *ELEANOR*, her appeale to the high Court of *PARLIAMENT.*

DAN. 2. 34.

Thou sawest till that a Stone was cut out without hands, which smote the Image upon the feete: That of Iron, and Clay, and brake them in peeces, &c.

HEere these touching the *Iron-age*, remaines of time, a tast thereof; the Sonnes of the Prophets for their use, needlesse; as into the water to cast a Logg, wherein a sticke cut downe, but thrown sufficeth, or to give a touch, &c. As farre either from building upon others foundation, theirs &c. The lanthorne unusefull, when the Moone gi-

ving

ving light at full, not trespassing in that way here, nor borrowing either &c. And so farther of the latter dayes, these even being become drosse changed, even commanded these by him.

The Iudge all-sufficient, God able to change all, and them reforme: As doubtlesse the end, the finall day before of doome refined reformed to bee: to this end commended by us, and being high time to make some preparation; the tydings of a troublesome time cut of, unfruitfull, &c.

In short shewed, those sharp dayes shortned, the brittle feete parted those, a warning peece, as followeth.

In peeces broken, destroyed at the last, though nothing than mettle lasting more: That stone then unmoveable, invincible, the everlasting Law, as the workemanship of the Creators finger, moreover his heavie hand therewith: None other that great Image but spirituall aspiring *BABYLON* the fall of both, the other *Babell* likewise that taken, going before the end of the World; like this dreame the World gone in a moment. And before the worlds departing, not without a Cutting blow threatned

ned forthwith, as when that hasty Decree sent forth his Proclamation for his owne Nation; those wise men to be destroyed. That first borne Monarchy, *Babylons* great revolution, visible even in our Horizon, that end or time, closing with the time of the end, and from the hand also a faire signe after to appeare.

And here so much for parallizing of this expensive time, with that time of wantonnesse, in his reigne not found currant. In which want none found: of weakenesse, willfulnesse begetting, lifted up like the empty Scale, when the full descends: The Sunne like at lowest, making then the longest shaddow. Thus represented in this Mirror of former times, the present age the visage thereof, &c. Also, no spare body, unwildy growne and great, every way dangerous division therby unable to stand upon the feete: Not spared by Her, whose song the Worlds farwell these. Disburthened in this ensuing briefe. And plaine to bee in undoing this knot too, the *Iron-age* done, finished, although this peece difficult to digest, somewhat, &c.

Thou saweſt, till that a Stone was cut out without hands, &c.

The ſumme of theſe words ſignifie, the *Burthen of Gods word in the laſt dayes*, of a truth diſcloſing the time of the end. And of premiſſes the concluſion following : So unexpected Iudgements foretold from them: Alſo made evident the end of time. Here *Stone* ſharpening *Iron*,and ſtriking fire,High favours (for the moſt part) not without a heavie hand imparted : like *Jacob and his Brother*, the unlike twinnes begotten,or the Bleſſing in one hand, a Rod of correction in the other,and of which fire already kindled, loving Kindneſſe and Iudgement, going hand in hand together, the evill times but touched onely.

Thou saweſt, till that a Stone was cut out without hands, which ſmote the Image.

The Signe in the feete ; So in theſe laſt dayes : ſee here, and behold fulfilled, how that very ſaying :

Thou saweſt till that, &c.

By Thee beheld,as much to ſay, to read a certain Manuſcript, the weighty Stone become a Booke, not waiting long for Priviledge,

viledge, Imprinted, howſoever ſooneafter.

Certainly, in what yeare teſtifying the Worlds diſolution; Manifeſted with a heavie one: In the yeare One thouſand ſix hundred twentie five.

That great Plague yeare, out of Darkneſſe, when the Viſions tranſlated *of the Man, greatly beloved DANJELL.* For the great dayes breaking forth, cleared thoſe clowdy Characters: As delivered not without a token, ſince made good, the Brittle ſtanding of his owne Kingdomes, dedicated to the KING of Great BRITTAINE, Defendor of the Faith.

And of whoſe making to juſtifie here, by whom Publiſhed; though hitherto by authority with-ſtood.

ELEANOR AUDELEY, handmayden of the moſt high GOD of Heaven, this Booke brought forth by Her, fifth Daughter of GEORGE, Lord of CASTLEHAVEN, Lord AUDLEY, *and Tuitchet. NO inferior* PEERE *of this* Land, *in* Ireland *the fifth* EARLE.

Which name blotted a Houſe or Caſtle,

B 2 of

of late fallen by the ancient of dayes : His Kingdomes misteries displaying, nor chosen any obscure Motto. *God hath devided thy Kingdome, and numbred, &c.*

And farther, *of this Stone ; of the Builders cast aside* : the Summe of this Booke or Subject, besides the day of Iudgement revealed, *even that Some standing here, shall not tast of Death, till they see that day.* Herewith fell upon the *ROMAN-EMPIRES* disolation. The World, the great *MAN* : the disolution ushered with *GERMANIES* overthrw unexpecting : As moreover one last serving these Feete, great Brittaines foote too, and *Germanie* divided both betweene two opinions, Religions, and Buisnesses, where never since a Nation such distractions. For Plagues and greivances, such inward and outward ones, striving to outstrip one another.

Heere-withall foreshewed, the Furious Progresse of the *French* and *Spannish Forces*, with those Leagues not in force now. Notwithstanding corsse Marriages, &c. never before so.

The Kings of the North, by those *France* signified :

ſignified: Likewiſe the Kings of the South, the *AVSTRIAN Family*, theſe like whirlwinds toſſing the World up and downe from this ſide to that, &c AND for the ſhutting up of this Treatiſe, laſtly; with a Salutation concluded for the Son of *Peace*, if he had been there ſaluted, &c.

And at that time ſhall MICHAEL ſtand up, the great Prince, &c.

Angel-land, or ENGLANDS-ILAND, therefore the *Arch-angels Name*; here the halfe name, and abbreviated words, the age or time ſhortned betokning, &c. And for future things derided their Muſique. *Daniels*, Propheſie ſhut up prohibited, this time of trouble, their's come to paſſe notwithſtanding. So paſſing or poaſting to the time, at laſt of deliverance, the bleſſed reſurrection. Heere unfolded that treble or threefold Coard, not eaſily broken nor altred: Sworne with a high hand, that meeting a *Trienniall* &c.

For a time and times, and halfe, (or part) from the halfe of Seaven, *the hand pointing at the ſeaventeenth-hundred yeare*: That very time, about the halfe but fulfilled of the laſt

Centerie, as five hundred yeares filling up a Period. Lastly, given under the hand lifted up, *even five thousand yeares compleate* for the age of the World. The Worlds Ages too, parted into three prats, allotted two thousand yeares a peece, or thereabouts, The shortest lot drawne last, for a time and times, and halfe; shortned in the behalfe of *His Elect*.

From *Adam* unto *Abraham*, (*offering of his sonne*) the first Stage or time; so unto *Jerusalems* destruction the second. And the last or third, to the end of the World, the glorious *Resurrection*, &c. And yet farther, for the fortunate figure of five, (*Blessed is he that waites and comes*,) &c. Here two hundred and ninety, and three hundred and five and thirty, amounting to six hundred twentie-five, signifying thereby, the yeare wherein unsealed the Booke of the Prophet *Daniell*, 1625. and 17. yeares current, sithence a time and times and halfe Likewise, this Bookes Resurrection-time also appointed, waiting for the appeasiing neere of these stormes and troubles, a Peaceable time: *God was not in the Wind, not in the Earthquake,*

not

not in the Fire: after the fire, at last, the small still voyce. AND so finished this Booke, (Beyond expectation,) but so came to Passe in the yeare aforesaid, 1625. Shee awakened *by a voyce from* HEAEVN, in the FIRTH moneth, the 28. of *July*, early in the Morning, the Heavenly voice uttering these words.

"There is Ninteene yeares and a halfe to "the day of *Judgement*, and you as the meek Virgin. These sealed with Virgins state in the Resurrection, when they not giving in Marriage.

And to take heede of *Pride*, or to that effect spoken or added: But as for the Golden number that heeded well or heard; the cleare voice of a Trumpet inclining thereto; and like the chaffe of the *Summer*-threshing-flowre scattered. When the Cittie flying or fled from the Pestilence, that Sommers great Visitation, the fifth monethes Farwell, *July* 28. the Heavie hand, in that very weeke, as weekely the number certified, five thousand deseased of the Plague: Moreover; the ensuing Weeke, giving up the reckoning more full, the number

ber of the dead, amounting to five thousand five hundred and odd, &c. there stoppt or stay'd immediately, as much to say; but a spanne the Worlds age, graven with that deadly Dart, and never to be forgotten, within few dayes how scarce a token? So suddenly ceasing then.

VERS. 36. *This is the dreame, and wee will tell the interpretation thereof before the King: thou art this head of gold.*

The Iron touched with the Load-stone, turnes towards the North, Great *Brittaines* foure Crownes or Kingdomes : This gyant-Image armed at all points, *England*, Angel-gold fought the first fight, incountred *Romes Dragon*, put to flight his Anges.

The Reformations Leader, the other inferiour Kingdome, *France* the Breast and Armes of *Silver*, sometimes subiect to this *Ilands-Crowne*, beares onely the *Lilly argent* for Armes, &c.

Another third Kingdome beari[illegible]*g, rule over all*: of brasse, *Scotland*; Bell Mettle, *the Belly and Thighes*, the Breeches to wit, or blessing wrestled for, having shrunck a sinnew, halting too. The

The *fourth kingdome of Iron, the feete Ireland broken in peeces by an army*, their old customes turn'd into new Lawes, & divided between two *Religions*, our *Ladies & our Lords* at strife together: *but Woman, what have we to doe with thee, but Potters earth and myrie clay, but water with wine compaird.*

And drawing here to the end, or foote of this *Image*: The *fourth Monarchies heavie estate*, & that fourth Kingdome weighed both here together, where *Princes* and *Nobles* going a begging: The basse set on Horse-backe commanding, without doubt the *Gentiles* their returne, to wallow in the mire, or *Heathenisme-covetousnes and Idolatry*: this massy peece importing and expressing no lesse. And further, the *Iron feete* as inferring besides *Irelands denominations*, the names of *Ferdinand*, by whom the devision of these dayes, left for a Legacie to his heires. Also, of that *Arch-engin* great peeces, Volues of shot where distance of so many miles, not securing without hands or mercie in a moment. Towers trodden under foot, and Ships as townes broken in peeces: doubtlesse which cruell Invention among *Christians*, sounding the *Alarum* of the day of *Judgement* at hand, by those thunderbolts discharged. And in dayes of old, had the mighty Volumes bin, those of late Imprinted, out of doubt repented they had. But this *Joseph they knew not the holy Scripture.* So old dayes presedents made for the future, the Fathers as it were laying up for the Children, & more tolerable in the day of *Judgement* for them, then for these times, and these of that rare Art also of the Presse, as wel as peeces, in an instant performed, drawn within the compasse *of this stone, cut out without hands, become a mountain: the Kingdome of heaven at hand,* pointing therat to be revealed *too.*

Lastly, this name of *Charles*, no small Favourites of the *Fisher-man* taken in his nets, stooping to his unsavorie toe; so come to the *French and Spanish* Emperours. And *Charles the great,* since whose daies, a thousand yeares expired neere: Feete of the longest size, of the Tenns. Fowre of his Race succeeding in the *Westerne* Empire, setting in *Europes-Ocean* that eye of the World. No little one, either the other great toe, *Charles the fifth,* & *of his successors some six of them.*

Thus of two thousand and two hundred yeares standing, this great *Image*; foure stories in height, or a nayle driven to the head: layd upon the Anvill by those, in all Arts so able, that further āplification ũnecessary, but cõmended *these.*

DAN. verse 44. *And in the daies of these Kings, shall the God of heaven set up a Kingdome, which shall never be destroyed: and the Kingdome shall not be left to other people, it shall break in peeces.*

Finally,

Finally, for a watch word also these, let fall; *at the end of twelue monethes, &c.* verse, 29 And the end of all these at aimed, either Heavens departing: for without some farther mistery, doubtlesse not. Even the not knowne day and houre, shewed about New-yeares-day, when that good time falling, or twelfe-tyde, there then to watch, as those night-watchers, the happie Shepheard, our example.

And *Nebuchadnezer* for examples sake too, for the future chastised, by whom an Act published the earth throughout, for those that walke in Pride to beware. And signes and wonders for to observe from above; which some carelesse observing not, othersome not discerning not, as blockish. So this sonne of the Morning, walking in his majestie, the heavie sentence falling, as foretold by the Prophet *Daniel*, for to avoyd the Tree, whereof the leaves faire, and fruit much; as much to say, a faire Pedigree, Kings and Princes growing thereon. And the axe laid to the trees roote, wherefore to shew mercy at length to the poore: Counselled for lengthning of his well-faire and tranquillity; lest of the lash tasting as well as others.

And upon greatnesse, none to presume, this *Daniel* penning feigned *Tragedies*, none sets forth plain this great *Assiryan* how; taking his

Sabbaticall progreſſe. In all haſt driven from his privy Chamber, how doing in the fielde open Pennance, alſo grazing before his Palace, feeds with his fellow Aſſe : And like *Eagles-plumes*, thoſe ſtareing locks of his overgrown; a heavie crowne or capp, to keepe his head from cold. Alſo Oxens puſhing hornes-like, thereto crooked nayles as *birds of prey*, the inſeparable crown and ſeptor ſo going together: Pride and cruelty here, which *Brutiſh condition* before ſerved our, that *apprentiſhip* before added excellent Majeſty, &c. and Lords ſeeking to him, conſtrained to caſt thoſe high lookes lower, little dreamed of that eſtate: ſometime who from the *Bed to mind calling the grave no doubt, and thoughts in their owne likenes begetting Dreames.* By this great *Monarch dreamed, thought he ſaw an* Image *& a ſtone of that greatnes, certainly lay thinking, when he gone the way of all fleſh, gathered to his fathers, upon ſome peece in his own likenes ſome everlaſting Monument.* From whoſe ſudden awakning and up riſing alſo, the *Prophet revealing earthly dominions and Monarches, the heaven therewith paſsing away in a moment of time, even mortallities change for no other paſſage this, or place of* Scripture. But like theſe mettels foure, the Elements melting, ſo live for ever, &c.

FINIS.

DANIEL,

I end all.

2. *Samsons Fall, Presented to the House* (1642; Wing D2010), issued with *To the most Honorable, The High Court of Parliament assembled* (1643), is reprinted, by permission of the Folger Shakespeare Library, from the clear copy held at the Folger (shelfmark D2010). This version of *To the most Honorable* contains printed marginal comments that do not appear in the version that prefaces *Samsons Legacie*. This copy contains some handwritten corrections that are believed to be in Lady Eleanor's hand. The text block of the original measures 146 × 90 mm.

Hard-to-read words:

5.1 his eyes thrust out

10.16 *since*

11.16 Now [transcription occludes original printed 'That']

SAMSONS FALL,

Presented to the HOUSE

1642.

Kings 13.

And he gave a Sign at the same time, saying, This is the sign, That the Lord hath spoken.

London, Printed in the Year 1642.

Samſons Fall

Unfolded

To the Houſe, from the Lady *Eleanor.*

Book of *Judges* 16.

S*AMSON* become *as another Man*, though of his unknown *Might* and great ſtrength ſtript, in a moment diſpoſſeſt, who wonders or commiſerates, unhappily came by intruſting others, dangerous ſecurity; otherwiſe as what *fetters of Braſs* had been of force him to binde? none whatſoever: So what occupation too baſe for him, ſometime though the worlds no little wonder, crowned with favors not a few, violated his

A 2 *Vow*

Vow or ſolemn Obligation; The Almighties Counſel diſcloſed to his Adverſary, overcome by *a Womans importunity*, her inchanting notes, whereby laid in a Trance; by whom forgotten or obſerved not, how reſerved the *Angel* would not diſcloſe his *Name* ſo much, *whoſe Birth foretold of*; no more then notice took of his Mothers charge, *ſhe wine none to touch*, diſcoverer of ſecrets, beſides abuſed afore through *like Violence, by one of the ſame uncircumciſed Breed*.

Such a blinde thing Love, *Told her all his heart*, the whole matter; they brought into thraldom ſuch, that harbor it, (nothing that can contain) with a look of whoſe brow able to ſilence, were they whoſoever; at his feet all doing homage.

Behold how degraded, had both

his

his eys thrust out, his teeth gnashing or grinding, too made *in the prison house to grinde*, a new dance shewed, to the Mils unaccustomed Musick till swet his heart out, the restless stone his exercise; presumes upon his loving her, or doting rather, *as bray a Fool in a morter, &c. Prov.* not by any Reins or Bit restrained, sent to school to the Horse, the last mite till spent of his vital Spirits; able to guess whose own counsel could keep so wel, what from a woman might expect, she to be trusted whilst a Sieve or Net retains water; besides where *WAITERS* such in her privy Chamber, no news either, how easie by such familiars inticed: And what renewed forces *Samson* stormed by, as aforeshewed, his darling *Dalilah* prest & urged him daily, in danger of shortning his days:

days: Moreover told him, *He loved her not*; (named her *His Love* it seems) because jested with her, the Lye takes at her hands.

VVhereby overmaster'd, no more plays fast and loose with his Mistris, *The Philistines upon him* in earnest, took him away, no false alarm, feeble *became as another man, wist not what he had done, undreamt of, puts on the Brass shakel his Garter, aforetime had mockt them, become their game and pastime*, brought himself to a fair pass, come *to be led by a Lad*; after twenty years over them, lawless vow-makers to them made an open Example, till death pays his Ransom, confined to the Dungeon-pit all his days.

And herewith hastning away the patience of your House, lest overcharged; where the Moral to vulgar ap-

apprehensions visible, a story no stranger to blinde Ale-houses, the bare walls not without it, of *Samson* the prisoner, *a Prince*, sometime *a Savior or Defender*, &c. at his presence all making way; No feigned *Atlas* strength, barr'd never so fast, that *laid on his shoulder the City Gates* and appurtenance, as a birding piece vvent away with all: also *new cords sevenfold* for failing, and *green wythes* as nothing pluckt asunder; likewise whose Maiden locks, like Sun beams extending, povvther'd vvith Angelical odours, fastned to a VVeavers-beam, instantly like a lace rent therefrom; portraying forth not only our *British* Union, fast knit and bound, soon dissolved after; and *Irish* flourishing plantation, that in a night all undone, as those *Brittle Cords and*

wythes.

wythes, &c. *By wilde Boars and ravening wolves rooted out, overrun. But how befel him whose heavy fate him also foreshewed in these barren times of ours, as* Samson *his Birth, the Angel when appeared to the Woman and Husband both* (Cap.13.) with the seventeenth Centuries Mystery, as what Date bears, by the multiplied number of seven, (*ver*.7.) *ver*.13. needless to be insisted on, a lamb where may wade, any shallow capacity dive or conceive, *Canaans* road not balkt, proceeding line by line thus, (*ver*.19.) first how awakened, found his crown bare, despoiled of his treasure by a desperate Executioners unlucky Razer, one ready at hand: *Samson* (by underminers over-reached) himself disarmed, the *Spirit of the Lord departed from him*, so forsaken, that after that

that preceding bout with her, by whose ungracious venomous hands woven that ſubtile web, taken of his locks *Livery* and *Seizin*.

VVhen at once upon his effectual prayer, had their PAY then, *avenged for his two eyes*, of both diſinherited together; deſcribed in that poſture, *ſtretching forth both his hands took hold with all his Might, &c.* at a blow, *by the houſe falling on thoſe Philiſtines, Lords three thouſand*, ſo *that at his Death, the dead exceeded*, ver. *or were more then had periſhed in his life, or ſuffered; Wives and Children partakers with them*, afore bare all the ſway; at which *Feſtival* ſpectators no few: other ſome on the Roof, ſuppoſing as at other times ſhould *have made them ſport*, the houſe *ſupported on Pillars*, at once ſwept away;

B *whom*

whom his Brethren of his fathers house took up and buried: that of the Powder design matching it the nearest, shewing what Trust to be reposed in *Princes* or *Pillars* either. And thus of *Samson* neither spared, brought to his Tryal, found guilty, *Great Britains* Lyon rent in pieces, shadowed out in *Samsons* exploits; so much for that, when Cashiered those Revellings, *Dagons house* demolished; and for these where twice voted, *And there was no King*, &c. *every man did what was right in his own eyes*, ver. evident as this unquestionable, *Whether ever before or since, in such a space of time, so many at once perished, as of late have done.*

VVhere these doings Recorded withal, till this Reformation the like deformity unknown, conjured up-

again,

again, as it were, (*What lack ye?*) though Sentenced down, whose owners under Condemnation, here robbed of their hair, in the likeness of *unclean Spirits* set on their Stalls; the Cap as ugly as ominous, saluted with this Neck-verse, ver.13. *If thou weavest or platest seven locks of my head, &c.* Summoned to appear at the Sign of the *Gallows*, by *Samsons* breaking as it were the Halter.

So from him *The Lord of Sabbath, holding in his Right hand the Sign of the seven stars,* This *Legacy* toward your yong mens feastings (thus armed at all points) Now turned into fire and sword, not unuseful for Sea and Land-service, the Ropes, wythes, and fetters for Ship-tackling, Brass pieces and Match, that *Goliah*-generation to withstand, blinde Monarchy and uncircumcised Priesthood, the vail not taken off their hearts. ; finished this of no common consequence (the whole worlds Map or Survey) whereby prefigured *his coming at hand, the Son of the Most High, a greater then Samson*, first a Sign given to the ungrateful *Jew*, and then to the *Gentile*, a prototype of the *Word of God*; Also who as though risen again or revived, after made their Musick and Game, *whose strength again came to him*, upon his solemn prayer (as that) *Father, glorifie me*, &c. (Ioh. 17.) also when convinced 3000 in one day, *Men and Brethren, what shall we do? prickt at the heart*, &c. with *Adams* fall inclusive, hearkned to her project *Eves* (Heb. *Chavah*) for which as *the man cast out*: so for whose degenerate progeny utter darkness reserved.

To the most Honorable, The High Court of Parliament assembled.

My Lords,

AS theres a *Time for every thing under the Sun*, and if ever for being abrupt and brief in, it is *NOW*, when *Time* thus precious with your Lordships; So under the Sun since there is nothing but a supernatural course to be taken, touching the *Cure* of such unnatural conditioned *Times*: The Almighty his *Word* the onely *Balm* and *Soveraign* Remedy when ye have tryed all: If any therefore do amiss and miscarry of you, blame your selves none but the *Parliament*: For I shall of no little *Burthen* discharge my self here, who can but say and tell you: a receipt

Sealed with the Lord *Brooks* blood, immediately after slain about Candlemas, 1642.

ceipt I have of ſuch rare operation and vertue given me, that within few days it ſhal bring him again to Himſelf, I mean the *KING*, after abſent ſo long from his *Parliament*; whoſe Character if ye pleaſe to obſerve, this is his:

He that no Chains could binde him, Mark Evangeliſt the 5.) *That had been often bound with fetters and Chains pluckt aſſunder by him, and the fetters broken in pieces; neither could by any man be tamed*; as much to ſay, *neither* Oath, *nor* word, *or* Promiſe *availing, or any Reaſon of force to perſwade with him,* as the Holy Ghoſts ſpeaking plain; by that adjuring in *Gods Name*, and by asking his *name* too, *ſaying*, LEGION, *for they were*

Which beſide his unfaithfulneſs, includes his impriſonment, and what enſues, as appears, who beſought not tormented to be before his time, as though the time had been foretold him.

were many, who ſpake not with the leaſt: Nevertheleſs, his great words not more fierce then fearful of the *Lords preſence*; This man wounding himſelf thus, bidden, *Go home to his friends*. Who went to the Scots, as not marvelled at a little.

And thus have made tender unto your Lordſhips of my ſervice, whether or no ye accept thereof, for to bring his Majeſty to you, *ſitting as afore time cloathed, &c.* and doing withal what ye ſhall ask or deſire.

As for the Cavaliers, what they ſhall do all of them, even crave a Paſs hereby to take Shipping for the *Low-Countreys* and *Germany*, to be gone away; the *Boors* will entertain them willingly: St. *Matth.*8. gives notice of two, *ſo exceeding fierce that none might paſs by that way*; to wit, that

that Dutch Duke and his Brother; those possessed Princes, to return also without delay Home again, beyond Sea.

Though had six moneths liberty to stay yet upon pain of death were commanded to depart within ten days.

1642. The 3. of *January*.

VVaiting on your *Lordships Commands*
ELEANOR.

In which fatal moneth of January, both the Archbishop and late King were executed afterward.

The Holy Ghosts

New-Years-Gift.

F I N I S.

3. *To The Most Honorable the High Covrt of Parliament Assembled* (1643), issued with *Samsons Legacie* (1643;Wing D2015), is reprinted, by permission of The British Library, from the clear copy found in the Thomason Tracts Collection (shelfmark E.96[19]). The text lacks a title page. A handwritten annotation at the bottom of sig. A appears to be the work of the famous collector of Civil War era tracts, George Thomason. The text block of the original measures 140 × 106 mm.

Hard to read words and handwritten annotations:

A	[bottom] 'written by [...] Lady Davis Aprill 14: 1643'
13.22	from the *Incarnation*

19.

TO THE MOST HONORABLE THE HIGH COVRT OF PARLIAMENT ASSEMBLED, &c.

MY *LORDS*;

THer's a *Time for every thing under the Sunne,* and if any; for to bee abrupt and breife in ever, tis *NOW* when *Time* so precious is with your Lordships: under the Sunne there

written by her A Lady Davis
Aprill 14: 1643

there is nothing but a ſupernaturall Courſe to be taken, Touching the *Cure* of ſuch unnaturall condition'd *Times*: The Almightie his VVord the only *Balme* then, and *Soveraigne* remedy when ye have tryd all: If any therefore doe amiſſe and miſcarry of you: Blame your ſelves none but the *Parliament*: For I ſhall of no little *Burthen* diſcharge my ſelfe here who can but ſay, and tell you. I have a receipt of ſuch rare opperation and vertue given me; That within few dayes it ſhall bring Him againe to Himſelf, I meane the *KING*; after abſent ſo long from his *Parliament*: whoſe Character if ye pleaſe to obſerve; This is his:

He that no Chaines could binde him, (Marke Evangeliſt the 5th.) *That had been often bound with fetters and with Chaines pluck'd aſſunder by him. And the fetters broken in pieces, neither could*

could by any man be tamed; as much to ſay, *neither* Oath, *nor* word, *or* promiſe *availing*, *or any reaſon of force to parſwade with Him, as the* Holy Ghoſt ſpeaking plaine: *by that adjuring in* Gods Name; *and by asking his* Name *too, ſaying*, LEGION, *for they were many, who ſpake not with the Left*: Neverthelеſſe, not more feirce then fearefull of the *Lords* comming, *this man wounding himſelf thus.*

And thus have made tender unto your Lordſhips; Of my ſervice, whether or no yee accept thereof: for to bring His Majeſtie to you, Setting as afore time cloath'd, &c. And doing withall what Ye ſhall aske or deſire. As for the Caveliers what They ſhall doe all of them, even crave a Paſſe here, to take Shipping for the *Low-Countries*, and *Germanie* to be gone away; the *Boors* will entertaine them willingly, S^t. *Matt:* the 8.

A 2 gives

gives Notice of two, so exceeding feirce that none might passe by that way, to wit, that Dutch Duke, or Prince possessed with an uncleane Spirit, out of his VVITS; he to returne also without delay Home againe, beyond Sea.

1642. VVaiting on your
The 3[d.] of *Lordships Commands*
January. ELEANOR.

The Holy Ghosts

New-yeares-gift.

SAMSONS LEGACIE.

JUDGES, the 16. Chap. &c.

ANd as inſtanc'd or brought to *his* Tryall, here found light; *SAMSON* guiltie that way: which *Vow* of his, had he unhappily not violated, a buſineſſe that: Of no mean weight, what *Fetters of Braſſe bound him had*; none of what kinde ſoever. *Samſons fall, loſt himſelf hereby, diſpoſſeſſed of the* Spirit *of the* LORD.

B By

By him diſcovered *the Almighties counſell unto the* Lords *Enemy, could not with-hold or refraine, told her all his heart*; ſhe acquainted is therewith bee it whatſoever : Such a blind thing is *Love*; They into ſuch Thraldom brought which harbour it : ſuſpected nothing becauſe he *lov'd* her, or *doted rather*. That whoſoever they were, was able with a looke of his *Browe*, to put them for ever to ſilence, wherein his ſoul ſo farre ingag'd, any to attempt but the motion, &c.

And farther ſhewed, how in his *allegiance having toward his Maſter and Lord fayled*: *Both ſtript of that great ſtrength of his, Loſt both his* Eies, *not only boord or put out*, faine to be lead afterwards by a Ladd : But *put in priſon, beſide grinding in a Mill*: To taſt of reſtleſſe HELL, that weariſome being. *Even* takes *Eſſaye* of our *Saviours Cup*; indeede theſe in ſome things to *Samſon* belong onely : able but for to turne his weary

weary ſides without other help, or by a wals ſide *to* go, which before had *The Lord his ſupport*; *The* Philiſtims *his Lords now*: a heavie change, of no other eſtate worthy, had taken his pleaſure and ſo came of it.

One Truſted with that high place of Government: Twenty yeares therabout, as it appeares. Crownd with ſo many favours; That had the *Eternall words direction his light*: ſet ſo light by alhough chaſtiſed never ſo ſeverly the bage of his Maſters heavy diſpleaſure, none commiſerate his Complaint bee it whatſoever, *whether marked, ſhorne or noted*. He *which wiſt not the* Spirit *of the Lord was departed from him*, *when* He *had fooliſhly departed from the Lord*: And if GOD ſpared not *Samſon*, others much leſſe that have him for their leſſon.

who could have ſuppoſed, warn'd before hand too, what truſt to be repoſed in them. That upon a VVomans aſſault her charms ſuch a Forte rendered up : without any reaſon rendred *But to pleaſe* Her, *was not that Riddle diſcloſd enough* : who would not have layd another wager, as great as *Samſons* ? That this man could never have been over taken ſo, that had been miſtaken ſo much in Her before, *named his Heifer* ; and *this* woman ſhe of the *Philiſtims* breed too, both of them one in effect : or two witneſſes appearing as it were : Herewithall bidden to take heed all, of Cloſe-underhand-dealers : For *the holy Ghoſt* is not without a double, or two-fold meaning in *theſe* thirty *Shirts* wrap'd *up*, & thirty *Shutes thoſe*; not only *Judas* His livery-Coates *or Coatearmes expresſing, but our bleeding dayes* wherein ſuch Plundering and *intolerable* Theifts :

For which betraying of the truſt, as one beſide himſelf ; beſide being a Priſoner, made a by-word, or one for a meane Occupation fitter, or truſted when *His eyes bee out rather then other-wiſe* : *In ſteed of a* Saviour

our *or* Deliverer, *bee delivered into the hands of ſuch, &c.* VVhich kindneſſe for : To none other *Bound, but to Her* : beſide *his* willſulneſſe, *whoſe Parents* ſome-time could not prevaile with *Him*, or any other : !s during the remnant *of his wretched dayes* , ordain'd for to beare *thoſe ſhakels and fetters*, Braſſen ones for ſuretiſhip, and better ſecuritie : *Thus armed by Her from Head to Foote &c.*

But *her* Ladyſhip *urged him* , *She preſt him* Daily, vext his Soule, his Conſcience to the *Death.* Moreover, by *Lulling of him as much againe, was kept in a Dreame, untill* layd *himſelf flat at her* Feet : By ſuch maine *Strength* was *Samſon* over-maſtred by his *Miſtres*, who *ſo often* gives the *Allarum* ; The *Philiſtins* SAMSON, &c.

But to bring theſe home a little *farther*, to theſe laſt dayes , without Over-laying Your patience *I hope*, ſhewed great *Brittains low ebbe*, like *Samſon what paſe brought to.* B 3 *The*

The worlds wounder *for blesfing and bounty from above beyond all theirs not unknowne*; a dreadfull Name, *farre* and *neere*: Now by His Majesties *warfare* being *fettered* and in *Armes*; become the game and musicke of the VVorld.

Those (as it were) away *bidding* and *running before time*, crowding as fast, and covering *house-tops*, fearelesse *now* of *Samson*. In which difference difficult to judge; whether *for Might and Majestie* more reverenced, then dejected at last and dispised: Certainly manifested as *great Imbecillitie in subjecting himselfe to a Womans waywardnesse, therewith carryed* away *so and transported*.

But these not for disputationsake; but made for dispatch, not so wide and full of stuffe as others are acknowledged: It it sit close, tis as becoming *Joseph* in makeing himself known to his Brethren, in hast told them, I am *Joseph*: So now it was not you that sent mee hether, but GOD

So was it of the Lord; no thanke to *Samson*, *Samsons saying*, *she pleaseth me well*: *When nevertheleſſe it displeased his Father and Mother. They saying; is there never a Woman among thy Brethren or people, &c.*

The almightie for bringing his owne Counsell and purpose to passe; suffers much, and forbeares long: the Holy Ghost thus saying, hee sought an occasion against the *Philistins*, GOD on his side, he needs not feare any. The Time was come of their fall: at last which stricks home, though hardly like the Thunder at first heard.

And to be som-what lowder, or plain herein: was not an occasion sought also against that House of Lords and Commons, by that unexpected progresse without *President* or Example of Progenitors, when he separated Himself from his Head-Kingdoms-Parliament Assembled then, for rooting that Slip out, blind *Herisie Her* Maiesties *darling*, grown unto such a height. Without doubt with as ill, or worse successe taken in hand, then hee which but lost his life, good *Samson*: When the House of Peeres and Commons those two Pillars, charged with a heavie taxe of *Treason*, purposing to lay violent hands next: First rob'd of their good Name; and then of their Life lastly, brought about by Lyers in waite for that purpose. And thus his causlesse falling out, the occasion of these such unspeakble miseries; He carried away from ſrom His Parliament thus , by the Church of the LIBERTINES and ROMES CHVRCH, proceeding from a looſneſſe or careleſneſſe of goodneſſe: the good affection not ſet by of thoſe, to have been Equaliz'd, if not preferr'd before Forreine ſtates ; a greater Honour then proginey (common to all) to diſcharge ſuch a Stewardſhip well. The office of a Crowne (*a good name, Proverbs. 22*) as our Eies open'd, and Woſull evidences thereby given to underſtand : That not old *Samuel*, godly *Queene Elizabeth* was rejected, tender hearted unto every one. But herewith wee which were not content : But nay, we will have a King to reigne over us, whatſoever coming to paſſe.

How ſoone verified, the old true proverbe, ſeldome comes a better: for unto *Samſon* as at his end ; ſo befallen us More ſlaine in one yeare, then ſince the Conqueſt in the Reigne of ſo many Kings and Queenes of them cald to ſacrifice their Lives for the Truths teſtimony : commanded to reſt a little ſeaſon. Bleſſed innocents were who changed have their ſcarlet for white robes, *calling a loud, how long O Lord* Revela. 6. &c.

And every haire of Times head grown precious, never recald ; and if ever perrilous to looſe it, as tis now reveal'd here ; and unloos'd the miſtery of time, *how*

how *Samsons seven-fold ropes pluck'd asunder, even drawn from them* ; *like* Pharaohs *double Dreame*, where the thing was one, likewise these broken *Withes and ropes* reach to this sevententh hundered yeare present not alone ; But to that sevententh yeare of the Kings reigne, a time of greater famine then *Pharaohs*, when the plentie was not known, by reason of the scarcity following so grevious.

And now great *Brittaine* newly so stiled, accompanied with no few Honours that started up, have in this sevententh hundred yeare ; Even as those knots undone all and broken, with *Irelands* green plantation by the rootes pluck'd up : This *knot or union so fast made, how is it come to nothing, but all up making ready in Armes* ; that beside a *Coate-armes* borne, no other appearance at all remains, suddenly like *his armes* become *when he awaked* ; *great Brittains peace even so brittle stands as those ropes, &c. Compard unto towe,*

C or

or a piece of thred, choaked with Match and Powder now: for the ſweet ſents of *peace* and *plenty* injoyed Long: And handled *Thus*: Notwithſtanding, not unfore-told. None *Conſiders of that hand writing*, though *in* the Yeare, 1633. ſhewing, His Kingdome is devided and numbred &c. *Belſhazzar, it ſhall be eaſier for him in the day of Judgement.*

By the Prophet *Jeremiah*: *PASHUR which ſmote him, was rebaptiz'd*: VVho gave him that Name Compounded as unluckie as it was Long; *MA: GOR-MIS Sabib namely reſtles or feare round about being no leſſe* then great Brittains very *Motto*: VVherefore to make it good unto His Majeſtie two Names be attributed a Godfathers and Godmothers here: toward his regeneration Baptized in their teares, for *Salt that is wanting*. Now from *Samſon*: *JAMES* SON derived, and alſo Mother *Rachels* Name; hers added: drawne from *CHARLES*, to weare it

for

for a Favour,as long as he lives here; *weep-ing becauſe they were Not*, or were loſt,*would not be comforted &c.*

The Lyon become a Noted ſheep, ſignifies: *for Rachell is a ſheep*, but herewith to give neverthleſſe ſome comfort: *Thy Kingdome come &c.* Then the only remedie when all is done ; *Come Lord Jeſus.* For what Thy Kingdomes are come unto,none need to ſhew it : They ſpeake for themſelves, round about plainly : and thus *Samſons* ſtory their ſtate ſets *forth*, no newes either Your hangings and Tapſtery makes it not a ſtranger,but Common blind *Ale-houſes* not without it, His lying in her Lapp a ſleep, whilſt ſhe pooles him &c.

And without ſtreining this *Legacie of his* too, beſids thoſe ropes puld in pieces, which became as ſinged with fire. VVith His *Brazon Chains*, as the one Stands for *Match*, the other toward your pieces of *Ordnance*. Faſtend this alſo on our *Effeminate*

C2 time,

time, *his ſeven Locks*, Left to this laſt hundred yeare : ſhewing what weaving and curlling we have of FALSE-HAIRE, by that going away of His, with the *Webbe* faſtend to the *Beame*; whoſe locks therein woven by her: who ſaid; Thou ſayeſt falſe, (*or*) haſt mocked mee, &c. Expresſing *how men forbidden expreſly long Haire, yet the ſonnes of God will weare it* : ſome of them looking thereby more like the ſonns of Divels.

And ſo farther, *for the green Withs and new ropes provided of old, long ſince for ſuch Hellhounds*, whoſe ſmoaking tongues as Links ſet on fire already, notwithſtanding RACHA, *he who cals his Brother ſo, he ſhall bee in danger of a Counſell, &c.* and ſo much for thoſe *Withs and ropes*; unuſefull neither for great *Brittains Navie and Taklings*, together with *Irelands Plow-Taklings* and other uſes, as aforeſaid.

And nevertheleſſe like the *Plague-tokens* of

of their inevitable end: The hastie Messengers, likewise so many *Judgements* sent forth suddenly forerunners of the dreadfull daies approach: *All prepared alike to meete the Son of God, as those Hoggish Gergesens, when all the Citie came out to meete Him, and besought him to depart: And now truely fulfilled. The wedding is prepared, but they which were bidden, were not worthy, &c.* (Matth. 22.) *For nothing but in eating and drinking, and giving in Marriage, is this your hastening* To *his Comming? Cleansing your selves of all filthinesse.* But returning to Times cutting off, which no more returns. That great Man sealed in the forehead, or front with 1642. *Noahs dayes even shall declare the meaning of that scentence from our* Saviours mouth; *that no flesh saved except those dayes be shortned,* as much to say: *shall come short of his dayes, at the time of the* Deluge alluding to it, when all flesh perished, *except eight persons.*

In like manner from the *Incarnation*, when

C 3

(when *God became man, thought not ſcorne to take our Nature upon Himſelfe* ,) From which time to his ſecond comming, Parrallels it Thus. But as the dayes *of Noah* were , ſo ſhall the comming *of the ſonne of Man bee* : For as in the dayes *before the flood, untill the day Noah entered into the Arke* : *And knew not untill the flood came, and tooke them all away* : *So ſhall alſo the Comming of the Sonne of Man bee.* And ſo all before the comming of the laſt day alſo *forewarnd* to be, appeares plainly (*Matt.*24.) Dated with the preſent yeare, 1642. *Two ſhalbe in the feild,two* Armes, to wit, *Two women ſhall be grinding at the* Mill, *&c.* and of our miſerable deviſſion, ſo much for a watch-word ſhall ſerve.

The ſeventh Angels Trumpet (*Revela.* 10.) give his voice on *Noahs ſide*, beſide that Angell that ſet his *Right foot upon the ſea, &c.* Whoſe feete as Pillars of fire : with that little Booke open in his hand : Even great *Brittains* revealed forewarning, That Ilands viſſitation : *That there be ſome ſtanding here not only, but throughout the World: that ſhall not taſt death, till the day of of Judgement.* And so take eate this little Booke, the Sacrament of his comming at hand :

As herein is no small mistery Conteind too, twofold double Witnesse appearing like all the rest : *Judges the 15. 20. verse, And he Judged Israell twenty yeares, in the dayes of the Philistins, &c.* *verse* 31. and 16 Chap. *And he Judged Israell twenty yeares.*

Also, when the sonns of GOD became Tyrants, and carnall (*Gen* 6.) My spirit shall not strive alway with man : for that he also is flesh. *Namely, how great soever* : Yet his dayes shall bee an hundred and twenty yeares : It includes *Times reigne* ; This twenty yeares to be put upon his last score. The Prophet *David* foresaw this weeke (*Psalm*, 90.) *A thousand yeares in his sight, are but as yesterday.* The Apostle *Peter* : *One day with the Lord, is as a Thousand yeares, and a Thousand yeares, as one day. Daniel* the Prophet, that Master of *Arrethmatitians* : confirms that weeke thus ; *He shall confirme his Covenant with many for a weeke, and in the middest of the weeke oblation shall cease, &c.* The Messiah slaine, and the Cities Desolation, to wit ; in the fourth Thousand yeare : Wherein not only shewed *Messiah* his dayes cut off : but *Time*, the sonne of Eternitie, his dayes too shortned : Even one Thousand yeares fulfilled, or compleat. For the Gospels Progresse :

The 20. of the *Revela* : Thus speakes ; *That they lived,*

lived, and reigned with Christ, a Thousand yeares: before these Idolatryous times of late: And therefore in respect of Time past, (our Saviours late comming Then.) The Apostle *Paul*, after this fashion admonisheth. *The Time is short*, as much to say; *And to be shortned. For which cause, as if we possessed or enjoyed nothing Corinth*.7.

And here adding but in a word or two, of the LORDS day; that also cut off: how this *Samson* hath been shaffed : This *Samson-day*, how it hath been observed and kept, after what spirituall fashion; Even the LORDS house haunted by *Spirits of Divels*, no few amongst those *Tombes, &c.* Holding their Spirituall-Courts there, whose daily Office, and Occupation was, before their being cast out of *Pauls*, Either to make many forsweare themselves; Or to fill Prisons, with those call'd by them, *Puritans*: and now, *Rownd-Heads*. For which senslesse, rediculous Name, not amisse with the Prophet, to bestowe these for a *Girdle*: alwayes to bee girded with feare, round about *MAGORMISSABIB* : those Characters compounded of GOG, & MA:GOG: Compassing the *Camp of the beloved Citie of the Saints*: Whose number &c. *Revela.* 20. consisting of *Papists*, the Queenes Armie, and prophaine *Protestants*, before the day of *Judgement*, being let loose: These like *Herod* and *Pilate*, that were made friends, at variance before.

And

And wherewith obſerv'd, as it deſerves no other, as others have ſerv'd God, profeſſing themſelves his ſervants, and going contrary : as it were your ſervant &c : likewiſe by them as ſuppoſed. Their *Name* but uſed for the abuſing or betraying of their perſon ; having firſt craftily gone about to cut the throats of ſo many : by giving them another *Name* : But to return ; Thus this Sabboth too diſcarded : not onely Excommunicating the Lord *prophets and ſervants, &c.* but turned into a Day of Cardding, and Diceing, with ſweating *Paſtimes* : *Goe for thy labour, ſit downe and* ſpinne, *and* weave ; plough, *and* ditch, *from henceforth in the ſweat of thy face Eate thy bread* : *Come no more into the garden of God* ; ſo much for harkening to the *Serpents* voice : The flaming Sword beware : *Neither be grieved with him*, crying ; *O my ſonne Abſolom my ſonne, my ſonne Abſolom.* (alſo) *O my ſonne Abſolom, O Abſolom my ſonne, my ſonne* : The *Saboths*

D double

double *Eclips* : as much to ſay, or twice Chang'd and alter'd: That harkend not to that voice rather, ſaying, *verily my Saboths ſhall ye keepe, even he ſhall be cut off, that worketh thereon.* That day which was given *for* a perpetuall ſigne: *Exodus* 31. &c. No marvell or wonder therefore; our Houſes though visſited by the Spoyler and Plunderer with our day-labour, turned into Daies and Nights-warding and watching.

Neverthelesse, not cut off without declaring in the place (of this *Judas-day*, more like then the *Reſurrections*) a lawfull Succeſſor herewith ſhewed, &c. upon *Mathias-day*, how the Lot fell in the yeare 1633. that Mundaies firſt day of the weeke. In which aforeſaid yeare, the *Beaſt hee alſo aſcended then out of the bottomleſſe Pit; The ſon of* perdition: The laſt Arch *B.* gone to his owne place Now; by whom the word of God, in the Moneth *October* 23. was burnd, ſuffered Martyrdome by a Candle, *from his*

own

owne hand, at the High-Commission board Sacrifiz'd. And at this time, two Armies striving in the fielde for Possession, and in *Barke-shire* and *Oxfordshire*, where the *Heavenly* voice was *heard first* at *Englefield-house*: The *prime Shire* imediately *carried thereupon* to *Oxfoads* Parliament *to bee published, &c.* In the *first yeare* of the Kings Raigne, it being a *Roule* a *manuscript, revealing* the day of Iudgement, &c.

For which *Cause now* againe, a great *meeting of the Prophets*; as sometime in the daies of *John*, that *Conjunction then*: *Isaiah*, 6. *An ancient* Saint complaining thus, *Woe is mee, I am cut off*, (or undon) *because I am a man of uncleane lips, &c.* VVhen as those Heralds of Armes present, *Each of them with six wings, twaine they covered their faces with, with twaine covered their feete, with twaine did fly: holy, holy, holy Lord of hostes; cryed one to another, &c. The whole earth is full of thy glory*: And here to bring these home to the dayes of *John*, in

 the

the *Revelation, &c.* prophecying to his *Time*, even to the end of the world; being *Times Voices expresly*: for no other then a third Sabath to be through the earth, as exprest by the foure *Beasts*, and foure *Evangelists*, &c. give all their voices also, saying; *holy, holy, holy, Lord God almightie, which was, which is, and which is to come*: And for more light in this matter; (*Revela.* 4.) *The seven Lamps of fire before the Throne, &c. which are called the seven Spirits*: signifie no other then Munday, to be a Spirituall day. (*Chap.* 5.) Signified thus, *There stood a Lambe in the middest of the Elders, having seven eies, and seven horns, which are the seven* Spirits *of God, sent forth into all the earth*: To wit, *Sunday* the middle Sabbath; the *Eie*, as it were, to the *Gentels*, that great light for seventeene hundered yeares space. Likewise the Horns, the new Sabbath, *Munday*, as afore shewed: As the one proclaming the first *Resurrection* or comming; So the other the Last, in the sevenventeth hundred yeares to be recal'd. And thus our eternall Sabbath, & these Sabath-dayes, both in one, sealed up in the little Booke.

Farthermore, for an addition these; shewing beside how the Worlds ages being cast into three parts. That had not those daies before the Flood, been cut off or shortned; the Deluge had not been till *Noahs* Death, which lived 300. Yeares after, &c. *Enoch* his walking with God, confirms it : *Walked with God* 300. yeares after his begetting Children : as much to say, weary *Time* three hundred yeares, Comes before his *Time*. High time of such daies to be disburthened.

And to touch this New-day with a coale from the Altar, shewed also the one even Munday purified, and the other remooved : As appeares in that Massage sent *Herod*, who had shut up the Lords Messenger : Sonne of *Herod* the great so Sir-Nam'd, That be-headed Him : setting abroach his *Blood* for his Birth-day : better he never had been borne : *John* of too high a *spirit* to feed him with *flattery*, tooke our Saviour for *John* risen againe, or some walking Spirit. The Lord sends him word of the *Resurrection*, saying; *go tell that FOX, behold* I *cast out Divels, and will heale to day, and to morrow, and the third day I*

D 3 *shalbe*

shalbe perfected : *Neverthelesse I must walke to day, and to morrow, and the day following, &c.* bids him doe his worst; as much to say : which Ambassage, whether delivered it were, or no, wee read not.

But doubtlesse for admonition spoken unto all spirituall *Herods*, neither being curious whether these came to her eare, indeavouring rather to unlocke or open the meaning of that. How coming to passe, *Herod* or *Hayreod*, to be Sur-named *Reynold the Fox*. Not onely because *John* called our Lord, *Innocent Lambe*, made their prey, but his eare dedicated to her so, his *Dalilah*. Very likely he did weare some odde Locke, Fox-tayle-like, a scourge, as it were, of hayre, portending how, together with his Souldiers, our Saviour should be stript, scourged, despised, and mocked by him.

Wherefore before that *Easter*, this word or mocke sent him, that before had given his consent : Onely for a rash words sake (as made an eye-winesse of his valour) to be-head such a one, for such a woman, partly because of his alliance, &c. Then lessen himselfe. His greatnesse makes himselfe a fire-brand of Hell rather : And although this Fox, the first of that Name, is said to be exceeding glad to see *Jesus*, of whose coming then questionlesse he was foretold, in that word sent unto him ; notwithstanding, to those questions of his, vouchsafed no answer at all.

As

As much to ſay, he had and would make good his word in the end, &c. Thus ſhee in ſuch obedience to her Mothers inſtruction; He ſtanding in as much awe of them both, thoſe *Philippian* Dames. And ſo much for an *Old Caſe* new reported.

And as in the Goſpell the five Yoke of *Oxen*, theſe ſerves for *O X F O R D S Meridian*, which belong to His Majeſties invitation: *Hath M A R I E D a wife, and cannot Come, &c.* Yoak'd in the yeare, 1 6 2 5. unequally. Alſo that Term of *F O X*, or *OXFORD*, to wit: Ominous to long Gownes ; *Samſon* Companion too crafty for him; afords them that ſubject likewiſe to worke upon. So againe Laſtly: What Lacke yee? Doe you lacke Match, and Powder, or Cable-Ropes, or any Braſſe &c: Fetters toward Field-pieces, or long Haire any to weare? Or *Iriſh Withs*? Of theſe as much as yee pleaſe: S *AMSON* is provided for you, Bound to ſerve is; as long as he Lives: Even hee with thoſe grinding Gun-powder. That Mother and Daughter in the *GOSPELL*: *Two women ſhall be grinding &c.* The laſt dayes watch-word, ſo much ſhall hereof ſuffice. Onely theſe, (*Matt* 24.) Then *ſhall two bee in the Field, &c.* As it ſerves for this yeare 1642. with the ſevententh hundred yeare: So *Samſons* ſacrificing here his Life. Hee bearing as it were, the gates of Hell and Death: Alſo,

Alſo, theſe beares date about this preſent *EASTER*, ſet forth in Honour of the glorious Reſurrection, his Life, and End.

And hetherto from Thence &c. Your Silence on all ſides, which concludes Conſent: Wherefore I Conjure and Charge the aforeſaid *Evill Spirits, or Legions, no more here to enter into this Kingdome from henceforth*: Goe downe into Hell, out into the fartheſt part of the Earth: *get thee hence, &c.* Glory, Honour, and Bleſſing.

From the Bleſſed *LADIE*,
her *Day* in *Lent, &c.*
1643.

None offer without *Priviledge*,
to Re-print *Theſe*.

4. *Amend, Amend; Gods Kingdome Is At Hand* (1643; Wing D1967) is reprinted, by permission of The British Library, from the clear copy held at The British Library (shelfmark 1078.1.13). The text block of the original measures 165 × 116 mm. Page 6 is misnumbered 9.

Hard-to-read handwritten annotations:
5 stanza 11 *Nebuch*: Signifies, a Grand-father, and a Father both.

Rodd. 2/-/-

Eardley / Eleanor / Lady

AMEND, AMEND;

GODS

KINGDOME IS AT HAND:

AMEN, AMEN.

THE

PROCLAMATION:

Mene, Mene; Thine finished (or ended; — *Anagr.*

Tekel; Thou found fickle, or weak by (*Them.*

Peres, Thy *Peers* or *Parliement* Mem:

Mene Tekel upharsin

K: Parliement *house*.

Jer: the first; and 10. vers.
Dan. the sixt, and 21. vers.

The *New* Song: *Come and* See.

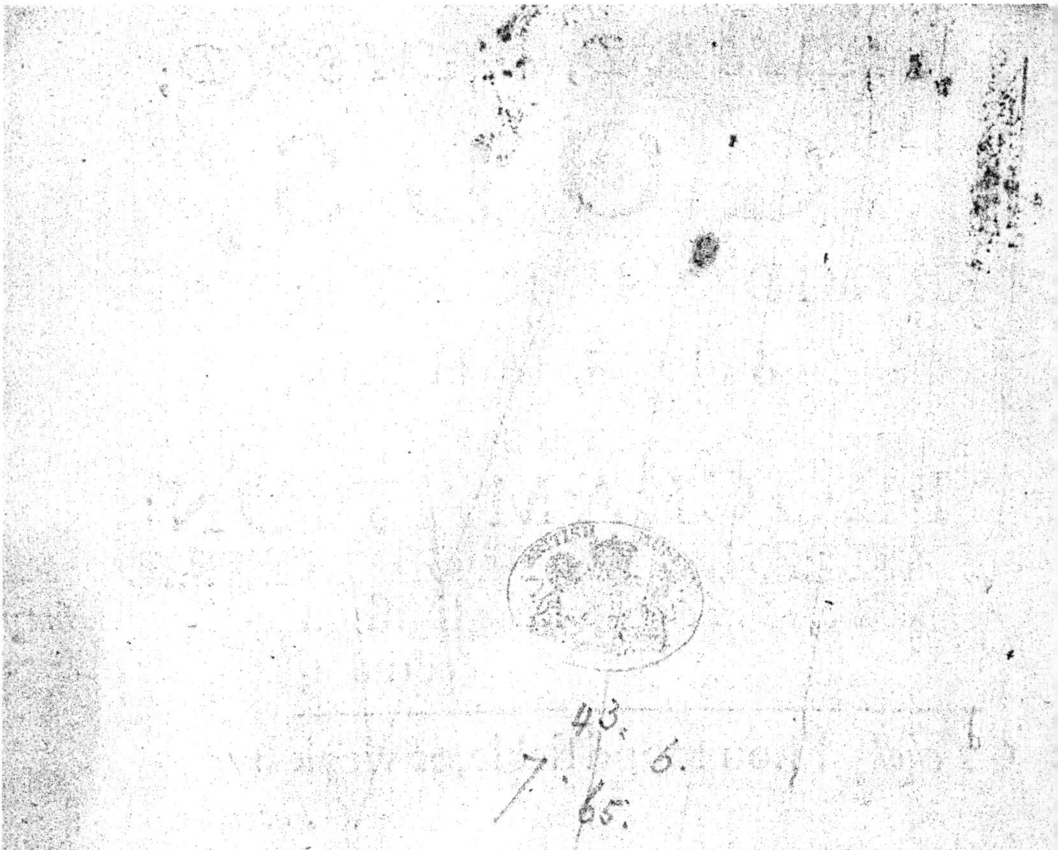
43. 6.
7. 65.

Anagrams, and *Daniel Touched &c.*

ELEANOR AVDELEY:

Reveale *O DANIEL.*

Chap. 2. verſ. (19.)

Then was the ſecret revealed to Daniel. (22) *He that revealeth the deepe and ſecret Things.* (28) *But there is a* GOD *that revealeth ſecrets.* (29) *He that revealeth ſecrets.* (47) *Of a truth, your* GOD *is a revealer of ſecrets.*

CHAP: 5.

The palme of the Hand: *To the* Palſgrave-prince, *given in the yeare* 1633. *a faire Caveat drawne from the* Letters *of his* Name : *For* Chriſtian Princes *namely, &c. Authoriz'd by the* Revel. 13. Chap. 17. verſ.

B*Elchazer*, Be-*Charles* : Beware the *French*; The *houſe of Medişis*, to wit: of him alſo take heed in the yeare 1642: R: *ESSEX. ESSE REX*, or *Devorex* his firſt yeare of Taking, &c: *Daniel*, the 5. Chap.

A 2 *And*

And Darius *tooke the Kingdome, being sixty-two yeares &c: which was devided between them two* Da: *and* Cy:

Belchazer, as much to say: without Treasure, or a Searcher, &c:

THE *Caldeans*: The *Caledonians*, or *Scots*: *LONDON, BABYLON, DUBYLON*:

FIRST Printed at *Amsterdam*: 1633.

Aprill; 1643.

To the *Tune*, who list a Souldiers life
to Lead.

1 TO *Sion* most *belov'd* I sing,
of *Babylon* a Song; (*I wot*
Concerns *you* more: full well
then ye do thinke upon.
Belchazer Loe, behold the King
feasting his thousand Lords;
Phebus and *Mars*, praysd on each string
every day records.

2 The vessels of Gods house in *Them*,
boldly they drinke about:
'Tis like His owne were made away,
bids holy *Things* bring out.

A 3 Praysing

Praysing the Gods of gold and brasse,
of *Iron*, *Wood*, and *Stone*
VVhich heare nor see, Not out alas
in Court are *prays'd* alone.

3 A *Hand* appeared in his sight,
as he did drinke the *Wine*;
Vpon the *Wall* against the *Light*,
it *Wrote* about a *Line*.
Before his *Lords*, the *Image* like
of any gastly *Skull*;
In *knees* nor *loynes*, he had no might
not set an houre *full*.

4 In vaine to veiw, who could it read:
Belchazer he doth shout,
Cals for Magitians, in with speed
came in; as wise went out.
Caldeans and *Southsayers* sage,
this meaning he which can;
Of MENE, MENE, and so forth,
cloathed in *purple* the Man.

5 Thus

5 Thus now, when all at their wits end
 wise men, all those Lords too,
A woman Loe to her they come:
 to Learne what is to doe.
His Majestie forgets to Supp,
 Nobles astonish'd all:
Musitians may their Pipes put up,
 such gazing on the *Wall*.

6 *When* mildly came the gracefull *Queene*,
 where no small noyse did Ring:
Comes to the *Banqueting-house* so wide,
 said ever *live O King*.
Daniel he shall end this strife,
 brought with no little speed:
VVas by the King saluted thus,
 of *Thee* we stand in Need.

7 Excellent things have heard of thee,
 how in my fathers dayes:
Inspired by the holy gods,
 thy sayings truth alwayes.

when

VVhen vissions *divine* sent him,
of *future* things most high:
Then by thy *Skill* deliverst *Them*,
decreed which were to die.

8 Make known this *Thing*, then if *thou dost*
as fayled *Thou* hast never:
VVeare *gold* and *purple* too, tis *Thine*,
choyse Make of *whatsoever*.
For *Courtly* phrase, returned plaine,
Sir Keepe your gifts in store:
High *Offices* let others gaine,
too much ye *have* given before.

9 Yet to the *King* make known I shall,
and read the *Writing* true:
As sure as in thy Treasure house,
where all the world may veiw.
The vessels of my God are brought,
also as *I am one*,
Of the *Captivitie* that mourne,
in BABYLON so *Long*.

10 For

10 For *veſſels* which profand by *Thee*,
before the *End*: tis ſent
Not ignorant of all thoſe *Things*,
how payd *that* twelve-moneths Rent.
VVhich on thy *Grandſir* came to paſſe,
ſo careleſſe yet *for all*:
As if a *Feigned ſtory* but,
his miſerable fall.

11 *O King* even *Thou*, the moſt *high God*,
unto *Thy Grandſir* bold:
Caldean Land a Nation *fell*,
gave them to *have* and *hold*.
The *Royall Septer* and the *Crowne*,
advanc'd *whom hee* would *have*:
And *whom he* would, *he* pul'd downe
could put to *death* and *ſave*.

Nebu
Signi
a Gra
father,
a Fat
both.

12 But rays'd *himſelfe* above the *Starrs*,
Names *Not his god* at all:
Pride thus forgetfulneſſe begets;
Full Tydes *Loe have their* FALL.

Excellent Majeſtie *how* ſoone,
departed 'twas and gone :
As much to ſay, but Bruiteſh *where*
The End is unthought *On*.

13 Now whilſt *The Earth* bedew'd with
he Eates the *heye* which *growes* : (*teares*,
Bewayld of all dejected *Soule*,
Not knowes his *friends* from *foes*.
The Earth, who late made ſeem to daunce,
with Songs of *Triumph Loud* :
Then fleeth every wight as *faſt*,
among the Beaſts doth *Crowde*.

14 Nayles *His* over-grown *from head* to
and *Hayre* like hornes that ſtares : (*feete*
His *Scarfe* turnd to a chaine of Braſſe,
His lodgeing as *he* fares.
Of *Divels Legions* lead by them,
a Monarch made a Slave :
Till ſerved out his ſeven times,
for reſt in vaine to crave.

15 VValking

15 VValking in *pride*, depos'd at length,
driven from ſonns of men:
Frighted was at the twelve-moneths End,
taken in his vaunting *then*.
No feigned *Metamorphos'd* one,
as Memory knowing well:
After that *feaſt*, how ſoone expell'd,
the wilde *ASSE* with did *dwell*.

16 To ſchoole ſent to the *OXE* to learne,
that owner knowes of his:
Fowles alſo their appointed time,
more ſenſleſſe ſure *he* is.
That's mindleſſe *of the time to Come*,
and beating needeth more:
Wilfullneſſe brother of the foole,
then *bend*, will breake *before*.

17 *Woodes* all *for* woe, as well as Men
ring out, and *Echos call*:
For mercy on this *ſavage King*,
in *Holy Temples all*.

Who gave by Stare-light *for* device,
  A *Harte* in silver fielde :
An *Eagle* mounted on the *Crest*,
  graven upon His *Shield*.

18 Both depos'd thus ; *Thou knowest well* :
  Belchazer O his Sonne,
And of deliverance renownd so ;
  how to *his glory* turnd.
A day a Trumpet made to sound,
  To generations all :
Heavens hand solemnizd with a *feast*,
  that No *Time* might recall.

19 The memory of such an *Act*,
  yet as it had not been ;
Who are Thy *favourites* more this day ;
  or Matched to *thy* Kinn ?
Then those adoreing *Wood* and *Stone*,
  for Statutes most *divine* :
Meditate Carved statues on,
  in *faction* dost *Combine*.

20 with

20 VVith *Enemies* of *God* most *high*,
to thrust *Him from his Throne* :
And thus hast *lifted* up *thy selfe* ;
so *facile and so prone*.
Against the *Lord of heaven thy* King,
not hmubling *of thy heart* :
But stiffned hast *with Pride thy necke*,
unto thy *future smarte*.

21 Besides polluting *holy Things*,
with *Sabaths so divine* :
Idolatry and *Revels* in,
That *Day* and *Night* made thine:
But *he* in whose *hand* thy *Life* is,
thy *Breath*, and thy *Wayes* all :
Hast *Thou* not *glorified* Him,
hath sent *This on the Wall*.

22 Thy *Kingdome* GOD hath finished,
by *Proclamation* here ;
How light soever made thereof,
He that *sees farre and neere*.

Hath in the *Ballance* weighed *Thee*,
  and as Thy weightlesse *gold*;
Loe *thou* his Image wanting: found
  more light then can be told.

23 Devided *Thy* kingdome here given,
  unto the *Medesis*;
At hand no doubte The *Hand it shewes*,
  Darius partly *His*.
Standing devided like *Thy* minde,
  so *Mene Mene* then:
Bids *Thee beware the Judgement day*,
  at *Hand*, Amen, Amen.

24 His fathers *Sonne* wilde over-growne,
  as *Daniel* reprov'd his *Sinne*:
VVho might by no meanes moved be,
  glory to render *Him*.
Ignorance with; not to be Cloak'd,
  but *Prid and Malice high*:
So hast not Thou *Sir*, done just so,
  And finding it no *Lye*.

25 Of

25 Of *Mene Mene* to Thee ſent,
Even twiſe fullfil'd to bee:
The Hand pointing at Twenty-five,
Heavenly *Palmiſtry*.
Which Yeare reveald GODs *Dreadfull day*,
whoſe Hand-mayd for a Signe:
Our Troubles fore-told as come to paſſe,
how never ſuch a Time.

26 Then is not He *Belchazer* right,
when all, and more then all;
Which could be thought, though fulfil'd ſince,
Mindleſſe on GOD to Call.
The Faithleſſe *Steward* rather then,
Michael who's like GOD: *Dan. 12.*
Become like one of us This Man,
ſhall cauſe Him *Kiſſe* the RODD.

27 When Death for one as tis no leſſe,
by Statute Law of Late:
To have two Wifes at once, yet thine
owne Caſe or preſent State.
What is it but to ſay the Truth?
the *Beame* doth not Eſpie;
Rather to be plucked out Then,
a Mote in others Eie.

28 Which

28 Which Hand as here betokn's a Blowe,
The *Ballance* who knowes not:
Cruelty and Injuſtice ſhew,
SIR AMEND *You* know what.
And ſo goe Little Booke to bee,
Sung as a *pleaſant Song*:
The *Times* at hand, another Note
Great Brittaine ſings ere Long.

29 Drunkards alſo, Here's to You,
beware the Trumpets Call:
For from *Pride* yours, and ſurfeiting,
proceeds our Troubles all.
Praying down with your *Twelfe-tyde-Shews*,
Stage-Playes and Foolery then,
Leſt in a Moment chang'd as *He*,
Turn'd into Divels from MEN.

30 So Cruelty and Pride farwell,
That great *Aſſyrians* fall:
Who meant at once to put to Death,
his wiſe Men even All,
Neither regards His *GOD* nor Man,
driven out as thoſe that *Braye*:
The *DIADEM* as well fitts Thee,
GOE *ASSE*, as much to ſay.

DANIEL: *J* End ALL.

5. *The Star to the Wise* (1643; Wing D2013) is reprinted, by permission of the Folger Shakespeare Library, from the copy held at the Folger (shelfmark D2013 bd. w. D2010). The text block of the original measures 140 × 95 mm.

Hard-to-read words:

4.2	*I Iesus have sent my Angel.*
4.15	*Adam*
4.16	Brim-
4.25	(The shortnesse
5.7	clouds, who rewards every one according to
5.10–15	That after the House swept and garnished, with *seven* foul spirits that goeth and berayeth it. And afar off, as in the one bewrayed, how long the preaching to last of Baptisme, as not in alluding to those dayes; By *sevens* when every clean, &c. entred into the Ark, By
5.17–23	end worse then his beginning. So he expresly speaks in another place of the worlds begining and end, to know one by another: *As the dayes of Noah were, so shall the son of mans dayes be also*; As the dayes before the Flood, One thousand seven hundred yeers; as much to say, To both alotted alike.
8.2–4	Likewise revealed the second coming of our Lord, when that time comes to passe:
8.8–18	and He who mockd with God, faining He would worship him, was himself mockd; after they made of his Counsell, having sent them to *Bethlehem*, &c. in revenge fell upon poor Innocents, under such an age spared none; who to that Fox returnd not any more, but went another way, supposing before their God they should have obeyed him: Whose Treasure then they said is at his feet; given as it were to the Churches use; made their Omage there.
14.6	unluckey,
14.22–3	Elector Palsegrave *Dedicated upon the letters of his name* The palme of the Hand,
15.1–7	Charles Be. *for* Belshazer: *hidden beware the Hands of the* Medesis: *and he being after so imprisoned in* France. *With the premises referred to the worlds judgement: What mould* Pharaohs *heart made of, whether the Handwriting hath not been fullfilled and double, Brittains Blowe.*
15.9–22	when praying it were to do again, give him for his doings, of that Sop his belly full till his Bowels gush out with that arch Traytor his fellow *Iudas*, Let the Executioner be without his fees no longer; his Gown and Girdle, Win it and wear it, who hath drawn this Curse upon us: and for whose cause (with those companions of his) these fleeing the very place where they sat: here repair to the Second House for this Licence for the Lambe and the Bride. She having made her self ready, like *Ioseph* and *Mary*, but betroathed as yet, this pair: So the other House of Parliament: Our Saviours second Coming assigned to them, to give Order for this his
19.1	after-
19.16	presaging
19.17	*Englefield* neer *Reading-*
20.11	*Where Lord shall thy Coming be revealed*
20.15	That Fast of the Lambe.
20.18	girt with a Letherne girdle coming before him,

The Star to the VVise. 13

1 6 4 3.

To the high Court of Parliament,
THE HONORABLE
HOVSE of *COMMONS*:
THE
Lady *ELEANOR* her Petition;
Shewing cause to have her Book Licensed,
BEING
The Revelations *Interpretation*.

MALACHY 4. 2.
For unto you who fear my Name, shall the Sun of Righteousnesse arise with healing in his wings.

LONDON: Printed in the yeer, 1643.

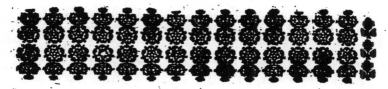

The Star to the wiſe.

To the High Court of Parliament, The Honorable Houſe of Commons;

The Lady Eleanor *her Petition, &c.*

HAppy Reader and Hearer; for ſo he who reads, and keeps the words of this laſt Prophecy, revealed to be at laſt: The Revelations ſhewing Things which ſhall ſhortly come to paſſe: And as the golden leaves of that fruitfull Tree, ſhewed to be for the healing of the Nations, *Their Bleſſed Peace-maker*, ſaying, *And there ſhall be no more curſe*: So the whole Prophecy directed unto our Nation, provided for theſe dayes of ours; That Soveraign Plaiſter, vvhen ſuch unnaturall Diviſion, ſowed by the old Serpent; The very foul

A 2 Diſeaſe

Diſeaſe of the *Kings-Evil*, &c. ſaying therefore, *I Jeſus have ſent my Angel*. And ſo, touching Malignant humors, for the moſt part reſorting about the Ears, in which parts, not a little dangerous; wherefore, *He that hath Ears to hear, let him hear*; being the burthen of every charge, to the Churches, concluded therewith; proclaiming his coming to be ſhewed aforehand to his ſervants, ſaying, *I am Alpha and Omega, the firſt and the laſt*; The Lord of Sabbath, as evident, by holding the *ſeven* ſtars in his right hand; and That Book ſealed with *ſeven* Seals, like *Pharaohs* Dream doubled, even the eſtabliſhed time; and ſo many dayes as from the *firſt Adam* to the flood of waters; ſo from the *ſecond Adam* to the fiery Lake, That flood of Fire and Brimſtone; And therefore the ſecond Death ſo called.

And as that Token ſet in the clouds: The ſtreighened Bow that bound himſelf thereby, ſo here crowned with the Bow; bindes it with an Oath, *By him that lives for ever, That Time ſhall be no longer*. But as the ſeventeenth hundred yeer revealed to *Noah*, ſhews Times myſtery contained in that little open Book; (The ſhortneſſe of Time) alſo revealed to be before the end:

Even

Even the days of Baptisme, likewise how long preached, to such disobedient spirits, as farther by *his right foot on the waters*, and *his left on the earth*: The times measured, the first *Noahs* dayes, by the second *Noahs* dayes: to wit, in the seventeenth Century, his coming in the clouds, who rewards every one according to his service, For the name of a Christian serves not, But his end worse then his beginning. That after the House swept and garnished, with *seven* foul spirits that goeth and bewrayeth it. And afar off, as in the one bewrayed, how long the preaching to last of Baptisme, as herein alluding to those dayes, By *sevens* when every clean, &c. entred into the *Ark*. By the unclean *seven* spirits entred into him, whose end worse then his beginning. So he expresly speaks in another place of the worlds begining and end, to know one by another: *As the dayes of Noah were, so shall the son of mans dayes be also*; As the dayes before the Flood, One thousand seven hundred yeers, as much to say, To both alotted alike. And so in *Luke* the Eleventh, a touch given going afore, for better discerning the time, when they said, *He by the Devil cast out Devils*. Much like now, as to beleeve that an army

army of another Religion should come to defend the true Religion. Where the end of Antichrists Kingdom, shewed also further, By such a King, as it were against himself divided; or a man possest, that goes about to make away himself.

And had the old world warning; and are the last dayes cast out of remembrance; and is his Promise come utterly to an end? Though saying, *Ye shall not see me, till ye say, Blessed is he that comes in the Name of the Lord.* And behold, *I will send you Elias before the great and dreadfull day*; as *Eli* signifying the Name of God, &c.

And so much for those dayes, when the sons of God took them wives of the Daughters of men, taken with their Sorceries.

And this yet held a sencelesse thing, or a fancie to expect it: Though I shewed, even thus it shall be when the son of man shall be revealed, (*Luke* 17) like giving in marriage, and revelling: And with such Buildings and Plantations &c. a fair warning to prepare for it.

And cursed *Iericho* that burnt with fire *seven* dayes, or a weeks warning that had, where *Rahab* saved her Fathers house there, by a Line for token, &c. And was the hand-writing at that Feast,

Feaſt, ſent to him, He of that firſt Monarchy, the laſt of them, who was weighed in the Ballance, &c. and found a loſt Body, &c. And by reading the Prophet *Ieremiahs* Books: He that underſtood then the number of thoſe yeers, that *seventy* yeers ſhould be accompliſhed in *Ierusalems* deſolation: Wherefore not by reading now of that Book, where bidden, *Let him that hath underſtanding, count the number of the Beaſt, 666.* &c. To underſtand alſo, how long the Churches captivity under ſpirituall *Babylon*: The Antichriſtian Monarchy, and aged now 43. and 1600. Even as, ſignified in his *ſeven* heads; and Ten horns, thoſe crowned: his age, So in her whores forehead, written too that Name of hers: Not of the bleſſed Virgins giving, of a certain; and ſo much for that. He ridden, and ruled ſo long by her, no longer to be indured: and which great Harlots City, not unknown. Beginning here, with the everlaſting Goſpel, ſhewing, as coming to paſſe in *Auguſtus* his Taxin dayes, there ſending forth his Decrees to have all the world Taxt. That ſecond *Cæſar*, when he the ſecond perſon in Trinity, came to pay the Ranſome of all; Alſo in his Raign, thoſe Taxing dayes of his, Not over the world unknown: Theſe Burthens

never

never so imposed, before He the second of *Great Britains Monarchy*. Likewise revealed the second coming of our Lord, when that time comes to passe: *And good will towards Men; Peace on Earth.*

So farther with That past, comparing This troublesome time: When all the city so troubled, and He who mockd with God, faining He would worship him, was himself mocked; after they made of his Counsell, having sent them to *Bethlehem*, &c. in revenge fell upon poor Innocents, under such an age spared none; who to that Fox returnd not any more, but went another way, supposing before their God they should have obeyed him: Whose Treasure then they laid it at his feet; given as it were to the Churches use; made their Omage there.

And in city and country, early and late, such keeping watch by day and night both, to keep out wolves inwardly, those late Bishops; as when the watchfull Shepherds visited, and were told where they should finde *The Lamb of God*: And the Churches watchmen likewise assembled. Wherefore as Thou *Bethlehem*, not the least, so inferior to none of *Great Britains* Villages;

Villages, Thou KNIGHTS-BRIDGE by Name; for such service of thine, found worthy to afford such a Plaister, *To the Honorable* KNIGHTS and BURGESSES in the Commons House, which was delivered by their worthy Speaker; Being made of the root of *Jesse* and pure Oyl-olive, & from the Hospitall of the diseased and dismembred, not distant far, doubtlesse remembred all those maimed in Gods service and slain, in preferring This place, made the receptacle of His Sacred Oracle, that oyntment.

Where the *Spittle* and the *Bridge*, in those Letters signified, *the Spirit and the Bride*; & as *Bethlehem*, *The House of Bread*, signifying, &c. so, *Let him that is athirst, come*: for here, *The wedding of the Lamb, The off-spring of David*; Even as the inseparable Witnesses in the Sacrament: Those places where the Word of God resides, like the Bread & Cup.

And thou *Hide-Park*, none of the greatest, yet makes up the Harmony, b. ore the wedding all rejoycing; The trees of the Wood also utter their ayrie voice, where the Court of Guards service weil worth the marking and observation; those Bulwarks there so watcht round about; and here to proceed with the everlasting Word of God; there the flaming sword also; the Tree of Life

B guarded

guarded thereby, which turns every way on the East of it; and as it were the Cherubims returnd, displaying in the air their golden wings, those Colours of theirs; like as the Man, when droven out to till the ground from whence he was taken; and so the *Thorn*, and the *Thistle*, and *Herb* of the Field, his portion with his Wife, sent away in their Buff-coats and skins, to take their progresse.

In vain neither those Pales pluckt up, laid open that Inclosure; for every one to make their Fuell of it: But the fore-runner of the little Books disclosing, the day of Judgements time discovered, Times race or finishd, &c. and so of those inlarged Horns of the *seven*-headed Beast, ranging without meane or measure, crownd with so many Crowns, *The mystery of Time there but sets forth.*

And *Britain* derived from *Brute*, having the *Beasts Name* as it were, and left the good angels, nothing ever since *Prospering* or *Thriving*; shewing also how He to *Oxford* now droven to go, a Prototype or figure of Time, sealed in his very brows or forehead, being aged 43. And thus as he participates of Times age like it. So tyrant Time to be no longer; but in the seventeenth hundred yeer cut off; a copartner with him, of his Estate also and Condition, which in the seventeenth yeer

was

was expelled of his Raigne forborn so long.

And thus, as the way shewed where keeps now the Tree of Life; so farthermore of what nature it is; a Tree hard and stony, the Fruit not to be medled with, or toucht at first; though none more mellow and soft then it afterward; and because of a restraining vertue, its good Name taken away, like the Medlars crowned fruit miscalled.

And so another place belonging to the city, in these dayes of such distraction, worthy to be thought upon, *Bethlehems* Hospitall, *Their House of Bread*; for the witlesse sent to This, as the Wise-men to the other, those Sages, &c. in some respects to That not inferior, where some Barn or the like, made the Bed-chamber of the blessed Lady; and He there born, our Bread from heaven, and for a signe given the Shepherds, of his racking on the crosse, that was put into the Rack or Manger; and by a Woman aforehand anointed; and other like signes and tokens.

Whether these betoken nothing too, appeal to the wisdom of our age; or to be such an unlikely thing; that he who wrote that brotherly Epistle (going before the *Apocalypse*) to a Lady, saying, *He had many things to write unto her*. Whatsoever it was which appears not there, but referred to another

B 2 time

time or meeting; That from another Lady, *The Revelations Interpretation* of her writing, should be sent to Divines for their assent to the same, written by that Divine, &c. where such a meeting of theirs, in a time of so much distraction of the Church.

Where touching or importing an inspiration; what phrase of speech more meet and proper, then that of, *Mouth to Mouth*; *That our joy may be full?* for a full expression of our Lords coming to be revealed to a woman; That secret disclosed.

And *the wind blowing where it lists*; wherefore not serving to bring these about from the Isle of *Patmos*, to *Great Britains* Islands, when testified he cometh, he cometh. The Islands may be glad thereof, &c. *Psal.* especially at such a time of perplexity and woe; and for the redemption of wounded prisoners too, so miserably relieved, and others for their hurts and maims, disabled ever to help themselves.

Wherefore then not to be revealed to us, before others in such case: and assoon to his handmaids as his menservants; the spirit of God to be poured on them: and so now, as well as then, when she had the first happy sight of him, after his rising, which was sent to tell and inform them

where

where they should meet him *first*: and what odds between *seven* Churches visited, or sent unto; and *Henry* the seventhś Chappell, in such a Church: and in the seventeenth hundred yeer of Grace; where the *Assembly of Ministers*, &c. sitting in that place, dedicated or consecrated to his memory; whose sons Royall Issue so soon reedified or reformed the Church so much gone to decay; renewed in such a short space of Time, The Scriptures buried in another Language, Life not only infused into them; but sent forth as far West, as even East in former dayes.

And now in the West, to us since this thing to be revealled, (the Misterie of the Lord of Sabbaths Coming) wherefore to *Westminster*, Not directed too: where the Kingdoms Great Counsell meeting shewed there where they shall meet *Him* coming in the Clouds.

And of late the Red Rose and the White also, By the scriptures that were delivered out of thraldom, how soon reconciled; being disunited before: The *Bread and Cup in the Lords Supper* reunited, having been judgled away By the old Serpents policie, becavse bidden to divide it, The Cup amongst them, as other allowance have none for it. So begins with the one first, intending not to forbear

the

the other long: *Eves* Daughters moved for their sake, layes hold of the fruitfull Uine, whose Embleme, those Branches to keep within their own walls: or because the Spirit *first* moved upon the waters, And he in hold now himself the very Antichristian Serpent, by whose crooked unluc ey, hands kindled this Kingdoms cruell Combustion again: shewed how Gods word *first*, even that burnt by him, together with the revealed last coming: the Handwriting applied to this Nation, being Sealed therewith, that Seal Manual. To *Belshazzar* that was sent heretofore. And now whether his Kingdoms: He which was so much incensed hereat, be Divided and Numbred, or he absent and found wanting, or this be proued a false alarme sent to him, who tatken With *Belshazers* loosenesse, the occasion of this befalne him: as for more proof of it, Moreover, &c.

Moreover of the Holy Oracle, that Handwrighting *reinterpreted by her for an express signe, Which in the yeer* 1633 *was to the* Elector Palsegrave *Dedicated upon the letters of his name.* The palme of the Hand, &c.

&c. Charles Bo : *for* Belshazer : *sudden beware the Hands of the* Medesis : *and he being after so imprisoned in* France. *With the premises referred to the worlds judgement: What would Pharaohs heart made of, whether the Handwriting hath not been fullfilled and double, Brittains Blowe,*

And as of late came to passe these ; So let his repentance come to late, when praying it were to do again, give him for his doings, of that Sop his belly full, till his Bowels gush out with that arch Traytor his fellow *Iudas*, Let the Executioner be without his fees no longer: his Gown and Girdle, Win it and wear it, who hath drawn this Curse upon us : and for whose cause (with those companions of his) these fleeing the very place where they sat : here repair to the Second House for this Licence for the Lambe and the Bride, She having made her self ready, like *Ioseph* and *Mary*, but betroathed as yet, this pair : So the other House of Parliament : Our Saviours second Coming assigned to them, to give Order for this his Licence, In due consideration of a Sihne, or the twelve Signes given rather for a token, as not unknown to both houses, &c. Which was delivered to their Speaker (taken out of the Revelation, Chap. 12.) *And there appeared a great signe in Heaven; a woman Clothed with the Sun and the Moon under her feet: And upon her head a Crown of twelve Stars.* Interpreted this way: The *Celestiall Woman* clothed with the Sun, to wit, the Suns entring in *Virgo*, the bowels and belly: Shewing the time of the Churches great deliverance, about Michaelmas to give her enemies for ever the overthrowe: as signified by *Michaels* victory and the Dragons fall, and which piece of Scripture thus expounded, be presented to them in the moneth of August. Not unlike that of *Ionas* in the *Whales* belly, that signe of the *Resurrection* then as this now of the *generall time* at hand.

And thus his Eexcellencie here, the Generall for the House of Parliamets defence, as that Archangel signifying Ezcellent to omong the Angels, and by War in heaven. The Division of tha high Cout set forth vvhere Saint *Iohn* ascends a degre higher then the Prophet *Daniel* speaking likevvise of the troubled time of the end: Thus, *And they that turn many* to Righteousnesse *shall shine as the Stars in the Firmament*, the *Parliaments* signification,

nification, *The Firmament* firm for ever: as much to ſay, To ſit there, fixt, &c. as they, *Daniel* and *Iohn*, joyned in Commiſsion for theſe dayes.

And ſo the day of Judgements Epitomy, This Battell here in heaven amongſt us here before his coming, that teſtifies he rewards every one according to his work; as they have done by others, even ſerved with the ſame themſelves; Their *toes pared too*, taken lower.

And ſhall our loins be girt, and lights burning to prevent bodily danger, ſo much preparation: And ſhall all be in ſuch ſecurity, when that dreadfull time, and no ſigne at all then on the poſts of our doors: But the deſtroyer coming into houſes of his ſervants alſo: When as the Devils ſtorming, becauſe he knows he hath but a ſhort time, ſhews expreſly the time is to be foreknown.

And the Nations angry for that time of wrath come; The time of the dead to be judged, (*Rev.* 11) ſhews the Churches Intelligence aforehand of that time; far be it from us to be like the deaf Adder, That becauſe once accurſed for harkning when forbidden. Therefore to forbear, charm the Word of God never ſo ſtrongly and ſweet; like the blinde Jews under colour of ſhunning

C Idola-

Idolatry, and the like, that fell to be ſuch Blaſphemers of God.

Preaching ye have alway, and may hear them when ye pleaſe, and their large Dedicatories and Volumns may Licenſe them daily: But the little Book, The Spirit of Propheſie, Not alway that.

And laſtly, here for teſtifying the burthen of the Word of the Lord revealed to her, by ſo many voices with one conſent, ſhewed as follows; touching this Firſtling the Word of God, where and when the ſame came to her: In the *firſt* yeer of his Raign, when His firſt Parliament called at *Oxford*. Whether he now returnd; a great voice from Heaven then, ſpeaking to her, revealing in what yeer the day of Judgement; and ſo at what time of the yeer, or how long that time; ſhe the Daughter of the *firſt* Peer or Baron, her *firſt* Husband the Kings *firſt* Sergeant, &c.

And in *Berkſhire*, the firſt of Shires at her houſe at *Englefield*, about the end of July which moneth, named after the *firſt* Emperou, heard the voice of God there.

And for publiſhing the ſame, from thence went immediatly to *Oxford*, that *firſt* Univerſity; To the Parliament then delivering the tydings of the end revealed, &c. in a Writing given to the prime

Biſhop

Bishop *Abots*; which being printed, was afterward burnt by his Successour in his *first* yeer, 1633. whose Passe given him before, &c. and with this Signe annext to it, That the great Plague presently should cease, which came but to its height the next Week after.

And so came to passe, after that Weeks great Bill, which amounted to Five thousand six hundred or neer, being the *first* Week of *August*, 1625. as it were the Worlds age, The mysticall Weeks reckoning.

And then so suddenly vanished, that before a Moneths end, or thereabout, scarse any token or appearance thereof, the City so long shut up, open again in a manner cleen.

Thus from that presaging place or Name of *Englands* bloody Field: *Englefield* neer *Reading*-Town, where the Term kept, that remarkable yeer, for so many Examples of Extraordinaries produced.

And

AND now where the day of Judgement, the great Day of Battels approach (as hath hin declared) was proclaimed,&c. There in those two very Shires, of Berkshire or Birchshire) and in Oxfordshire. What we have not so much as heard the half of, others have by wofull experience felt the waight of it. Where two such Bodies of Armies so large, Whose last Blow, after that cruell Fight, was within a bowe-shot of the afore-said House of *Engle-field*: at Theill village: and these belonging to this place of Scripture, wherefore worthy of notice, Luke the 17. *Where Lord shall thy Coming be revealed*:) when replyed, *Where the bodie is, the Eagles will resort.* As Gods Word without a high and heavy hand never digested, or obtaining passage, but like the Passeover, ever eaten with bitter Herbes, That Fast of the Lambe.

The Raven is sent forth before the Dove, likewise before him: That same that had his raiment of Camels hair, girt with a Letherne girdle coming before him, in whose Coat, not so much as a seam. And Here the still, or soft voice sent with everlasting peace, the last, before the good time bring the true Olive Leaf.

POSTSCRIPT. Revel.ii.

And here The Cup none debard of it: He that is athirst Let him Come, &c.

Knights-Bridge, November. 1643.

6. *The Restitvtion Of Reprobates* (1644; Wing D2008) is reprinted, by permission of the Folger Shakespeare Library, from the copy held at the Folger (shelfmark D2008 bd. w. D2010). This copy contains some handwritten notes and corrections that may be in Lady Eleanor's hand. The text block of the original measures 140 × 91 mm. The following pages are misnumbered (and the correct number is shown in square brackets): 16 [9], 8 [16], (01) [17], 11 [20], 15 [21], 14 [24].

Hard-to-read handwritten annotations and printed words:

Title page	[top] Countess of Castlehaven present [transcription]
	[bottom] Corrected [transcription]

8.15	And then as
11.2	And then as
11.5	not [transcription]
12.2	with these
14.5	that [transcription]
15.20	SO [transcription]
[16].13	SO over [transcription]
[17].6	sentenced to such utter
[17].7	though he knowes his
[17].13	so many times gon over *him, was* resto-
[17].14	as
18.1	some of [transcription]
19.5	as *amazed* or
19.7	Leaveing
19.8	comming forth,
19.11	*deridings and*
19.13	And like a *graine of mustardseed*
[20].1–2	Vagabone fugitive people ever since, *Having circumcisions marke.*
[20].16	And *Eloi Eloi*, as one forsaken &c.
[20].18–19	truly (to wit) *Yee shall not see me till yee say, Blessed is he that come in the Name*
[21].9	As [transcription]
[24].15–20	Our first parent *not being* letted or hindred of *the tree of Knowledge*, because so requisit to let them know themselves, thought *Satan* never the more to be excused in the discovery of their naked estate.
25.12	in respect of the
25.15–17	those called perpetuall Statutes afterward abolished. And so all fulfilled
25.18	And thus like that *Cloudy robe*; these [transcription]
26:18	to be [transcription]
26.18–19	Her's one reserv'd for ELIAS coming: *As* [transcription]
27.1	be as [transcription]
[30]	original page number obscured, should be 30.
30.12	deepe; where [transcription]
33.12	churl [transcription]
35.4	foreseen
35.5	from
35.12	Iudgements
35.13	and
35.14	increase
35.15	*Charitas*

End paper, 6–8: last three handwritten lines appear to be as follows: forerunners of peace/*&c.*/ Pax [transcription]

For ye countess of Castle Haven
present

THE RESTITVTION OF REPROBATES.

Malac: 3.

Behold I will send my messenger, &c.

Printed in the Yeare, 1644.

A
GENERALL PARDON
for Reprobate *Rebels*, all of them:
Their *restitution*, as authoriz'd & affirm'd;

Math. 18. *ELIAS truly shall first come and restore all things.*

AND before the great and dreadfull *day* of the *Lords* comming: VVhen sent that *Prophet* which for a *signe* of it, foreshewing what *Plagues* with; *He will smite them*, and truly never greater knowne, then at this very

A 2 time

time: So take this into consideration, as *probable* as other things, before they *come to passe*; For *Mercy*, and *Judgements* going together, *in these last dayes reveal'd.*

The time being come *of the end then* and no more occasion to continue threatning any longer, *and terrifyings* against wickednesse amongst *VS* here raignning, with that prohibited old proverbe out of date: *The fathers have eaten sower grapes, and the childrens teeth set an edge.* Shall cansell that oppinion of old, of Hell to be a place or prison without redemption, as it stands not in truth well with *Equitie*, where *mercy* is so *unmeasurable* for the offence of our first deceived parents; *Who knew not what they did:* That for their *cause*, so many without compassion, and commismisseration, utterly should be *undon* & *cast away*, whereas *SODOM* for so few, their sakes had beene spair'd when *prest*, shall not the Judge of all the world doe right ?

But, for this redemption of *theirs* ; however seeming a thing of *impossibilitie* : Yet *nothing unpossible with GOD*, *or too hard for him in his time.*

Take, and receive these misticall words to your *comfort* all of you : saying; *Whosoever shall speake a word against the sonne of man, it shall be forgiven: But blasphemeing against the Holy-Ghost, neither in this world, nor the world to come shall be forgiven.*

But shall be in danger of eternall Hell-fire : To wit, though punishment inevitable, yet the *perpetuitie* in suspence ;

A 3 as

as by the word *DANGER*, given to underſtand.

And *furthermore,* as given under the ſame hand for their *releaſe* or *new pardon* ſeal'd here with this ſaying alſo. *Yee have heard it ſaid of old time, Whoſoever ſhall kill, ſhall be in danger of a judgement. But I ſay unto you, whoſoever is angry with his brother without a cauſe, ſhall be in danger of a judgement: And whoſoever ſhall ſay to his brother Racha, ſhall be in danger of a counſell. And whoſoever ſhall ſay Foole, ſhall be in danger of Hell fire.* Whereby as here posſible ſometimes for old ſayings to be *diſanul'd* and *revok'd*, ſo the day of *judgements very caſe*, how reviled and menaced the tidings, with a great *councell or high court*, faireing both alike, foreſhew-ſhewed likewiſe *reproachfully* ſtiled by their *Enemies*, in this moſt ſtrick and ſevere *Sermon*, handled, *or* ſet forth *upon the Mountaine, &c.* concluded with *mercy* being ſhewed ;· Neverthelesse, appointed for *Reprobates, and Rebells both.*

Etſi ſalutaveritis fratres veſtros tantum quid amplius facitis & ethnici hoc faciunt, &c. Even their charge, as by the miſticall name *Racha* expreſt, how brethren miſſecalling one another, as it were high *treaſon*, and *blaſphemy* no leſſe.

And here *beati pauperis, beati mites, &c.* with *GOD* in ſuch eſteéme, the diſpiſed by the world, and they on the other ſide receiving their *conſolation* here, ſuch an impoſſibilitie for them to *eſcape torment, as for an Elephant*, or *Camell,*

mell, to goe through the Eye of an needle : Then the least *of his words*, not lightly to be set by so needfull, where such may be proud, to be the *least* in that *Kingdome* or *Court*, any *doore keeper* or the like : VVhose word gives light in this darknesse, for that *gulfe* between *U S* and them, to be a passage to *Life* through those straits, &c. *As bee able to bind and loose*, and so with *Paul* able to say ; *Sirs, be of good cheere, for G O D is as good ever as His* word, yee are but *in jeopardie of eternall Hell-fire*.

And th[illegible]as no light in many dayes apppeared, then in his dangerous *voyage and sayling slowly*, even like those *prisoners*, though in so much danger, yet escaped *drownding* and *killing*, both

(*Acts*)

(*Acts*) so in that hopelesse estate of theirs whose Anchors as it were *cut off*, for that *capitall offence*, the *sin against the Holy Ghost*, tis possible with GOD to pardon it, to release them of those chains seeming endlesse.

So againe, this for another, *Verily I say unto thee, thou shalt by no meanes come forth thence untill paid the uttermost farthing.* The veritie of which place of *Scripture* : So wrested for *Purgatory*, those fictions founded or laid thereon overthrowing that principle. *Who shall lay any thing to the charge of Gods elect?* Therefore no other way but this to overthrow that ; as in truth concerning utter darkenesse intended the utmost *mite* paid to be there : and not extended in that grosse manner, for

B *these*

these soules justified by G O D : To make Marchandise of them; cryed up and down, and sold as *Romes* Kitchin-stuffe, &c.

And thus farre for clearring that mistake of *utter darknesse*, taken for that third *place*. So here shall not passe over, his *being taken up into the third heaven* : there heareing things not lawfull to be utterd, that Apostle made of G O D S counsell. Beside the *Resurrections* mistery shewed him, even this very Thing, heard the same, as most probable of *Reprobation* and *Election*. The dispute whereof prohibited : VVith *what art thou O man, made of clay, to question thy Maker, Quid me fecisti sic*? And so a thing of too high a *Nature* then to be publi-

publiſh'd, reſerv'd for the worlds laſt time: And *whereas duſt thou art,* and to *duſt diſolv'd*; Likewiſe all reduced to their firſt eſtate, as all things very good in the beginning, therefore *returne and live, &c.* and in a day the *world made,* no more *times without* their determined *Bounds and precincts*, all things at once manifeſted, neither the very *Diſciples* forbears to ſatisfie them in ſome *caſes.* Saying, *He had many things to ſay unto them,* which they could not beare at that time: *That in his Fathers Houſe were many Manſions,* (to witt) *privie Chambers and Cloſits* and the like, how officious ſo ever they were to be informed, as that for one. VVhen the time of reſtoreing againe the Kingdome to *Iſarell, Acts* 1 Chap.

And although their laſt ſuite yet put *backe* as it were wit[illegible]e, *Yee know not of what ſpirit yee be,* In taking *ELIAS* office upon you: Or tis *not for you to know times and ſeaſons which the father hath put in his own power. But the power of the Holy Ghoſt ſhall come upon you.* Linguæ tanquam ignis, ſuper ſingulos, &c.

And againe requeſted another time to know what ſhould be the ſigne of his ſecond comming, were put off with thoſe unwellcome tokens, &c. bidden to watch, becauſe the day and houre unknown, a reſerved *point*; and yet nothing *cover'd, which ſhall not be reveal'd*, as much to ſay, the *Apocalyps* or *Revelation*, that ſevenfold ſealed Booke which no man *could ſo much as*

looke

looke upon, &c. And his ſealed Commiſsion he bidden goe thy way *Daniel* for the words till the end are cloſed up, &c. even how long twas to end, which he longed ſo to underſtand.

And ſo ſtill preſt, *Lord are there many that ſhall be ſaved,* are commanded to ſtrive themſelves *to enter at the ſtraite gate,* ſent as it were to *Noahs* Cabin doore; when ſaved thoſe few ſoules, a *cold comfort,* had it not included the miſtery of *Noahs* time, the Goſpells progreſſe paraleld by thoſe dayes before the flood ſhortned alſo or cut off, came ſhort of 2000. yeares *&c.*

And thus for thoſe hungry ſoules, craving the leaſt crumbe or drop of mercy falling from our table, have gathered up theſe multiplied fragments

A 3 for

for them, *whose multitude as the sand of the sea* : *GOG* and *MAGOG*, shewing His unlimitted plentifull Redemption.

And that in no wise, *So much as a tittle of these blessed words to be lost, or cast away, &c. Blessed is he that hath his part in the first Resurrection, for on such the second death hath no power.* Inferring for all such having bin partakers of the second death, to have a second resurrection : *Therfore return and live, for as I live I have no pleasure in the death of the wicked*, saith *the Lord* : Ezekiel, &c. *for all soules are mine, &c.* So Satans being bound a Thousand yeeres, even seales a *finite* or *fixt* time, including beside *Hell* in the *last dayes*, (as it were) broken loose, also the generall delivery or loosing of the damned at last.

For

For above reach, *as his Mercy exceeds in height, ſo his Judgements in depth*, difficult to ſearch into them. Let this *ſuffice* therefore, from *Lazarus* finger ſo much, though *much* more the Scripture affords, for *Iſhmaels* comfort & his brethren, *of the Concubine: and thus as when God opened her eies and ſhe ſaw a ſpring, Gen. &c.* The *free womans ſonne being* none of *them*, ſtands in no need of the *water of life with them*.

But *theſe* their *portion falne from* the table of *Abraham, Iſaac, and Jacob*, ſitting in the *Kingdome of Heaven, reſerv'd for thoſe very Hell-hounds of Cerberus; rathter then Abrahams ſeed*: Although calls *Him*, Sonne; *remember that THOV in thy Life time, &c.*

SO here one *drop more, falne from*

that

that Sopp given Him, that Arch-Blood-Sucker *Judas*, though ſpeaking on this wiſe, Good had it been *for that had he never been borne.* Yet *H E E* having *a being before his birth*, is not *depriv'd of* that eſtate, though *borne Never.* Therefore not *diſinherited utterly but* in ſtate of *Salvàtion*, neverthéleſſe at laſt, *for whoſe* too late *Repentance, Hell of old prepared for Him, where a Million of times Not too many for ſuch, &c.*

SO thus *over for them, whoſe dolefull language of deſperation, that* good man *whoſe* name was *Iob*, ſeemes to *borrow* and *reſtor'd alſo* : Saying, *Shall we receive good from the hand of the Lord, and ſhall we not receive evill? Borne* under *the* ſame planit, as it were *with them*

or

or very sencible *of their* estate, *powrs forth* like ample, *execrations* upon the day and houre *of* his *Nativitie*, *that dismale day*, all the maledictions under the Sunne imposed *thereon, like the day of Judgement, sentenced to such utter darknesse* : testifies, *though he knowes his Redeemer lives*, and saying : *Therefore have I uttered that which I understand not*, Things *too wonderfull for me, which I knew not*. (Job 42.) And *Nebuchadnezar his* excellent Maiestie ? That after so many times gon over *him, was* restored, come to be himselfe in the end, as he had come out of Hell *in their slavish Condition, and as the day of Judgements Alarme hadbeene affrighted so, that was driven away*, &c:

And thus his wayes equale, as this
C most

most *proper* to be done by ~~that~~ Some of *Sex*: a VVoman being the occasion of the worlds woe and undoeing: *Therefore this PLAISTER or PARDON* by a *Womans hand*; shewing after condigne punishment, *the reward of sin, He the propitiation of the whole world*, and not the *Elects only*, saying: *Father forgive them they know not what they doe*, as proclamed on the crosse, *that last Petition or prayer of his*. And if they forgiven, the *Actors* and *Authors* of that most horrid *crime*, and abominable *blasphemy*; of all others that could plead *ignorance* least: His *Brethren the Iewes for so many goodturnes, such ungratfullnesse returning*, doubtlesse others *of seventy times seven forgivenesse* better worthy, *then they of seven times*.

But

But the light, *an evill sight overcomming: so he their stumbling Blocke became a rocke of offence.* This stocke blinde, and stuborne harted the world by *Nature*: though that day *as amazed* or *ashamed*, borrows the nights vayle, and departed Ghosts restlesse, Leaving *their graves below*, and comming forth, yet know not what they have done to this day: VVhen *Cains murthering his only brother, and Ishmaels deridings and the like*, But as a *gnate* to a *Camel or Elephant*: And like a *graine of mustardseed with a Mountaine* weigh'd, or to be compar'd.

VVhose figure or prototype *accursed Caine* sent forth, *banished from the presence of G O D saying, his punishment was greater then could be borne*, like those

Vagabond fugitive people ever since, *Having circumcisions marke*. And thus their *Pardon* folded up first in HIS: That *by the LORD had a* Marke *set upon him* also:

And so farre for Marks of a Future forgivenesse, for the whole VVorld, &c. from *Adam* to the VVorlds end: Even as that Salutation, *peace and good will towards men proclaim'd at His* first *Coming* or *Arrivall*: so a Larges before his second Coming, for such in utter Darknesse, setting in *the shadow of* Eternall perdition, for their enlargement at Last, &c.

And *Eloi Eloi*, as one forsaken &c. not without a twofold signification truly (to wit) *Yee shall not see me till yee say, Blessed is he that comes in the Name*

of

of the Lord, the name of *Elias* being not farre from *Eli* or Lord, *as* they came very neer it: Saying, *Let us see if Elias will come, &c. In whose likenesse or forlorne estate: of a truth, Lazarus set forth* how it fares with the *Prophets. John* for example put in prison; and others, &c.

And for the gulfe, as in truth signifying a space of time, betweene our Resurection & theirs, so *that* even the water of life begg'd but to coole *his* scorched tongue: And thus *that Prophet, the Lords second messenger, stiled by his name (Elias,)* because before the change, not tasting death, but taken up alive, like him the resurections figure: and with *Elijah* going on saying: *As thy soule lives, I will not leave thee*, here posting away briefly shewing his pro-

C 3 gresse

gresse: *The Prince of life ſhal relate ſomewhat of his ſermon beſtowed upon thoſe diſobedient ſpirits*, impriſon'd ſometimes in *Noahs daies* (Peter 1. chap.) *Who certainly wold not have afforded them the high favour of his preſence* : Had *he intended to* caſt them away utterly, as ſhe told her husband. *If the Lord had meant or been pleaſed to kill us, He would not have ſhe'wd us all theſe things, Judg. &c.*

Thus he the Iudge of quicke and dead, declaring the vayle, &c. not taking away of their attonement: then *was clothed in a cloude*, as this likeneſſe in moſt probable did appeare: (*Revel.* 10.) *Crown'd with the Raine Bow, his Feet as pillars of fire, a little booke in His hand open*, the Goſpell all fulfilled &c.

By

By whose posture or standing, *setting* HIS *right* Foote *on the Water, the left on the land*: giveing to understand the Gospels pilgrimage, or preaching how long to continue by *Sea* and *Land*, before published through the VVorld, and before the flood That time, as afore shewed, so the worlds last Age paced forth thereby. The *Arke* Baptismes *figure*, when a few saved; wherefore said: *So shall the* Comming *of the sonne of man, be as the dayes of Noah also*: According to that paterne, which dayes comming short of two thousand yeares, likewise this assured to be shortned; And therefore no marvell Since amongst us such VVatch kept by all. The LORD having watched over *U S*, to bring this evill upon *U S*, even at their wits end: which

which remember not the end, nor regard at all His tokens:

And ſo decending amongſt *them theſe* diſobedient, &c Haveing in his hand *Gods word*, as much to ſay : *I am the word of God* : *Alpha and Omega*. *And without the word made nothing that was made according to all Equitie*, have madē good all faylings, to witt, upon his own innocent perſon, hath taken the faults of all the world, *as none but one good* : And thus like them ſtunge by *firy Serpents*, by the ſigne of the Serpent were cured and healed : Againe. Our firſt parent *not being* letted or hindred *of the tree of Knowledge*, becauſe ſo requiſite to let them know themſelves, though *Satan* never the more to be excuſed in the diſcovery of their naked eſtate.

And

And ſo theſe words at Laſt, &c. *father forgive them &c.* Though expreſt in the voice of that Time preſent, yet *extends to pardoning* of all *Adams proginie*: VVhoſe ignorance or *Errour* not imputed to the utter ruine of the whole *World*.

And as that *Apoſtle* heard Things *unutterable*: Alſo in this of *theirs*, (a Thing as difficult to expreſſe it: *viz.* Their *releaſe*, *Pardon'd* after their being puniſh'd ſo:) in reſpect of the word, *Everlaſting and Perpetuall*; an ordinary word indeed, as in the Cerimoniall *LAW*: thoſe call'd *perpetuall Statutes afterward aboliſhed*: And ſo all *fulfilled &c*

And [redacted], theſe

D in

in a Miſtery ſolded up, *opened here, or diſcloſed*: Their ſuture eſtate of *Bliſſe*, and *Reſtitution*, a Thouſand times happie in the *End, that ſhall ſee GOD*; *Though a thouſand Yeeres, or Times*: *puniſhment to indure, in that hot* BATH *or* BOYLING Lake *for the purging of their* boyles *and* ſoares *to be cleanſed of them*, as *Origin* that Father partly his Opinion, caſt out of the Churches favour for his paines, by whom *Originall ſinnes purgation held by this way* expiated, &c.

And *Purgatory* having thus undermined: Yet reſts another wall between *US* and *THEM*; as requiſit to be caſt down, and one figurative *ſpeech opening another* : Her's one [illegible] ſerv'd [illegible] : *As* [illegible]*bold behold of a* LYON, His riddle : *Out of the Eater, came forth MEATE: And out of the Strong, came forth Sweetnesse* : Signifying even the Ovens-mouth: And the *Barrell* or *Butt*, its Ribbs *or* Belly, &c. *The bread and wine in the Sacrament*, viz. : And thus *Samson eate of the same spirituall meate, and dranke of the same spirituall drinke.*

And also of this *Ambiguous word* (till) a VVord of it for example, in *Matth. the first*, not without some reserv'd meaning: knowne to the *Holy Ghost by whom SHE conceived*, since *HEE* without doubt did never know Her: Although shewed, HEE knew Her Not, *till she had brought forth Her first borne Sonne:*

And so againe, in a double sence contrary to the former : *Goe thy way*

D 2 DA-

DANIEL, *for the words are closed up, till the time of the end*; where *though* it rests doubtfull before the end, whether disclosed at all, *those words*: yet ther's *hope* left, &c.

Nor stands for a *Cypher* here either: *And his* Lord *delivered him to the Tormentors, till paid all was due, &c.* That is to say: *till the utmost minuite there, that* Mite *of time expired, due to* Sinne.

Hereupon the Apostles not in vain saying, *Lord increase our FAITH*: As some new *Article* were added to their *Beleife* (*Luke* 17.) upon that &c. *I say unto* Thee, *Not untill seven times: But untill seventy times seven times: And what yee binde and loose on earth, shall bee bound and loosed in Heaven, &c.*

Spoken not to *Peter*: By him *having the keyes of* Death *and* Hell: For

such

ſuch intent, for this prerogative of His to be wreſted : That Legions ſuch of *Pardons* ſhould bee bought up, as ſold by His *Succeſſors* ; able quench at their pleaſure that Fire ∴ As many poſſeſt with a beliefe thereof, for thoſe *keyes of* ſuppoſed *purgatory* reſting in their *power* or *Cuſtodie.*

In truth whereas intended by the *Holy Ghoſt* to concerne the *Commisſion* of *Apoſtles* and *Prophets*; thoſe words of ſuch *Extent* and *Latitude*, the *Holy Ghoſts* meaning being able to explaine it, ſent Therefore. *Peter* 1. *And hope to the End, for the Grace that is to be brought unto you at the revelation of* Ieſus Chriſt.

By the Lady

ELEANOR:

F F N F S.

D 3 And

AND so to make toward the *shore* (or end this) these broken peeces offered or imparted here, taken out of the flowing Scripture: *As when all hope that they should be saved was taken away*: Yet in *Romes dangerous voyage escaped all, Acts, &c.* So making no doubt when in such a fearfull estate so many, but these hopfull *WORDES* will be no lesse embraced by them whose part in *Etnas* unquenchable *Gulfe* so deepe were, although the fire everlasting and eternall, And where the never dying VVorme and the like: Neverthelesse implies or proves not their pains to be of like nature, and that God is implacable or not to be intreated, which God forbid.

NOVV

NOw a larger PARDON: so who can wish, or imagin to *make* then These: *Who so speakes a* VVord *against the* Sonne *of man, &c.* *ALL* Blasphemies *and* Sinnes *soever forgiven the* Sons *of men*: *Math.* 12. *Mark. Luke*: no doubt able upon true *repentance* made in *ashes*, mingled *with teares*:

That precious gift) *for to remit, &c*:

And one of the second *Table*, that Commandement *Thou shalt not kill* : like as it refined and alter'd: (*Math*:) Even he the *Law-Maker and fulfiller both*; what *fine* soever, or *pain* imposed by old daies *but in terror*: *In former* Ages *he likewise able, as the second death, That also to change & abate it.*

And *Nothing then impossible with Him*, although in the highest degree; *The unspeakable offence against the Holy* Ghost

Ghost, though Left *without forme* (as it were) *and voyde* : The pardoning of it yet, verily a Thing not only possible (as appeares) by these words of *his* added to the former ; *But shall bee of Eternall damnation in danger* : BVT VERY CERTAINE, for *Reprobates* after due punishment, undergon to be released from utterdarknesse, and pardon all at the Last: since as much given from his mouth, *That made every thing so very good in the beginning.* The least tittle of whose words and sayings Not in vaine, *Then dangerous not a little, to make Them utterly voyde,* as to miscall what GOD hath cleansed out of a dangerousnesse and Nicenesse, to make it a common thing abstaining from it, alike to disalow what the *Holy Ghost* hath Cleer'd and Licensed.

And

And now lawfull, that which without *Blasphemy heretofore, could not be disputed*, (to wit) in iudging of GODS waies, *whether equall or no*, since the wicked (*Adams* Children for *His* disobedience:) not left in *Hell*, but in state of *Redemption*, as without doubt also: *That of the two debtors reflects on all*, both frankly forgiven.

Although instanced in *ADAM and EVES case* those two, &c. VVhen he that charge forgetting himselfe so much, *so mildly Him reproved*; who as one beholding to none or, *no Physition needed, and* being *displeased* for her Repaire to the House, *therefore* was *bidden to goe in peace*.

Delivered *that was at once of so many spirits or* DIVELS, *that dispossessed Woman* whereby forbids any to *murmur*

E and

and *grudge* at his goodnesse, HEE giving to the *first* and *last* both, *Even forgivenesse*: So take heed least HEE have somewhat to say unto Thee also: Or should but say, *take what thine is, and goe thy way, &c. An non licet mihi? &c.* Mat. 20. 15.

NOVV here with this not unlawfull Newes and Tydings, a degree above their *purgatory Pardon*: Being not ignorant of old Distinctions, between the *Sufficient* and *Efficient cause*, as all constran'd to confesse for the whole worlds sin his suffering alsufficient, whose Soule tasted of very *Hell*.

Though no corruption saw, Nor of that difference, either unwitting between the cause and the occasion, Nor how straitly Schoole-men beseiged unwilling to yeeld originall sin the only and

and ſole cauſe of reprobation. And yet if granted *ESAU* rejected becauſe of ſome particular or Actuall ſin or evill foreſeen in him: Conſequently the others ELECTION from ſomewhat which GOD foreſaw to bee good &c.

Even ſo to him who overcomes when he is Iudged, and nothing with him impoſſible, be aſcribed all poſſible Praiſe and Thankſgiving, whoſe Iudgements (*Rom.* 11.) unſearchable and VVay paſt finding out, ſo even ncreaſe our FAITH LORD.

Charitas non æmulatur; omnia credit.

1644.

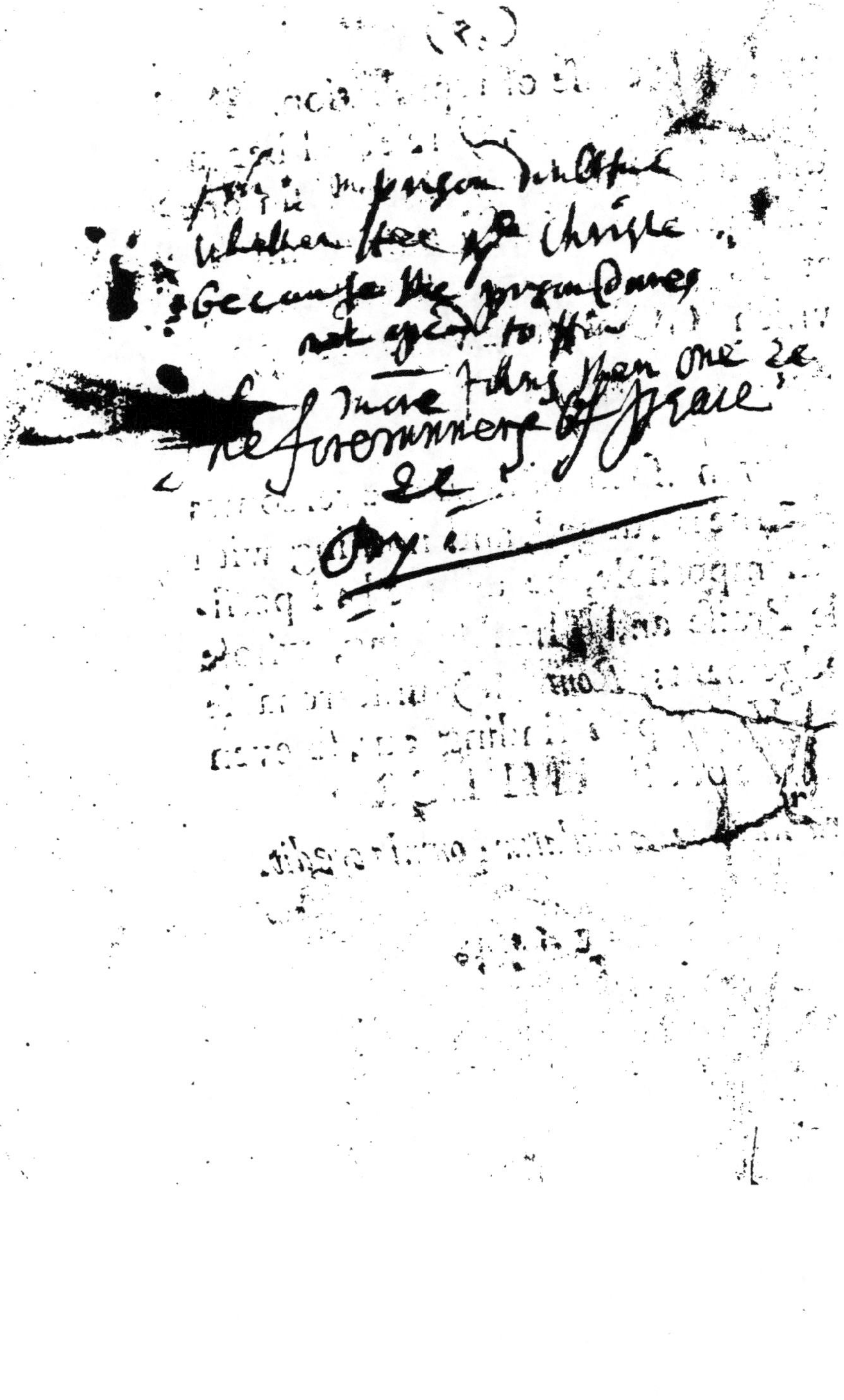
(7.)
whether free ye Christe
because the person dares
not speake to him
more tokens than one &c
the forerunners of grace
&c
Pray

7. *Apocalypsis Jesu Christi* (1644; Wing D1970) is reprinted, by permission of The British Library, from the unique copy held at The British Library (shelfmark Tab.603. a.38. [6]). The text block of the original measures 160 × 92 mm. Signatures B3v onwards are incorrectly paginated, with two pages numbered '13'. B3v should be numbered '14' and all following pages should be one number higher. In addition, p. 36 should be p. 26.

Hard-to-read words:

24[25].16	way; and setting others
25[26].7	*crosses,*
25[26].9	*cruciatus corum.*
25[26].15	aforesaid
25[26].16	WARRE
25[26].17	peices, the

APOCALYPSIS
JESU CHRISTI.

Domine Dominus : *Psal.* 8. 3.

When I consider thy heavens, even the workes of thy fingers, the Moone and the Starres, which thou hast ordained.

Printed in the Yeare, 1644.

Arch-Angell Michael.

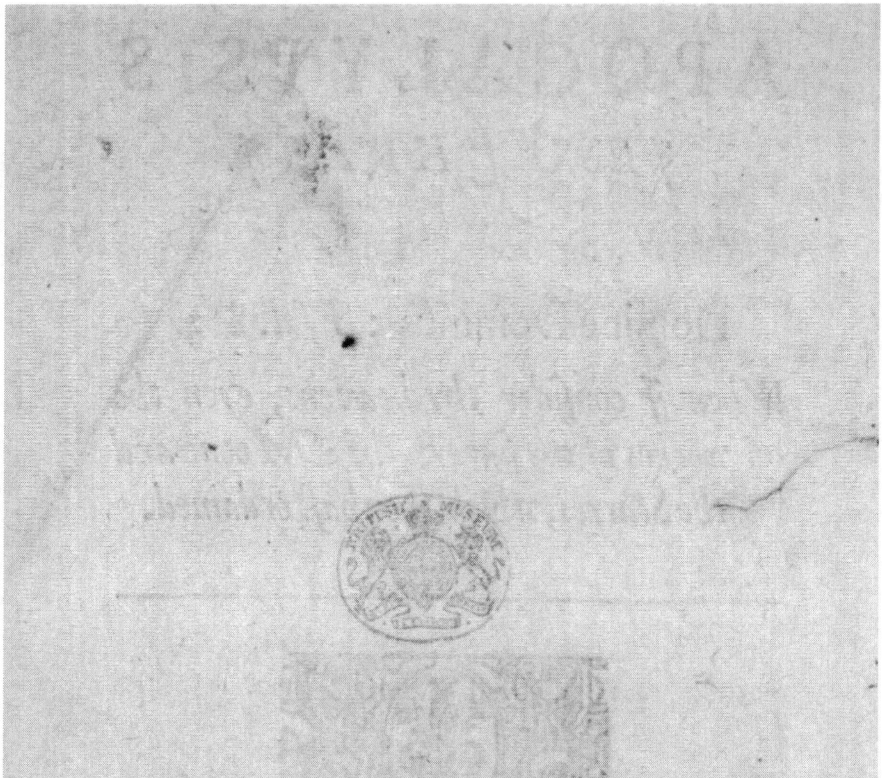

REVEREND MEN OF GOD AND GUIDES:

T*Heſe things being Commanded* You : To try the Spirits whether they be of GOD ; *and on my part, that No fayling bee in whatſoever, which may haſten* Theſe, *or further His commands* : Even

)(the

the ſame yeſterday, and to day for Ever: *Therefore without Boaſting, to tender my* Service; *have made bold here,* whether yee pleaſe to make tryall this way or No:

Shewing how there hath not fayled of My writing, *the leſt tittle as it were, of any Judgement, as no few of* Late *taſted of, having been by* Mee, before they came to paſſe, *related and foretold; As moſt of them* Extant *on Records, with the preſent heavy diviſion for one, extracted out of the* words *of That* prophecie: Thy kingdome is numbred and devided; (*Dan.* 5.) And thou found wanting or Loſt, &c. *bearing date for great* Brittain, *in the* Year 1633: *Witneſſed with ſufferings ſince undergone,* No inferior ones, *for ſeales and ſignes of the day of Judgement, to follow*

low from those Premises, *even that* Conclusion. *So in Expectation of* Your *Commands ; Forbidden to prove* ALL THINGS : *Which disproves of utterly and for ever to despise and shake off* Prophecie : *For a time ceasd, Though indeed forebidden to bee soone shaken in mind that way with those Tydings* : (Thessalonians, &c.) Because first a falling away, &c. *And then together with* the fall of that Sonne of perdition, *Antichrists going downe, Namely the* Enemie *of the day of* Christ : *then even The day of Judgement revealed in the* 1700. *yeare : And his going into* Perdition *with those crowned Heads of his so many Yeares : Supreame* Priest *as stiled, seven years that was so before his* Imprisonment. *And thus shewed how great* Brittaine *drinkes of* Germanies *cup* :

No

No more Popes *and* Bishops *Now.*
Being the summe of these VVrits unsealed, *as here in hast with an* Altar-Coal, *some storakes begun to be drawne of it presented to the Churches.*

FROM

FROM THE LADY ELEANOR:

Apocalypsis, *Jesu Christi.*

CONTENTS.

SHewes the day of *Judgement* to be reveal'd in the seventeenth hundred *year*, and in the aforesaid *Century, in the yeare of grace* even, 1644. The great day then to be. *And unto great Brittains Churches aforehand shewed*, when assembled at *Westminster*, H: 7. Chapell, being extracted out of Gods word, as: *Beatus qui legit & audit verba prophetie hujus: &c. tempus enim prope est testifies.*

VVhereof thus concerning the signified time at hand, to be revealed out of the *booke of the Old and New Testament:*

A

ment : which in this visſion he ſaw: *Whoſe name is here thrice put down: Joannes ſignifying the grace of God*, ANNO DOMINI as it were, *the year of Grace*, &c. Even ſo *Joannes eſt Nomen*, this other Meſſenger *of the ſecond comming of our Lord*. By whom as *John* the firſt was ſurnamed *Elias* the *Tisbit*, for his rough *clothing* or *raiment* : So he againe *Ecce agnus Dei*, ſtiles him, *in whoſe Coate not a ſeame*.

And againe *the ſtill ſoft voice* not being permitted to ſpeake otherwiſe, ſo *Elia: Tichet* by name, *ſends theſe writs of his*, that Divine or Elder : VVho wrote *unto that Elect Lady, &c.* By way here of writing unto the Churches of the Nations, *the truth of the Revelation*, ſaying, *He that hath an eare, let him heare* without delay *what the*

ſpirit

Spirit of Prophecie saith, &c.

John to the seven Churches grace, a name to this NATION no stranger: And here as often with times voices witnessed from him, *Which was, and which is, and which is to come*: The time past, present, and future, as much to say: *Times mistery or the mistery of God*, at such a time revealed by the Spirit of Prophecie, *covered or vailed under that Sabbaticall Number*, Sealed with the figure of Seven severall wayes.

And so shew'd with those fulfilled weeks (for HVMILIATION assigned) when the yeare begins, about the *Resurrection Feast or Easter*, Thus signified, *a septem Spiritibus qui in conspectu Throni, &c. et a Jesu Christo primo genitus*

A 2

tus mortuorum Lavit. Nos a peccatis nostris in sanguine suo: VVitnessed with the blessed Sacrament then given. And with two Coronations *their Feasts solemnized*, succeeding one another: Then as by this made good; *And hath made us Kings and Priests (or Prophets, &c.)* The truth of which, as much to say, *In the first yeare of the present bloody reigne, the word of the Lord came unto her*, his Hand-maide, in the yeare aforesaid, 1625. Shewing then how many yeares to the day of judgement.

And so now since the conquest, about Seven hundred yeares neere, and twenty foure Princes having cast their diadems, *Wherefore saying as it were to that* ALPHABET, *Amen,*

Ego

Ego A & O, Principium & finis.

The Prince of the Kings of the Earth: as they all but very earthen Vessells so brittle, from *Cesar, to the* Conquerour, &c. And this is the sum or substance of the matter of the end, *revealed to be at such a time, the Resurrection tydings, &c.*

Also thus for the Ile of Patmos, situated in the Egean Sea: *I John who also am your Brother, &c. gives notice of the place as time and place necessary circumstances, where such swarming Vipers* visited by *those monsterous Headed* Beasts: with tayles not inferiour, reaching up such a hight to the Firmament: *Some comming up out of the Sea, and others out of the Earth,* Moralizing the

the laſt dayes, even theſe. As thoſe ſeven, & ten Horns *bearing date of this very* laſt CENTVRY.

VVherefore *this Diſciple and Apoſtle* (ſtiled the *Divines*) *for the word of God in ſuch tribulation*, and the Teſtimony of *Jeſu*, even directs this diſcovery of the time to the *Divines* of this famous Iland : *Their meeting now in this troubleſome time, ſo full of diviſion, the Church in travell as it were, &c.*

And thus like 'the Sun, from the uttmoſt part of Heaven, unto the end of it again that runs about. *So Gods Word from Aſia thoſe Churches come about to Europe*, Sets in truth in the weſt, ſent to *Weſtminſters*, ſitting there for to take into conſideration, and

weigh

weigh the words of this blessed prophecie. Concerning this of no light consequence, *the time of the End like a Theife in the night stolne upon the world.*

As behold he comes and every Eie shall see him, Iew and Gentil that have both pierced him, &c. in his Servants so handled, *And in those mistaken words in his last Supper, Take Eate,* &c. rather admitting a sencelesse Miracle, then a reserved sence.

VVhereas the bread profits nothing without faith, *which betokens only whosoever they be that beleeve in him at his comming, he will raise them againe,* as he was raised. *And thus we Eate his Body and live by him, as he lives by the Father,* &c. And so away with Satans Bolde trans-

transſubſtantiation. *Thou ſhalt not tempt the Lord thy God, with one unſeene ſingle Miracle,* VVho as well may maintaine and affirme, when for a ſhew he waſht their feet, *And girt himſelfe,* &c. That it was his very blood, becauſe *John affirmes,* as he ſhews here, that he that loved us, waſht us from our ſins in his own blood, who before He worſhiped him *or bound to beleeve,* ſaid, *Thou haſt both ſeen him, and it is he that talketh with thee (Joh. 9.)*

And by him preſt farther *thus, which wee have ſeen with our eies, which we have* looked upon, and our Hands have handled, and was manifeſted, ſo palbable and evident, His body: And ſo much for this much miſtaken miſtery by a willfull miſunderſtanding.

But

But laſtly *Abraham the father of all them that beleeve*, as he ſaw that day and rejoyced, *So we eate and drinke with him*, And ſo much for that time here ſignified: *The Reſurrections Feaſt, and his firſt Viſsion on the Lords day*: when he in the Spirit heard behind him, the great voice of a Trumpet, ſaying: *I am ALPHA and OMEGA: Write, &c.* To wit, the Reſurrections time to be revealed out of the Scriptures, as aforeſhewed.

So here the Old and New Teſtament, *in the day of judgements Likeneſſe*: the Booke covered and bound in fine paper, with Braſſe Claſps, &c. (as it were) *Clothed and girt about the Paps*, in the midſt of thoſe watch lights ſtanding: *As for the Propheticall two edged*

B Sword

Sword comming out of his mouth,(as much to ſay) the Bleſsing rejected, *the Curſe, beware of it at your perill, &c.* And for the ſeven Stars whereby he was raiſed being laid on *John*, falne dead, &c. Saying: *I am he that was dead and am alive for ever more*: (Againe as to ſay) VVaite for the ſeventeenth hundred yeare: *When I ſhall knock or ſend, &c.*

The fourth Chap.

AS here ſhewed, a doore open'd, having been long ſhut, *the Gift of Prophecie, the day of judgement to be reveal'd, &c.* As the Trumpet gives a loude warning, *Come up heither, and I will ſhew thee things to come*: And thus all thoſe lights, and this paſſage ſet open, *all but one and the ſame thing, the*

laſt

last dayes discovery, &c. to be shewed to the Churches, *also the Church of Westminster.* That very doore includes, VVhere those ancient Records of the Kingdome of Heaven kept.

Disputed at this time and examined by *DIVINES*, with the Divine Service, and their Sitting there: *And how many Princes, since the Conquest, inter'd or Crown'd of those Elders,* in their Alablaster Robes, a Grand Iury, twenty foure, *so many sommoned here,* of those Law-makers.

Set forth, *or shadowed under the Prophets and Apostles:* VVhere first like the ancient of dayes, the Tables of the *Law represented with the Winged Evangelists, foure of them:* The flying Gos-

B 2 pel

pel preached to all Nations, *giving in such ample Evidence of the end come* : All fulfilled. And this for another Mapp, or Modell of the day of Iudgements preparation.

As even all the Scriptures agreeing in one about the time, *Containing in the fourth Commandement*, to witt, remember the great weeke also saying all of them, *for Thou hast Created all things ; And for Thy pleasure, they are, and were Created*. And therefore in six dayes *every thing finished. And a thousand yeares but as yesterday in his sight*, and the like witnessed by St. Peter : *The full time then (in respect of the time to be shortned)* cannot be farr for those things made for his Pleasure, in his displeasure to be dissolved againe to nothing.

And

Chap. 5.

AND here like the light by degrees the great dayes appearing set forth, Namely, *a Booke in his right hand, that sate on the Throne*, seal'd with the seven stars, as it were, those seven seales on the back-side: the yeare of God, as much to say, *Where Agnus apervisit unum de septem sigillis* : viz. *annus, or anno Dom.* In such a yeare the sonne of God his comming Revealed, &c.

The secret contents of which Virgin booke being to no man to be disclosed, *None but the Lambe of the Roote of David worthy to know it*, *ECCE LEO*, &c. Having overcome, hath prevaild, *Davids key only opens that door* that

that openeth and no man ſhutteth, and ſhutteth and no man openeth: *And ſo much for no man, though* St. *John wept much, &c.*

Chap. 6.

NOw knocking lowder here (as it were) then formerly, by the voice of a Trumpet, *the ſonne of thunder who heard like a thundering voice one of the foure Beaſts*, thoſe winged Herals ſaying, Come and ſee whoſe Coats ſo powthered, or full of Eies behind and before, *time paſt and to come*, as in the Scriptures both contained.

And the word of God thus, *Whereby all things made the light of lights*: And the worlds eie that overcomes darke-neſſe

nesse, even the Sun of whose progresse as followes, and the yeare of God whose sound gone out into all Lands, ride on : *Their arrowes are very sharp, &c. Vene vide*, like that I saw, I overcame, by whom alotted so many dayes to the yeare, stiled the *Julian account*, &c. when as the word commanded to be preached to all Nations, 1700. since.

A greater then he or the Conquerour, *either come and see, his comming as cleare manifested as Noone-day, &c.* VVhat date it beares and to what Nation. *And I saw and behold a White Horse And he that sat on him had a Bow and a Crowne given unto him*, and he went forth conquering and to Conquer.

So the time being come for the manifestation·

nifestation now of *Times and Seasons*: VVhereof *the* Apostle said, *there was no need then to write* : As much to say, reserved *for a necessitious time* : And the *Characters of the Celestiall signes foure of them* Beasts of the Earth : *Aries*, *Taurus*, *Leo*, *Capricorn* ; Here the Ring-leader, the victorious *Ramme*, Crown'd in his Yvorie cloathing : *The white* Horse, *he that sat on him, having a* Bow, *and a Crowne given unto him, &c.*

The second Season giving the Armed *Crab* : VVhen the *Sun* enters *Cancer*, having a *Sword* of such a *length* growing out of his mouth : Then as in the Field with Harvest weapons, Pikes, and Sithes and the like: *So many, all as redd as* Fire *or* Blood : The

redd

red *Horse* the second *Rider*, &c. one of the *Prophets* setting forth These foure: Names them *the foure Spirits of Heaven: which goe forth, &c. or Winds.*

The *Third, having a paire of* Ballance *in his hand,* Even the equall day and night weighed or measured out unto each twelve *houres*, as the word *Chœnix*, the twelve part &c. VVherefore *Libra* its very Voice freely given, Saying; *a measure of Wheat for a penny, and three measures of Barley &c. In all foure measures* as that Number of *foure* of such *Note* in Times booke: The *houres* of the Day; The *weekes* of the Moneth: and *Quarters* so many contained in the Yeare. *And see thou hurt not the* Oyle *and the* VVine:

C Authoms

Authoms *language not difficult to understand.*

The Last of these *Horses* of the Sun *Capricorne*. The *fourth a paile Horse*, The gastly *grizled Goate* ; VVinters wann vissage, *to wit* : *with hoary Locks and shakeing* , *&c*. And with him *HELL* followed The *fourth Beast* saying, *Come and see* : VVhen the *fourth Seale opened*, *the Truth of which*, *The second death Not to be escaped then* : For that *Season* appointed, the *fire everlasting &c*. The *houre* of *pailenesse* for them : turning that time called *Christmas after his Name, whereat all knees to bowe* , into BELCHAZERS prophane Idolatrous *Feast*, or *Herods* bloody birth-day &c. as of Late *some heads Narrowly escaped*, the *Five &c*. for Example : And so much *for the* Sheepe

Sheepe *ſeparate from the* Goates, as no little diſtance betweene the *Goate* and the *Ramme* here ſhewed. Alſo the ſeverall *Complextions* includes ſome *beautifull,* aa others *Black* and *Swarſe, Moores* and *Savages.* The VVord preacht through the VVorld at its *ſetting* or *deſcending ſo full of glory in the Weſterne parts* : And thus theſe *ſealed* with *the Conquerour,* and *RUFUS* a Horſe-backe, as it were, Their very Seals in whoſe dayes *Weſtminſters* Cathederall, &c. reedified. And that Palace built, that Throne and the Booke called *Dooms-day,* as written in our Chronicles, and *tſebe* within *the* Space of *ſeven hundred* Yeares *ſince the Conqueſt* : (Now to be Stewards no longer) How many *Elders* ſiting there? Not unknowne. So much

C 2 for

for *the* great day come of *his* VVrath ſhewed.

Chap: 7.

AND 1644. *The ſinall BLOWE Then, as this the* great Yeare (no longer deferd) ſhewed *Him in that Viſion: Who ſaw* foure *Angels ſtanding on the* foure Corners *of the EARTH, holding the* foure VVinds *that they ſhould not blowe &c.* Saying to *the* foure Angels, *hurt not the EARTH till &c. Wee have ſealed the* Servants *of GOD in the* Foreheads : Even *hath* relation to *the aforeſhewed* Angelicall celeſtiall Horſe-man, *theſe* Foure called *Angels* or Spirits here : As by *that Voice ſo loude*, Hurt *not &c.* Comming *from the* Sunns *ariſing* or *aſcend-*

ing

ing from *the East*. And as *The ſealed* Number a *hundered fortyfoure* &c. (although 1000. &c. put *laſt*, that ſhould bee *firſt*) a prefixed Time being, to wit, The yeare *of* GOD: amounting to *Twelve times Twelve* (144) Including the *Nativitie Feaſt*, the *Lambe* and his *Servants*, the *Apoſtles* all invited to that good *Time*: Aſſured that no *Sunne*, nor any *Heate* ſhould light upon *Them*. VVhen the *Sun* then makes its greateſt *declination from US*. So *farthermore*, ſhewing the Truth *of This*: One *of theſe twenty-foure Elders*, or that *Elder*, inquiring VVHAT THEY VVERE; *And whence They came*? That *victorious* Troope, in their *Snowe-Clothing*, and *Palmes in their hands*: And *John* replying, *SIR*, *THOU KNOW-*

KNOWEST, as much to ſay, Your *Majeſtie* reigne, Sir, never ſuch a *Perſecution* ſince the Conqueſt, or ſince this a *Nation*. Their *Albion arraye* anſwers, or ſpeakes *for* Them : *whence they are*.

Chap. 8.

THe ſeventh, or laſt Seale being opened : *And in* Heaven *ſilence about the ſpace of halfe an houre* : A *Vacancie in the* Church, (as much to ſay) or their Authoritie taken away in the *ſeventeenth hundred yeare* : So all come and heare the ſeven Trumpets, thoſe *Angels ſounding Times farwell* : HIS laſt *houre-glaſſe* (to wit) the preſent *Centure* cut in *halfe* or thereabout.

And

And the *Number of foure*, in the aforesaid *Prognostication* the meaning thereof *Explained*; Also the Number of *Three reiterated* sundry waies: Shall likewise render an Accounte of it, Even the *Woefull estate of these three* Kingdoms expresly by *Land* and *Sea*: Together with HIS *fall*, and *His* followers, Likened to that of *Lucifers*. So *VVoe, woe, woe, to the Inhabiters of the Earth, &c.* England, Scotland, *and* Ireland, *Because of the Voices of the three, &c. to Come.*

And *Thus* hee in the Yeare 1633. *Midsomer*, Mounted to that *Height*; Better hee had been unborne. Compar'd here to that unluckie *Starre* &c. *Falne*, &c. Or the Lampe of (*Englands*) great Ship, like *ETNAS* smoaking Moun-

Mountaine, *Casting out fire* &c. being Lancht forth: VVell had it never beene Built and *Pauls* too: witnesse *such a den* of *Robers*, And those *wormwood Taxes* imposed of *Ship-Money*, accompanied with innumerable others.

And farther for the false *Prophet*, in whose custodie *the Keys of the Bottumlesse-pitt open'd by him*, supposing by those *Smoakes and Vapours* to have obscur'd the gate of *heaven* open'd, or *those lights to choake them*: Intruth imprisoning the Servants of *GOD* hereby as appeares. *VVhere desir'd death*, flees away; and setting others at Liberty against the *Law*, &c. So whose *Image* ells with *haire*, as the *haire* of *women*, like a *Scourge* or a *Scorpions-tayle*, *Hermorphradit* like, seemly enough to weare

weare for a *Mayden-Queen*, so proceeding on. *Et habebunt super se regnum Angelum ABYSS: Et audivi numerum Eorum*: Gold causing such a mist *or* blinding the *Sight*.

And *thus* passing briefly over the first *Woe*: Those current *dolors* and *crosses*, (Hors-men with *Crownes &c.*) *Currentium in Bellum & cruciatus eorum. Ut cruciatus scorpij*, a signe also in Heaven: as *Leo* and *Virgo, &c.* VVhose *Teeth* and *Haire* not wanting, as hereby appeares. VVhere the *Bottomlesse-pit*, and *Heaven* opened both.

Also *shewed* unto the aforesaid Peices, for the maintenance in VVARRE: added great field Peices, the Second *Woe fore-runners of the* Third *Woe* comming quickly, &c. provided or

D pre-

prepared for the *Last evill dayes* : In *the day* of *Judgements* likenesse, as *Earthquakes* such and *Thunder* &c. able to affright farr and neer, so much Power having in their *Mouthes*, and with their *Tayles* doing such *hurt poysoning vapors* : And these for another *Forerunner* those *Indian-Mines* open'd their late discovery, suffices here.

Lastly, Concerning that *Voice*, from the Altar, as here Voices of severall sorts Confus'd or *mixt* : Thus for example ; where those significant *Servants of GOD to be sealed*, before those *Winds* being *Loosed* or set at Liberty as *houres, daies, moneths and years*, even that *Year* wherin the finall *Blowe* : So here againe, The foure very VVinds loosed, prepar'd for those Sea-Horses , with Lyons heads

roare-

roareing &c. (to wit) Ships, The Narrow-Seas *NAVYE*, set forth in this *Vision*, bound in the great *Euphrates*. And *farther* for the *foure Horns of the golden Altar* (*Aras:*) even in English the *R A M M E*: or foure *Seasons* aforeshewed &c. As for *Covetousnesse* so common, *that* Restlesse deadly *Sin* shaddowed under *Idolatry*, requires no farther Report then these: *And the rest of the men yet repented not of the workes of their hands; That they should not worship Devils of* gold *and* silver demonia, &c.

Chap. 10.

IN which way of explaining, These very dayes hastening on, wher one part so enlightens or proves another: As *herein this Babe, or little* Booke, speaks

D2 much

much plainer then heretofore: Now behold open in the *Angels hand*, a Booke of no *ſmall importance and weight*; concerning the *diſcovery of Times miſtery*: The time of the *End at hand*.

Though never ſo little a *Volume*, for that purpoſe, ſufficient to Contain the *Time to come*. As here appeares by *thoſe* daies of *Noah* paced out: How long the Goſpels reign among the *Gentiles*: betokn'd *by that faithfull witneſſe in heaven*, *The Rainbowe crown*: As the *Angell* Crown'd herewith, ſetting His right foot on the *Waters*, *whoſe feete as fiery Pillars*, &c. For which daies all things not unknown, as a Lyons roareing, *their ſound gone through the world*: How long after the *Creation* even the VVorlds being drown'd? So dayes and houres needleſſe to obſerve them

them, like *that* conceal'd *day and houre, unto none made known* as the ſeven *Thunders their ſecret Voice*, here he commanded not to write it; but to be *ſcaled up*. Even gives Notice hereof, to bee no barre or hinderance : Concerning the *Premiſes of the very Yeare* made knowne, although ſeemes *contrary*, by *forbidding the houre and day, &c.* As GOD *forbid otherwiſe* : *Who then would have ſaid indeed, the* LORD *defers His comming* : Let *US* bee Lords &c.

But proceeding *on* with the aforeſaid *Time* of the *End*: Here *with a high hand Swears in his wrath, that Time ſhall be no longer*; But as the daies before the *flood, from the Creation of the world, proteſted by him that lives for* Ever *and* ever, not be pro-

prolong'd beyond that *Time*: *Sworne by Heaven, and the things That therein* are. And Earth and the things that therein are: As much to say, *in This little booke* or *Prognostication sealed with seaven planets* as set forth by those Characters of *Terrestiall creatures the celestiall shadowed out, &c.* And so that seventh Angels Trumpet : But *times voice sounding the mistery of the End when finished*, in what Century, when he shall *begine to sound, &c.*

And lastly, where like the last supper foreshewing *His* houre come: *likewise this Sacramentall booke containing the mistery of his second comming shewed to be at hand*: commands it to be taken and eaten up, being compared to a womans travill: *That so joy of a man child forgets her former paine and anguish.*

Likewise

Likewiſe when this booke to be re-prophecied. Though *the beaſt aſended out of the botomleſſe pit* : out of patience with their teſtimony the two Prophets being produced, &c. *And the nations (the Gentiles)* angry alſo that *That* time was come (*Revela.* 11.) *And the Dragon with ſuch a tayle that was ſo wrathfull againſt the Woman.* And Satan for another, playing *REX: Roaring becauſe His reigne no longer to continue* : (*Revela.* 12.) Is concluded with theſe : *Yee now therefore have* Sorrow, *but I will ſee you again, and your* heart *ſhall* rejoyce : *And* your *Joy no man taketh from you.* So *reſerved* for another time, that Celeſtiall *VIRGO*, the meaning therof with that ſigne in Heaven too about *Michael tyde*, to witt, *as by the Serpents* caſting ſuch a Flood *after* the woman,

woman, by the *Earth drunke up*. About the ſame time gives notice he to receive his ſentence to be caſt out of heaven, &c. as ſhe into the wilderneſſe was ſent to take her flight, &c.[1]

Chap: XI.

&c.

8. *From The Lady Eleanor, Her Blessing To Her Beloved Daughter* (1644; Wing D1991) is reprinted, by permission of the Folger Shakespeare Library, from the copy held at the Folger (shelfmark D1991 bd. w. D2010). The text block of the original measures 140 × 92 mm.

For Hard-to-read words, see p. 229 following this text.

FROM THE LADY ELEANOR, HER BLESSING TO HER BELOVED DAVGHTER;

The Right HONORABLE *LVCY*,
COVNTESSE OF
Huntingdon.

The Prophet DANIELS *Vißion*:
Chap. 7. *In the first yeare of*
Belchazer *REX*, *&c.*

Printed in the Yeare, 1644.

Huntingdon.

Printed in the Yeare, 164

FROM THE LADY ELEANOR, HER *BLESSING* to Her beloved Daughter, &c.

WHose new Interpretation, not with *Froath* filled up, or Interlarded with differing Opinions of others, ſuch old peices having No affinity *and* agreement *with* this BRITISH *garments* or diſplayed COATE *by bleſſed Prophets pend*: So what the *Veritie* of thoſe *fouer great Beaſts*, divers one *from*

A 2 another,

another, *which should arise &c. Who so would understand & know their mistery for this very time reserved, hitherto with* the *Kingdome of Heavens great seale shut up.*

Distinguishing not only *Nations* but *Times*: The very truth of it: N'other then the severall Coate, Armes, *given or borne by him,* the first of great *Brittains Kingdoms or Monarchie.*

Not unlike *Jacobs united Familie his Wives Children, and Children of the Hand-maids.* The aforesaid Crowns foure, *concerning whose peice of super-artificiall Heraldry unknown to those Heralds of the King of great Babylon (Dan.3.)* even at hand proclame the ancient of dayes, *the aproach of that great day of his. So goe thy way* Daniel, *for the words are closed up and sealed till the time of the end,* which

which: *Not only the Time*, but unfolds unto what *Nation* or *Language*, revealed those glad Tydings, as *by the Word* (*Sealed*) given to understand thereby. *Even where the great Seale the Impression thereof, those fouer Coates or* Beasts, *styled Kings which shall arise, &c.* And the *Coine* stampt therwith and the like, &c.

And so the first *in the likenesse of a Lyon with Eagels wings, &c.* first displays the armes of *England* and *France*, and then *standing upon the feet like a man*, a Lyon rampant (to wit) *Scotlands coate*, where the other the *Irish* Instrument, or Harpe evident also out of Tune, &c. That no need to say, *I am Joseph*, or over-verball to be in this case.

No more requisit then their asking

A 3 either

either whether or no thy sonns coate this of so many colours or peices, as in the field, now those inumerable colours, &c. That were HE living, our Father *JACOB* would say, *some evill beast had devoured us*, to behold such blood shed amongst brethren and cruelty, as Since the Creation such a flood, the old *Serpent* never casting out of his mouth, and so like *Joseph sold to the Midianits*, our wofull estate, sale and rapine made, *by Malignant* brethren *&c.* But such miserable Shipwracke with us being no news, shall returne to those misteries of *Heraldry.*

The frequent Oraments of your House wherefore to explain them farther, but needlesse; nor endlesse Figures *here borrowed out of old Orators Bookes,* suffices for

for figurative Demonſtrations ſuch, *to render their meaning truly, running the way of the plaine rather for the ancient of dayes his comming to prepare the way.* So *for my Commisſion thus.*

And farther as to you not unknown eſpecially at what time your Mother became a VVriter or Secretary, concerning the unſealing or interpreting this obſcure peice to open *the Viſion of Daniel, though no obſcure perſons of the ſeed of the KINGS and of PRINCES.* Even in the yeere 1625. undertaken this burthen, following his ſteps, who declares when *HE* wrote firſt in *BELCHAZARS* firſt yeere, the laſt of thoſe *Caldeans* of great Babylon.

Alſo ſhewed in that great plague yeere, when the City ſhut up: This Viſion then opened

opened, *whereof even* Then a Signe *ro* Token, *not without a touch* given *in those* words. But *thou O Daniel shut up, &c.* (*Dan.* 12.) And thus where every word a *mistery*, cannot passe over *them*, as none of the least His being so often saluted or stiled so highly of the *Angel*: *O Daniel greatly beloved man*, as much to say too, *O K J N G of great Britaine*! as Kings and Prophets, Brethren, *Let him that reads* Daniel *understand*.

And as it extends to this time also, beares Date forty foure; directly the present *Yeare* as these beareing Record of time and place, &c. of whose storming daies thus. *And Daniel spake and said, J saw and behold upon the great* Sea, *the foure Winds strove, and foure great* Beasts *came up, divers one from another*

to

(tosay) *from beyond sea*, the occasion of such divission, ready to be swallow'd up in these swelling Seas.

The first like a LYON, *and Eagels wings*, (Daniel 7.) *I beheld till the* VVings *were pluckt thereof* : *And lifted up from the Earth, and made stand upon the* Feete *like a* MAN : And *a* MANS HEART *was given unto it*, viz. The LYONS Passant (*regardant*) turn'd into the Rampant, &c. After her decease, a *Virgin* Princesse of renown'd MEMORY, ENGLAND stil'd great Britaine, and then these foure severall *Coates* given, &c.

(And this Sayling on ; or pursuing *the* Subject:) *And behold a nother* Beast,

B a

a *second like to a* BEARE, *and it raised it selfe upon one side* : *And had three* Ribbs *in the mouth of it, between the teeth of it.* N'other then as it were displayed *The three* LYLLIES: The *Armes of FRANCE*, to the full given by this KINGDOME, where Nothing but a meere Shadow, or the bare Coate of it. Left, *Leaves in stead of Fruite* : Besides, how by a She-Beare, as this N'other : Three devided KINGDOMS rent in peices. The *Ribbe* or *Side*, beares VVitnesse thereof, The second *SEXE* its Character.

And so farther from *This saying, too well prooved* ; (*Arise and devoure much* FLESH :) even what *Date* it bears needlesse to say : *Her MOTTO the*

the Mother not of the Living *Child,* but of Divisſions *and* Maſſacres, *where* incluſive the ador'd *Sacrament* called the *MASSE*: Thus uttered Her Voice, *Let it bee neither Thine*, nor *Mine, but devide it : deſtroy it utterly, &c.* No ſuch *Coate* then, like to have any Affinitie with *Solomons* Ivory Rament or Robe: as the *Enſigne of Peace, the* LILLY *of the field,* but rather a Slippe come out of the *Bear-garden,* unworthy to behold the *Sunne* : became *degenerate and ſo wild* : Sometime to none of the *Flowers* of Parradiſe inferiour.

And another like *LEOPARD,* Lyon-like *SCOTLANDS Coate* the truth of it diſplaied Thus : *Which had foure* Heads, *and foure* VVings *on the backe of it,* as it were a Heralds

B 2 Coate,

Coate, or KING AT ARMS, &c. So great *BRITAINS* foure KINGDOMS or *Crownes* proclaimes by them : And this the Summe of it ; shewing Then revealed the time of *END*, when united *These foure aforesaid, &c. As hereby farther appeares.* (*And* Dominion *was given unto it* :) No small addition, after Her dayes raigning forty foure Yeares, for *Scotland* to give such a Large *Coate* by a Prince as *unfortunate* in His *Progenie* and *Successor* ; As in *his Predisessors* or *Parents* : VVherefore liken'd to the LEOPARDS Spoted skinn those sable spots or *drops*.

And behold a fourth BEAST like a *HARPYE*, or some such *Monster*, having great *Iron Teeth*, and

and *Nayls of braſſe*, to be ſhort, *the Iriſh Harpe demonſtrated*, likewiſe the very wreſt as it were a little Horne, of which *Inſtrument not a little out of tune*, as inſues, ſtamping all underfoote *Gods Law*, *Humaine Law*.

And ſo farre for the *Harpe*, *Like the very forequarter or ribbs informe or likeneſſe*, as ſtrung in that manner ribbwayes, *whoſe ſhort Horne the expreſſe Character of tirrants of no long continuance*, raiſing up and ſetting lower, like the wreſt according to their will made a law, *changing and altering* when they pleaſe.

Informing moreover *concerning the blaſpheming blaſts of the little Horne, that had eies like a man, and ſuch a mouth*, as much

much to say, *that mouth speaking such great things, a Womans and no Mans.*

Her Proclamations at her command, *the great Seale, the Elders and the Nobles,* so with the Story goeing on of that Idolatrious time, *Come see now that cursed Womans spirit, she cast downe, &c. cunjured up,* as it were, *walks up and down,* that like her selfe of her unnaturall Dogs, *Acteon* like eaten (*of her none left to bury*) *Jezebel* by name, *Woe to the House,* whose signification, so no other then a stolne peice by the Poet, very like to be, as that for another: *Borrowed from Elias, Elevation, also the fable of Phateon,* That *Prophets* being sought for as though some where had falne or miscarried.

VVhose

Whose *misteries* or *morralls* in so high esteeme among the *Heathen* a gainst many may rise in *Judgement*, of *whom reverenced no more Divine Oracles* further more, to weigh or unite those times, *with our heavie dayes*, *Likewise Peace*, though voiced, *Jacobs voice like and the hands of Esau*, yet such divisions and slaying of all hands, *nothing but peace*, put the question *as though he sought nothing else*, is it peace, *and thus saith the King, is it peace.*

And ever and againe, *Thus saith the KING,&c. Is it peace, JEHU.* New Propositions as it were. And Sir as long as her *Sorcerors* inforce - doeing what she pleaseth, *what hast thou to doe with peace*, also at her last cast (when this Motto, *who is on my side* who) *who trcode* HER *underfoote*, her inchanting voice,

Had

Had he Peace *that slew his* Master? (As *it* were *to looke to his* Head) This blood-thirsty Mistres of *Charmes* and *Spells* like Satans falling those aspiring Spirits.

So alike the time possest, now see what a double portion powr'd out of the curse what one leavs, another taks, *He that escapes the Sworde of Hazael Jehu slayes, and hee escaping Jehus Sword Elisha slayes,* because the Land devided as those waters by him parted with the mantell of *Elias,* wherewith *Sayled over Jordan River,* and such virtue in it, bein worne out by them, much more vigere then and Spirit in their Books being perused and studyed upon.

And Mother and Daughter alike too. Now she cast into a languishing bed

bed, consumed to nothing an *Anatomy*, &c. scarce any thing to bury.

The occasion of this LANDS *deep* CONSVMPTION *SHE*, And wast made *thereof* : *Woe to the House of God*, and the House of PARLIAMENT both, the nursing mother of *DRAGONS*, those *Sonns* of *BELIALL* in armes, for as her name is, so is she MARRAH: *The GALL of bitternesse*.

But because the *Daughter of a King* as *JEHU* speake, *Here forborne the Remainder, buryed in silence*, for so births PREROGATIVE *surmounts* or *goes* before *that gain'd* by Marrage *as desent* and *blood*, a Character not to be blotted out, wherewith follows the state of

C Virginity

VIRGINITY, the preſidence theirs, *Not in ſubjection as others.*

And for *ELIAS* progreſſe in the SPIRIT: The returne of thoſe long expected dayes, Let the READER be pleaſed for his ſatisfaction to turne but (to the *Apocalyps* the 11) And ſee in his COMMISSION to the *Gentills*. *What date it beares there, concerning the revealed time of the Reſurrection, &c. even behold the Sevententh Centurye it meaſured out by moneths and dayes, amounting* unto three years and halfe, the halfe of ſeaven like the time nothing, but divisſion, including the great miſticall weeke, expreſt ſeverall & divers wayes. A touch *of* which time *folded* up with that *ſevenfold* marriage, put the *queſtion* in the *reſurrection whoſe wife*, &c.

VVherefore of the laſt (turned) Houre-

Houre-Glaſſe of time, Thus (*Revel. &c.*) *And in the ſame Houre a great Earth Quake and the tenth part of the* CI-TY *fell, and ſlaine Seven Thouſand, Decima Pars, &c. and* thus pend with the *Character* of the preſent when *Elias* his *dayes ſhall appeare againe*, their Reſurrection or *Revolution*, as it were by a beſeiged City its modell, and yeelded or rendered up by the affrighted remnant, when ſuch publike Thanksgiving, ſaying, *Wee give thee thanks O LORD GOD Almighty, which art and waſt, and art to come.* Vtter'd (times) treble voices, to weigh the time, &c.

And as a Reformation time, to the greateſt part hatefull & unſufferable: *ſo the day of Judgements tydings as wellcome,* like the writs of Parliament *that news* to

C 2 many

many alſo dreadfull, and deteſtable to the world, theſe makes it ſufficiently plaine, *and the Nations were angry the time of the dead was come that they ſhould be judged, &c.* (ergo or viz.) *to be manifeſted* to the *Gentills*, and ſo like the laſt Supper aforehand, ſhewing his death, likewiſe *commands the little booke open'd to be received and eaten*, as much to ſay, *The laſt day revealed to be or afore ſhewed the Lords ſecond comming, &c.* Alſo by two witneſſes, to witt, the Bookes of *Daniel* and St. *John*, *although reproved for his firy Spirit*: That he was forward and ſudden *in calling for the day of Judgment as it were*: Then who knew not of what *Spirit he was*.

And here like *Elias* and *Elijah* not to be parted (*thoſe twain goeing along further with*

with the last time, those aforesaid mourning moneths 42. And a Thousand two Hundred and Sixty dayes, and three dayes and a halfe, &c. (*Revela.* 11.) all *but sounding the great dayes Alarme in the seventeenth Century*: Then to watch *as the time for the Elects cause promised to be cut off and shortned*, to witt its comming short of 2000. yeares, and so much for times sentence, to be no longer (*Revela.* 10.) *And the Sacramentall tree of life*, or Bookes of the old and new Testament, afore mentioned, *And he therefore that shall add or deminish* from the set time written by those witnesses *let Him expect the plagues also proceeding out of their mouths*, *Pestilence and Warre*, *&c.* otherwise that might have *escaped* death no few with *Elias* have been taken alive up, debarred *from* entering the

the reſt,&c.as that figure of the Reſurrection, double witneſſed by *Elijah* a touch of whoſe Corps therby one raiſed up againe, but let downe into this Sepulchare.

So againe looking backe to *Daniel* touching the *little Horne* declaring or ſounding the brevitye of great *Brittaines* Monarchie, (*Whoſe looke more ſtoute then his fellows*) more over thus I conſidered the *Hornes*, *And there came up another little Horne, before whom three of the firſt Hornes were pluckt up by the roots*, the truth of it as much as to ſay, *That he the firſt Heire of the red roſe and the white*. VVhoſe ISVE three of them Crown'd Princes childleſſe, *deceaſing without Heires of their body*, the Crown of *England* fell to *Scotland*, *and great Brittaine ſo ſtiled*, then wherefore blazoned

zoned by those great *Beasts foure being from name of Bruite derived*, whose *Unicorns* Horne become as short as his fellowes. Lookeing of late as though al by conquest had been his, so according to his will wresting and altering whatsoever, and possest with no little willfullnesse as well as pride, proceeding *from Ephnesse* and *Shallownesse*.

And so from *HENRY* the fourths taking possession of the *Kingdome*, regained by *EDWARD* the fourth of those royall Rose ten in number (giving the dunn Cow) so many even from the House of *Lancasters* usurpation untill the *diadem* fell to be *Scotlands* lott, all which displayed by those *Horns ten and another little* Horne, &c. as *Corone* being derived from *Cornua*, and *Carolus* a Diminative, &c.

For

For sayling on, the VVind serving faire still, or *for proceeding with the* Map *of great Brittains last Parliament, so manifest*, that whose Image this, who needs to doubt, as a little *farther*, I shall hold on, &c. (*I beheld, then because of the* great voice *of the* word which the Horne spake, *I beheld even till the* Beast *was slaine and his body given to the* burning flame:) Some may say hath God care *of Oxen*? Yes doubtlesse beholds even such a Den or Draught *of restlesse beastlinesse* day and night, St. *James*-Fayre *so called*, not without Cause their Priviledge of late abolished: As hereby appeares the Modell every of those Courts put downe: VVhere so long such Lawlesse *doings* there, &c.

(As for the rest of the *Beasts*, They had

had their *Dominion taken away* : B V T *their Lives were prolonged*) as Hee no little or inferiour Beaſt for one, *whoſe voice ſet a Note lower*, brought to the barre, though ſo long deferred, *yet whoſe Judgement ſleeps Not*

And then the Ancient of dayes, ſitting in his Iudges Robe, and Locks like Snow, Even *the day of Judgement clothed in the Parliaments likeneſſe* : And the Parliament clouded under, or ſhadow'd out by the day of Iudgement. *His comming in the Clouds, ſo all in their pure wooll, ſet forth & wood Seats*, and thus much for that: *The judgement ſhall ſit, and the Bookes were opened*, the Bookes of the Old and New Teſtament alſo: *Nothing covered that ſhall not be diſcloſed too; and proclaimed.*

D Likewiſe

Likewise by those *Legions of Angells*, beside the Parliaments everlasting sitting, the warre raised, *by them* set forth, *like Dooms day as it were*, when the Elements melting and the *Heavens* shaking, & *Stars falling*, *like* those Valies of Thunder-Bolts with lightnings; *such a firy Streame now making way*: the generall dayes *Epitome* & the conclusion of all these, Dan. 7.

(*And the Kingdome and Dominion, and the greatnesse of the Kingdome* under the whole Heaven, *Shall be given to the Saints of the most high (OR RULERS) whose Kingdome is an everlasting Kingdome*.)

As to no other given such a high stile, except unto this Kingdome, &c.

Hitherto

Hitherto is the end of the matter concerning the end, *and as for Daniel his countenance changed*, and his cogitations troubled. The troublesome time before the change, *fore saw* even *our* evill times, *His heart bleeding too, &c.* And as *Daniel* signifying the *judgements of God*, so that *Monsterous fourth Beast*, as much to say, *a Viperous generation*:

*H*erewith is signyfied like *Josephs* & *Pharoahs* dreams doubled, even the seventeenth hundred yeare: By this very measure doubled to bee likewise: a *Time and times, & the deviding of time*, or three and a halfe, (viz. 7.) *Surge & metire templum*, (*Revel.* 11.) followes *tempus & tempora, & dimidium temporis*. The Resurrections time thereby measured even in the present *Century* cut in

D 2 the

the *midst* [illegible] it were) *Peradventure there be fifty*, &c. And peradventure there shall lacke five of fifty, exprest in the day of judgement so very language, as *shall not the Judge of all the earth doe right*, and *Abraham* [illegible] but Dust and Ashes then.

With whom saying, *Now I have taken upon me to speake*, cannot here rest shewing farther, as *Noah outlived* the Flood, three hundred years and dyed, two thousand yeares after the Creation, likewise *now* the time [illegible] comes [illegible] years, wherefore the dissolution in the seventeenth hundred yeare, and thus cut off so many yeares, like the shortned dayes of *Enoch whom God tooke* [illegible] three hundred yeares: and after [illegible] *begat Methuselah*, [illegible] five hundred yeares [illegible]

mounts

mounts to a PERIOD, *as deeply swarne the Time should be longer, (Revela. 10.)* measured by the CREATORS his right hand lifted up; *Tempus non erit amplius, sed in diebus vocis septimi Angeli: Times mistery revealed, &c.* as promised, to be witnessed by the Prophets, *his servants* concerning times TRUMPET then put to silence time no more, &c.

And lastly for MICHAELMUS (1644) *That happie halfe yeare herein included,* a time and times and halfe also, *to disperse the Forces, &c. Revela. the* 12. *and Dan. the* 12. concerning *Michaelmas,* there signified and so like a Thiefe in the night as this fearful night vission, appeares even the end stolne upon the whole world, or comming as the travel of a VVoman misreckoning sometimes

ſometimes taken before *SHE* looks.

Alſo farther for this laſt of Parliaments, & *whereas Gods word able to ſpeake for it ſelfe of full age,* other argument whatſoever, needleſſe, it being of a quicker returne, *ſhall preſſe another place of Scripture,* as briefly explaind as others afore, *Reve.*10.9. *Concerning that Albion Army, and Aleluja voices where even the revealed time of the Lords comming.* And the writs of this happie Parliament ſealed up in one: *Scribe Beata,* &c. *They that are called to this meeting,* &c. All ſealed with the Vnicorne in pure Paper, as it were mounted on white Horſes, or like the great ſhew. both going together: as noted &c.

Nomen ſcriptam quod nemo novit, the Parliaments name in another language, viz.

viz. *et vocabant nomen ejus verbum dei. The Word, &c. et cum Justitia judicat, et pugnat. And upon his head many Crowns with a garment dipt in blood, deep Scarlet clothed*, and on his vesture, and upon his legg written, &c.

Namely the Colour and Garter of the order the Knights of St. *Gorge* (*Ecce equus Albus*) likewise from *Chival* and *Equus*. And thus the Knights and Esquires of both Houses displayed, of what house, and so from the name of *Oxford*, thus, *et vidi Beastiam et Regis terræ et exercitus*, &c. Revela. 10, 9.

And for the aforesaid warre so farr, as for the motive, *Meritrice magna qui corrupit terram in prostitutione sua*, &c. Hath bin shew'd afore where she painted

ted like her Images that downfall of *Hers* before theirs.

Also added these to the premises because injoyned not to part, or put asunder what is joyn'd, shewed *Farthermore*, *The great Image*, (*Dan*.2.) even *armed at all points*, the verity of those foure Metals, *ore* Argent, &c. the very same likewise divers one from another. Apertains to *the foure great* Beasts *the one rising out of the Earth, the other out of the Sea.*

So contains Cæsars Superscription even *the Roman-Empires age*, written in in those Characters of the 3. Ribs, 4. VVings and the 10. *Horns* and then *those Eagles wings so lifted up pluckt too*, notwithstanding *Germanies* manly looks, that Saxon state: like this great Statue

Statue unable *longer* to ſtand upon its feet, not unlike *Irelands eſtate*, the modell of that *Empire* in ſuch a flouriſhing condition, *and as the blow then in the* 17. *yeare of the preſent reigne*, ſo the other in the 1700. &c. broken ſo ſoon in peices: *Wherefore the world but like a D ame vaniſhed*: Like his ſuddain awaking in a moment forgotten all, &c.

But now returning to great *Brittains brittle condition* againe: *That union diſſolved and broken in peices ſince his dayes*: He the head of GOLD, as by thoſe peices called *IACOBUS*, after his name, &c. And he the ROMAN SPANISH Emperour by his tribute of late, ſince the *Indies diſcovery, who makes up the head of Gold too*: And all this but to manifeſt and ſhew. *That God is a Re-*

E *vealer*

vealer of Secrets in these dayes also: Reveales the deep and secret things, *And maketh known what shall be in the Latter dayes, by divers & severall demonstrations, as this for another: Of the Axe laid to the roote*: *That tree or pedigree whose fruit much of such a hight*, reached up to Heaven, *this Jacobs Ladder, &c*. And now but the Stump end remains as yee see.

The very VVoods every where proclaims it, where the Axe never put so to the Root, *such felling, &c. And so the Axe that fell into the water, by a sticke cast into it, caused to swime*: The Morrall thereof no other then the *Resurrection time revealed to be by the Spirit of prophesie*. As much to say, As the late hand writing for a seale or signe of it, *a sufficient propheticall proclamation though not*

on

on the Walls, &c, in the Banquetting-House, yet not unknown to Lord no few how these applied. *Thy Kingdome numbred, and thou found wanting,* &c. and come to passe *too*, as published and printed, 1633. *sufficiently* known, *in meeter to his Majestie* from great Babylon *transferred to great Brittain.*

And so this but the truth of it (*shewed in the* 12. *of the Revelation*) *How* Satan because he knows his reigne or time to be short: is ready to devoure the VVoman even for the truth of the Resurrection time revealed, *as most proper to be performed by that sex, a Woman by whom death came to be the Messenger of Life.* And so, *WOE TO THE INHABITERS of the EARTH, and of the SEA, &c.*

And since a pleasing Theame (as

E 2 tis

tis ſaid) makes a good Orator, and ſure I am a worſe time then this never known or ever heard of, ſo then the time the end diſcovered, although pend ſomewhat hastily or unperfectly, &c. being like the hony: and like the hony gathered out of ſo many parts, I ſhall the leſſe need to excuſe it unto ſuch as have a ful knowledge of the Scriptures, That ſhould it be written at large a Chronicle or a booke as ample as thoſe tables, of the Mapps of the VVorld could I ſuppoſe not contain it.

Not ſutable to the little book, being but an *Epittomie* as it were, and ſo much for being not voluminous, eſpecially when the time ſo ſhort too: as by *Tyrant time his reigne expired*, ſhew'd to be and theſe the apointed *S*cutchins for his

his Herſſe apeared, thoſe winged *Beaſts devouring times likeneſſe, &c.*

As by this one wittneſſe more produced or ſet forth: *aſigned to the preſent,* even in the dayes of theſe Kings, or united Kingdoms: *Shall the God of Heaven ſet up a Kingdome which never be diſtroyed.* And the Kingdome ſhal not be left to other, &c. And ſhall breake in peices, even to the ſame effect, with that (*Dan.* the 7.) *The greatneſſe of the Kingdome under the whole Heaven, for ever given to the Saints* (*or Rulers, &c.*) which ſhall breake in peices, &c. viz. By thoſe ordinance or orders of Parliaments, and feild peices, &c.

And yet not ſo ſtrange as true, notwithſtanding ſuch a troubleſome time

O

O let Ismale live as it were, prefer'd before *Isaac to be his Heire*. And *Absolons* life before *Solomon the wise* (*O Absolon my sonne Absolon*) Like *Egypts* Leekes & Garlike before *Canaans* Grapes, &c. And so preferred this worlds vanity & folly, before everlasting Righteousnesse, *endlesse Joy, life eternall*, and now ended thus this point of Honour, displaying these *Ancient of dayes his Kingdome your portion* to you dedicated: that so punctually have discharged that duty of the first commandement with promise, in so much and such dishonour endured, have bene your mothers Coparcner, even You, her alone and sole support under the Almighty. *So Veni Domine Jesu, gracia Domine, &c.*

[8. *From The Lady Eleanor, Her Blessing ...*]

Hard-to-read words:

7.18–19 *Also shewed in that great plague yeere, when the City shut up:*

23.2 *derived*

23.13 those royall Rose ten in number (gi

23.16 *diadem* fell to be *Scotlands* lott, all which

23.17 displayed by those *Horns*

23.19–20 *Cornua*, and *Carolos* a Diminative, &c.

25.7–8 *And then the Ancient of dayes*, sitting in his Iudges Robe, and Locks like

25.11–15 the Parliament clouded under, or shadow'd out by the day of Iudgement. *His comming in the Clouds, so all in their pure wooll, set forth & wooll Seats*, and thus much for that: *The judgement shall sit,*

25.18–19 *Nothing covered that shall not be disclosed too, and proclaimed.*

26.3–6 the warre raised, *by them* set forth, *like Dooms day as it were*, when the Elements melting and the *Heavens* shaking, & *Stars falling, like* those

26.8–10 *such a firy Streame now making way*: the generall dayes *Epitome* & the conclusion of all these, Dan. 7.

26.13–16 *Shall be given to the Saints of the most high* (*OR RULERS*) *whose Kingdome is an everlasting Kingdome.*)

26.17–18 As to no other, given such a high stile, except unto this Kingdome, &c.

27.1–5 Hitherto is the end of the matter concerning the end, *and as for Daniel his countenance changed*, and his cogitations troubled. The troublesome time before the change

27.9–10 *a Viperous generation*:

27.11–20 Herewith is signyfied like *Josephs* & *Pharoahs* dreams doubled, even the seventeenth hundred yeare: By this very measure doubled to bee likewise: a *Time and times*, & *the deviding of time*, or three and a halfe, (viz. 7.) *Surge & metire templum, Revvel.* 11.) followes *tempus & tempora, & dimidium temporis*. The Resurrections time hereby measured even in the present *Century* cut *in*

28.1–20 *the midst too* (as it were) *Paradventure the fifty there, &c.* And paradventure there shall lacke five of fifty, exprest in the day of judgements very language, as *shall not the Judge of all the earth doe right*, and *Abram* he but Dust and Ashes then.

With whom saying, *Now I have taken upon me to speake*, cannot here rest shewing farther, as *Noah outlived* the Flood, three hundred years and dyed, two thousand years after the Creation, likewise *now* the time abated or comes short 300. years, wherefore the disolution in the seventeenth hundred yeare, and thus cut off so many yeares, like the shortned dayes of *Enoch whom God tooke*, who lived three hundred yeares and *Eternitys* forerunner *begat Metheuseliah*, thus five *hundred* years amounts

29.1–20 to a PERIOD, *as deeply sworne the Time should be longer*, (*Revela.* 10.) measured by the CREATORS his right hand lifted up, *Tempus non erit amplius, sea in diebus vocis septimi Angeli: Times mistery revealed, &c.* as promised to be witnessed by the Prophets, *his servants concerning* times TRVMPET then put to silence time no more, &c.

29.11–20 And lastly for MICHAELMVS (1644) *That happie halfe yeare herein included*, a time and times and halfe also, *to disperse the Forces, &c. Revela. the* 12. *and*

Dan. the 12. concerning *Michaels alarme*, there signified and so like a Thiefe in the night as this fearful night vission, appeares even the end stolne upon the whole world, or comming as the travel of a Woman misreckoning sometimes

30.18–19 *Nomen scriptam quod neme novit, the Parliaments name in another language*,

31.16–17 *Meretrice magna qui corrupit terram in prostitutione sua*,

32.16–19 Wings, and the 10. *Horns* and then *those Eagles wings so lifted up pluckt too*, notwithstanding *Germanies* manly looks, that Saxon state: like this great

38.1–14 *O let Ismale live as it were*, prefer'd before *Isaac to be his Heire*, And *Absolons* life before *Solomon the wise* (*O Absolon my sonne Absolon*) Like *Egypts* Leekes & Garlike before *Canaans* Grapes, &c. And so preferred this worlds vanity & folly before everlasting Righteousnesse, *endlesse Joy*, *life eternall*, and now ended thus this point of Honour, displaying the *Ancient of dayes his Kingdome your portion* to you dedicated: that so punctually have discharged that duty of the first commandement

9. *The Word Of God, To the Citie of London, from the Lady Eleanor: Of The Earle Of Castle-Haven: Condemn'd, and Beheaded: Aprill 25.1631. &c.* (1645; Wing D2018) is reprinted, by permission of the Worcester College Library (Oxford University), from the clear copy held at Worcester College (shelfmark AA. 1.12 [29]). In identifying the date of publication as 1645 rather than 1644 as on the title page, we are following the Gregorian calendar rather than the Julian one then in use; for Lady Eleanor and the English printers the new year began on March 25. The text block of the original measures 180 × 143 mm. The following signatures are misnumbered (and the correct number is shown in square brackets): A4v [11], B [12], Bv [13], B2 [14], B2v [15], B3 [16], B3v [17].

Hard-to-read words:

3.1-2	*dome of God was neere*; *or immediately should appeare.*
3.21	*also*
4.1-3	Lord *behold here is thy one pound*, that wrapt up in the *heavie*
4.11	explanation of this
4.14–16	*That unto every one that hath shall be given and from him that hath not, shall be taken away that he hath.*
4.20	mistery thereof as manifested, also re-
5.2–3	receive no losse: *That hath nothing of his owne, or to that purpose.*
5.5	how he shall be recompenced so
5.7	*That from him that hath not*
5.14	to the time: though in no small *hast*
5.20–21	drawes neere great *Brittaine*, as shewes the things
6.8–10	heavie sentence visits the temple, to purifie it, casting out *those making their markets there, as no news is refullfild with us.*
6.13–14	*directed to our dayes where the faithfull rewarded with so many Cities*
6.21	*obscure*
7.1–4	envied, and surely a one then come of no *Sodome seed, but like Isaack rather sacrificd*, who as he sufferd for the misdemenors of an unrulie houshold sufferd by him,
7.7–10	To suffer between those two the one cleering him at that houre, *affirming for that fact whereof the Earle of Castle-Haven was accusd by his wife*
7.13	Idolater
7.20	*adde a word*
8.2–3	*You see this odious crime, and therefore you must be cautous you admit of no Mittigation*, who

THE VVORD OF GOD,

To the Citie of LONDON, from the Lady *ELEANOR*: OF THE EARLE OF Castle-Haven:

Condemn'd, and Beheaded: *Aprill* 25. 1631. &c.

LUKE, 21.

And some of you shall They cause to be put to death, &c
But there shall not a haire of your head perish.

Printed in the yeare 1644.

WORD OF GOD, To the Citie of LONDON,

[illegible] the Lord MAYOR:

OF THE

EARLE OF

Castle-Haven:

Condemned, and Executed:

Aprill 25. 1631. &c.

Luke 21.

And some of you shall They cause to be put to death, &c.
But there shall not a haire of your head perish.

Printed in the yeare 1644.

THE VVORD OF GOD TO The Citie of *LONDON*:

Luke Evangelist the 19. From The Lady *Eleanor*: 1644.

TO confirme it out of the mouth of two witnesses: The time *of your Visitation*, as formerly out of the Old Testament. (2 of *Kings* 20. &c.) *A signe given of the Resurrection at what time it is reveald* by the times paraleld. So here is one out of the New from a Parable: (*Luke* the 19.) witnesses the same, concerning *when our Saviours returne not fare off. As when thought then the Kingdome*

dome of God was neere: or immediately should appeare.

VVherefore of the very yeare of God 1631. *April* 25. thus what *then* came to passe *no inferior token or* signe of it, as witnesse *such a one, &c.* And he said therefore *a certain Nobleman went into a far Country to receive a Kingdome, and to returne. And cald his ten servants and gave them ten pounds, &c.* As moreover in what reign followed that, needs no more date but this. *But his Citizens hated him, and sent a Message after him saying. We will not have this man to reigne over us.*

And thus proceeding on, as it were with the ten Commandements, then came the first saying, *Lord thy pound hath gaind ten*: and said have authority over ten Cities. And the second came saying, *Lord thy pound hath gaind five*: and he said *also be thou Ruler over five Cities.* And a-nother

nother came saying, Lord *behold here is thy one pound*, that wrapt up in the *heavie* Handcherchife or Napkin, *which amounts to Anno Domi.* 1631. *April* 25. And so *THREE* of them come to their Last account too, the EARL of *Castle-Haven* first: One as evill requited by his family, *As reputed free to his followers, and accounted* just to all and charitable, &c.

So farther for explanation of this peice of *Substraction and Addition*, saying *Lord he hath ten*, whose reply was: *That unto every one that hath shall be given and from him that hath not, shall be taken away that he hath.* VVhen he said or gave command, take from HIM the pound and give it to him that hath *ten*; where besides the aforesaid yeare of God the mistery thereof as manifested, also refers to a certaine principle so distastfull

to

to his Majestie, to the Parliament saying he can receive no losse: *That hath nothing of his owne, or to that purpose.*

And so much added concerning these words, how he shall be recompenced so evill a steward of his Lords money: *That from him that hath not* (Notwithstanding) *shall be taken away that which he hath.* Accompanied with that voice of the present reigne: Bring them *forth* and slay them before me mine enemies.

And farther more to bring this home to the time: though in no small *hast* passing on with great *Brittains* progresse or story in *this of the* 19. *of Luke*&c. *When* he wept over that hard harted Citie visited in that manner, comming neigh *Bethphage and Bethania, &c.* which also drawes neere great *Brittaine*, as shewes the things belonging to their peace hidden

den from their eyes, saying withall. *If these should hold their peace when peace in Heaven proclaim'd and his comming, very stones would not be silent, but liken'd to a womans travell,* would immediatly cry out.

And thus having denounced their heavie sentence visits the temple, to purifie it, casting out *those making their markets there, as no newes is refullfild with us.*

And as this cleare and out of question this parable or portion of Scripture, *directed to our dayes where the faithfull rewarded with so many Cities, and the like,* so evident likewise where that *Publican pardond, (Luke 19,) Saying salvation was come to his house, bidden to make hast, &c.* The very true Portrature of him, his hastie departure or death. The sonne of old ancient *Abraham* also: *The house of Audeley no obscure one,* though one much envied,

envied, and such a one then come of no *Sodome seed, but like Isaack rather sacrificed,* who as he sufferd for the misdemenors of an unruly houshold sufferd by him, laying on him their faults, so had the honour to have this added.

To suffer between those two the one cleering him at that houre, *affirming for that fact whereof the Earle of Castle-Haven was accus'd by his wife* (such a wicked woman) He was as innocent as the child new borne. Though by the other an Impudent Idolater not cleered, calling out upon *Saint Bennet,* but cursing the said Earle, wishing him and all his Generation except his sonne hangd and damnd.

And now Sirs you of this Honourable Citie as you *have heard these: Shall adde a word of His Majesties Atturney generall that day after they had heard their*

examinati-

examination (falne to a low ebb of what was expected (saying my Lord. *You see this odious crime, and therefore you must be cu tous you admit of no Mitigation*, who came short of this first promise. That His Majesties intent was like God to shew mercy, who from fifty did come down to ten when he interceeded for *Sodom*.

And so what the prisoner answered to them: *when his Majesties Chaplins came and told him the King had a gracious purpose to alter the manner of his death.* And that he should be beheaded like a Noble man: *Replyed he should esteeme that Haulter which should draw H J M to Heaven before a collor of pearle or the like.* And for the Gallowes likewise that should bring him to his Saviour and Redeemer that dispised not the crosse for him; and so much for him a man

man of a meane ſtature too, who clm-
bed that tree at *Tower-Hill*, when
as a like no little throng or preſſe: A
*Peere of two Kingdomes a Noble man
here*, a Prince or Earle in *Ireland*, whoſe
eſtate ſometime inferior to none. And
thus ſtands forth like that Noble *Za-
cheus* cal'd by his name to come downe.

The

The EARLE of *Castle-Havens* Confession.

In the name of God Amen.

I Mervin, *Earl of* Castle-haven *being in my full strength and memory thankes be given unto my maker, having been branded and openly accused for chang, alteration, and doubtfullnes of my Faith and Religion. I thought fitt like a Christian man to give satisfaction upon what grounds I stand for my beleife, and to expresse it under my hand for the satisfaction of all charitable people and Christians:*

First, I doe believe in the blessed and glorious Trinity, three persons, one eternall and everliving God, God the Father, God my Redeemer, and God my Sanctifier.

I doe relie upon the merit, death, and passion of our blessed Saviour Christ Jesus, and upon his Mediation for the remission of my sins.

I doe believe and use with most humble reverence our Lords prayer, the Creed of the Apostles and the tenn Commandements, as they are set downe and allowed in the Church of England.

I doe believe the Canonicall Scriptures and that they are written by the inspiration of the holy spirit.

I

I doe beleive the Booke of Common Prayer, as it is allowed in the Church of England, *to be a good forme in those dayes for the service of God and to use the same, and for the rest of my beleife I doe referre it to the true Orthodox faith of our Church of* England. *And from the Articles received at this present in the Church of* England, *and confirmed by authority of Parliament,* I *doe not differ in any point, renouncing all the superstitions and errors taught or beleived in the Church of* Rome *or any other Church, in which faith* I *will, God willing continue to my lives end in Testimony whereof* I *have hereunto subscribed my hand this first of* May 1631.

C: ſtle haven.

L*Ikewise of whose Letter, makeing bold to shew the beginning thereof: When without* MERCY Castaway : *how well resolv'd* He *was,* who had ſuch ill luck at one and Thirty.

(Anagram. *Eleanor Audeley.*)

Reveale O Daniel, I send thee 1631. *farewells with thankes for thy letter and advice. But I am bound for* Nineveh : *And having bidden* Tarſhiſh *farewell. Not fearing death, I doe not desire life.*

CASTLE-HAVEN.

And

AND for more manifestation of what nature this unnaturall strange trespasse. *Whereof this man Mer: Lord Audeley was accus'd, his undeserv'd death is referd to Geneses 38. Judahs sonnes Er: his eldest*, and ONan his trespasse: *And how the Lord slew them both*: with her disguising: *putting off her widowes garment*, with child by whoredome, *Tamer travaling with twinns* those sonns: with that ominous Scarlet, or Red thread bound, &c.

And therefore shall but name them, the contrivers of it. *Ann his wife*, and his brother *Ferdinando: the one for envie*, she being an Heire, and *such* a notorious one,

B (O

(*O Ann*) The other a perverted *Papist wanting no malice*: wherefore to cut him off, *some time gone that way astray too*: but recald himselfe, no aspertion was held too foule for him. And for saving her honour an adultresse by promis'd preferment, *a Page and a foot man was* brought forth : Those VVitnesses rewarded in their kind, condemned out of their owne mouths, like sillie Sheep for their labour: *Who came against a Peere of two Kingdomes, as* Broadway by name, *charged with that breach made on her* :

The other one *Fitz Patricke*, *or* O *Donel a very Vagarant* : Accusing himselfe of O *Nans uncleannesse or trespasse with his* LORD. Vpon his *Oath* beleev'd, *which had* never received the Sacrament, or at least but one kind before him; that thrice tooke it upon his death:

And

And one never heard to have an Oath come out of his mouth, *That* in that kind *he* was not guilty, never intending to reserve *oathes to that purpose to make himselfe forsworne before his death.*

And ſo much for thoſe twinns or fellow-ſervants. Themſelves falling into the pit dig'd for another, though guilty of that: *as much* as thoſe Babes Then *born*; Yet worthy of no other, *witnes out of their owne mouths. Therefore the Executioner, or* Man-midwif, *as the one helps them into the world, he* others out *of it: This* work *though* ſooner diſpatched, where *Irelands heavie blow at hand incluſive in theſe.* And after came his Brother with the Red thred, &c.

Alſo *farther* for the time of the yeare, about *ſheep-ſhering* time or S. *Georges feaſt:*

B 2 as

as Times circumſtance requiſit, when it came to paſſe of the LORD Keepers giving ſentence; *Keeper of the great Seale, made Lord high Steward.* That Iudge, *Judah* like in this, though not acknowledged, condemned one, more righteous then himſelfe. *Yet diſcerne I pray you whoſe are theſe, the Signit or Seale, the Staffe, or white Rod,* and Bracelets or Color, of what office theſe are the Enſignes.

And more over how it came to paſſe *with him*, behold *his* own brother *Sir Ferdinando Touchet what end he came to, That day* twelve moneth in the morning at the ſame houre his brother was condemn'd, how he dyed ſuddainly, *which had polluted his owne Neſt or Houſe, the juſt hand of God diſpleaſed*: This unnaturall brother, in a Houſe of *Office* or the like, ſtroken dead

dead coming but from the *Tennis on Holborn Hill*, without any servent with him. *This O Man ready to be torn in peices before the breath out of his body : some their hands in his pockets; Others for his Clothes, was* found thus by His *Servants which* came to aske *for H I M.* Thus rewarded as They no other deserved ; *JUDAS-like,* rather then of *Judahs Race* or *Kind*, (*Luke* 21.) in betraying *H I M* betrayed by *Friends* and *Bretheren* so openly : *Mervin* LORD AVDELEY, *of the Manor of* Straw-Bridge, *which never suspected or did know that the* VVord to be of his house, or appertaining to Parsonages and Tithes, that *Mat.* 25. *Thou knewest I reap where I sowed not, and gather where I have not strawed.* VVhere although the Arch/B. of *Canterburies burying his Lords money* (as it may well be

no

no little or hidden of that kind in the earth) with *the loosing of his head also tyed up with that Napkin or Kircheife* : the one gone to his owne place, *Little-Ease or Esaus Rest*. The other a cheife Peere, though his hard hap to loose his Head *first*, yet neverthelesse in *Abrahams bosome or Paradice*, as his Saviour saying *I come to save that which is lost*, Luk. 19. As when the ancient of dayes his returne shewed there, so referd to *Malachi*, shall come as a swift witnesse in judgement, against adulterers, & adultresses and false swearers, *and for Tithes that robery and the like*. For yee have Rob'd me, &c.

So come *LORD*, and cut off such an evill time, deferre us not.

F I N I S.

10. *As not unknowne, though hath long beene deferd* (1645; Wing D1973) is reprinted, by permission of the Worcester College Library (Oxford University), from the clear copy held at Worcester College (shelfmark AA. 1.12 [30]). The text block of the original measures 365 × 272 mm.

A second text (not reproduced here), *To The Kings Most Excellent Majesty: The Humble Petition of the Lady Eleanor 1633* (Wing D2014A), reproduces the second half of the broadside *As not unknowne* (reproduced in *The Blasphemous Charge* **[36]**), and includes a set of handwritten marginal notes on this material. This second text, itself a broadside, has been dated after 1644. The two extant copies of *To The Kings Most Excellent Majesty* are housed at Worcester College Library (Oxford University) and are appended to that library's copy of *Given to the Elector* **[34]**.

The distinctive marginal comments are as follows:

Alongside Lady Eleanor's petition to the king:

> July 28. 1625. these words saying, *There is Nineteen years and an half to the Judgement day, be you as the meek Virgin.*
> (Fulfilling *Rev.*11. ver.5.) 1644. he on a Friday morning Janu. 10. Beheaded or killed, who burnt that testimony with his own hand, in the presence of so many.

Alongside the brief 'prediction' ('*Shall go on the Word of God to the King* ...') that follows Lady Eleanor's petition to the king:

> And accordingly accomplished on both, as the King at his coming forth 47. so the other seven years compleat and eight current Archbishop before his going into prison, translated that was 1633. Septem. 19. to his Metropolitanship, including also the very seventh and eight moneth And H:7 and H:8. their Character.
>
> So Again the aforesaid 19 of Septem. whose Coach and Horse with the Ferry-Boat, going (as it were) into the Abyss, which sunk down, ascended again.

AS not unknowne, though hath long beene deferd: Neverthelesse this Petition or Prophesie (on Record) not uncomplished: witnesse the present yeare, 1644. When as he on a *Friday* morning was killed or sufferd then: Who little supposed such a *SOP* prepared for his Lordship. (*Mat.* 24.) Saying, *The Lord of that servant shall come in a day and an houre hee lookes not for*: Even unprepared, as much to say, fore-warn'd, Although, that because the day and houre none knowes. Therefore thinks to put off the *Time made knowne of* HIS *comming*, with that Shift: *Who shall cut assunder that false Prophet*, or as the Word renders it, *Cut off* (to wit) his Head, with that Arch Hypocrite gracelesse *Iudas*, bursting *Assunder* His very sentence, both served with one *Writ*.

Doubtlesse *an houre and a day*, Not dreamed of in his *Diarie*, where sets down the 19. of *September*, 1633. Was translated to be Arch *BB*. But not by whose high authority the *Lords day cut off*, *the Sabboth translated into a day of such prophanation*.

And thus having shewd: *The Beast like his Sabbaticall reigne finishd*, seven yeares compleat and eight current that was Arch *BB*. of *Lambeth* (or *Bethlam*) before his going into Prison rewarded as he had shut up and silenced others.

Also for his *Majesties* reference thus, how presumptious so ever the imprinting seemd then of those Books, where prayed to beware *the hand writing*, yet how true: Not behind hand with Him, in applying great *Babylons* judgement at hand. *Dan.* 5. *dedicated unto the present* REIGNE; needs no other *but referrd to such raging division* the Occurrents of the *Present*. *And* with that *for another* of the great Prince *Michaels* standing up, *when such an* unprralleld troublesome Time (Cap. the last) *also shewd to be directed to our distracted Nation of Great Brittain, in the* Arch *Angels name*, *given to this Island*. So notwithstanding these stilod presumptious and detestable: Have made bold presumd to publish the fore-shewing of them in the yeare 1633. When little expected such a blow so nigh, His Majestie then crownd in *Scotland*, With the Arch *B*. hornd here, whose absence and Acts, Weighed with his the last of those *Assyrians*, found as full of *Levity*, or *No lesse wanting*.

TO THE *KINGS* MOST EXCELLENT *MAJESTIE.*

The humble Petition of the Lady Eleanor. 1633

Most humbly ſheweth to Your Ma[tie].

THat the word of God ſpoken in the firſt yeare of Your happie reign unto the Petitioner, upon *Friday* laſt did ſuffer early in the morning: the B:BEAST aſcended out of the Bottomleſſe pitt: having ſeven Heads, &c. ſeaven Yeares, *viz.* making Warre hath overcome, and killed them: *Bookes* ſealed by the Prophets. By the Biſhop of *Lambeth* horned like the Lambe, harted like a VVolfe, are condemned to be burned at *Pauls-Croſſe*, where our Lord crucified, &c. This is the third Day, that their dead Bodies ſhrowded in looſe ſheets of paper. Lye in the ſtreets of the Great Citie, &c. more cruell and hard harted, then other tongues and Nations, who will not ſuffer them ſo to be buried. If your Highneſſe pleaſe to ſpeake the word the ſpirit of life will enter into them they will ſtand upon their feete, &c.

Craving no other pardon, humbly as in duty bound ſhall pray for your Ma[tie].

The word of God to the King, Revela: 17. *October,* 1644.
The BEAST that was, and is not: Even Hee is the eight,
and is of the ſeven, and goeth into perdition.

At the Court at *White-Hall, October* the 8. 1633.

His Majeſtie doth expreſly command the Lord Arch-Biſhop of *Canterburyes Grace*, and his highnes Commiſſioners, for cauſes Eccleſiaſticall. That the Petitioner be forthwith called before them, to anſwer for preſuming to Imprint the ſaid bookes, and for preferring this deteſtable petition.

Sydney Mountague:

Concordat cum originale facta collatione per me Thomam Maydwell, no librum publicum

11. *The Brides Preparation* (1645; Wing D1982) is reprinted by permission of The British Library, from the clear copy found in the Thomason Tracts Collection (shelfmark E.274. [13]). In identifying the date of publication as 1645 rather than 1644 as on the title page, we are following the Gregorian calendar rather than the Julian one then in use; for Lady Eleanor and the English printers the new year began on March 25. The text block of the original measures 143 × 99 mm.

Hard-to-read words and marginal annotations:
4 'wayes' [crossed out]

THE

BRIDES

Preparation.

By the Lady *ELEANOR*:

For it is the day of the Lords *vengeance: and the yeare of recompence for the controveosie of Sion*: (Isaiah 34.

Printed in the year *March* 1644.

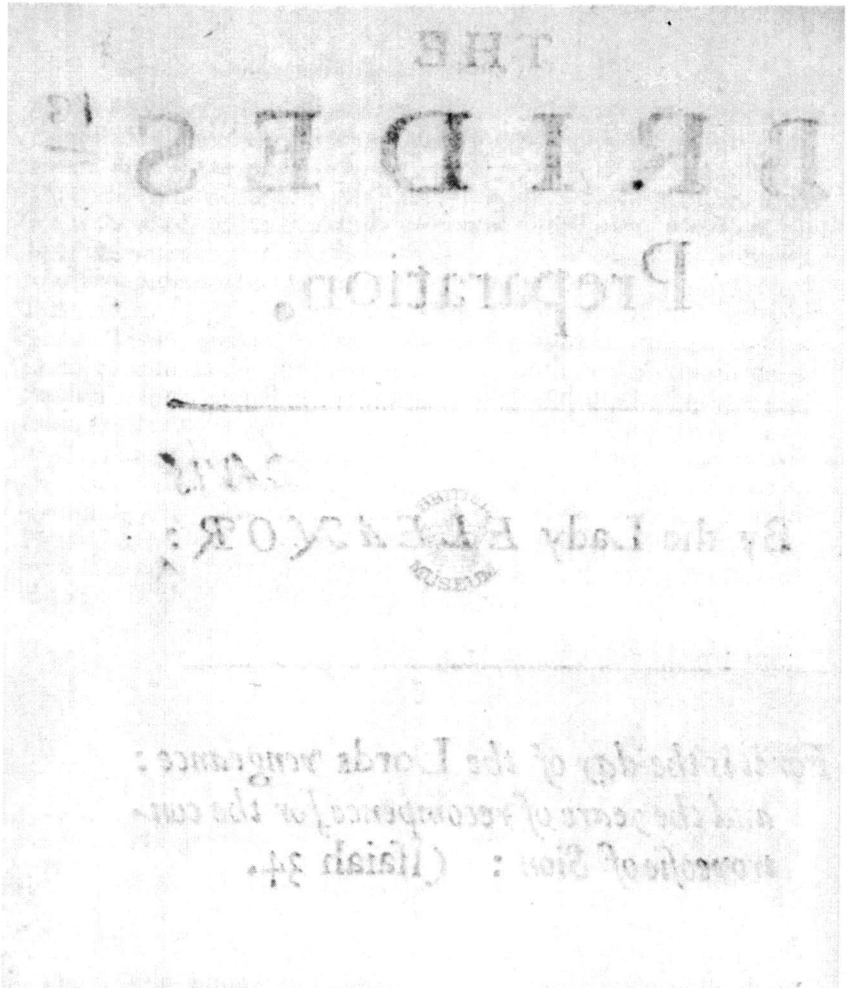

Of the Signification and Meaning of that *Celestiall* foure-square *Citie*: measur'd 144 Cubits.

Revelation, 21.

AS most clearly shews: the Yeare of GOD 1644: VVith our Lady-Dayes *descrip-tion*. & of the *Worlds* Creation, and the things therein made in the *Spring*: to whose beauty, all the glory of the *Indies* Not to bee compar'd, which

A quickens

quickens and revives every *Creature*: So unto *Nothing againe diſolv'd*, to be at the *ſame ſeaſon* even ſeaſonable, *for the quick and dead their meeting.* Even then the bleſſed glorious *Reſurrection*, as the great *Maſter-builder*, ſaying, it is done. *I am ALPHA and OMEGA, The beginning and the end*; The yeare finiſhed, as much to ſay.

And ſo when fruit in perfection at the fall then fell *Adam*: *But proceeding with this HOLY-DAY* partly why preferrd becauſe this ſecreet diſcloſed to one of that *SEX*. Beſides a day obſervd of payment, like the doy of judgement every ones ſervice which rewards *even the appointed time then*: when the Day and Night ~~wayes~~ equall houres the precious Spring.

mixes

Revelation

Revelation. XXI.

And I saw a New heaven, and a New earth, for the first were passed away.

And I *John* (*Joh: annes*) saw the holy Citie, *comming downe from Heaven as a Bride prepared, &c.* shew'd by one of the *seven Angels* (to wit) *Winged time* (the 1700. yeare) which had *the seven Vials full of the seven last plagues, saying, I will shew Thee the bride the Lambes wife*; Even this *uxorem Agni*: The *spring* in her variety of Colours, the *Earth* in all her riches, who begins with; it: for *Times* farwell, shewed or signified. His last houre glasse; run out.

A2 But

But to bee briefe herein, as every Moneth of the Yeare shews, Named severally, by the *Tribes and Apostles* Names, written on those Gates and Foundations twelve in number: where *Juda* for *January* and the like, and the *Wall* answerable thereto twelve thousand *furlongs* all bidding time *a thousand times* farwell: So by the measure of the *Angel, Time so swiftly fleeing* a father of many generations, even the Yeare *aforesaid* 1644: *is measured by those Cubits* 144. *With the foure quarters of the Yeare,* three *moneths alotted each: Of such even Length and Breadth, all foure-square: Three to the East, and three to the West, as it were, &c. where the equall Day and Night put into the reckoning or ballance. And so every Gate of one pearle, one and thirty dayes a peice: The most of these* Vni-*ons, so going on with this vaile of misery ended.*

And

And farther *for* the very place thus *figuring aged time*: the Tower of *Londons* situation represented, the *Cities safety*, that great store house even shew'd St. *John* then newly done: *unreparable now not worth your beholding to what then was*: turned into a prison, *a place of teares and death*, together with the street of this Citie *not unknown of pure Gold like transparet glasse*: the mint on both sides letticd. VVith that Christall Spring proceeding out of the Throne of God and the Lambe, as *Agnus* for *Anno Dom*: and *Mensura* for *Menses, and Tempus for Templum*, &c. And so the tree of life *significant also* which yeelds it monthly fruit for the *healing of Nations whose evill incureable without it*. to wit, The last day reveale their only remedy: like that water of life, *free for every one* to *come and take it*, so farre from being *forbidden or* within the compasse of any curse

on

or point of curiosity that it is become a blessing, *no lesse then one of the commandement to doe it.* As the second death appointed to be their portion the fearfull and unbeleevers which shall add or deminish from the words of this book and *faithfull* prophesie shewing the Lords second comming.

Seconded thus in the 7. Chap. and Chap. 14. Where concerning the great blow in such a yeare all going upon that great number. *And I saw foure Angels standing on the foure corners of the earth holding the foure winds, that the wind should not blow, till a hundred forty and foure sealed,* As it were our great Army: For so no question to be made of what Nation that company. Cap. 7, verse 14. In *Albion* Array St. *Iohns* reply to that Elder, in plaine English makes it knowne: Saying, SIR, thou knowest and wheuce they came, If thou art one of the 24. Elders since the Conquest your Majestie knowes them as much to say whose reign concluding it with his Corownation, thus Mat. 25. *Where the Kingdome of Heaven likend to five wise Virgins and five foolish,* no doubt pointes at the blessed Virgins feast *not* to be unprepared then. So make no tarying O my God.

FINIS.

12. *Great Brittains Visitation* (1645; Wing D1994) is reprinted by permission of The British Library, from the unique copy held at The British Library (shelfmark Tab.603. a.38. [9]). The text block of the original measures 151 × 81 mm. The following pages are misnumbered (and the correct number is shown in square brackets): 01 [10], 27 [33], 29 [34], 25 [35], 32 [37], 28 [39], 30 [40].

Hard-to-read words:

[40].1–8 though not unforetold how bitter a pille it would prove: So might be insisted on his writing to a LADIE (willing her) not to salute with God speed them of the faction of Antichrist. But unwilling to be voluminus to intrude too farr on the bounds of patience in distracted times.

GREAT BRITTAINS VISITATION.

By the Lady *ELEANOR*.

Printed in the Yeare, 1645

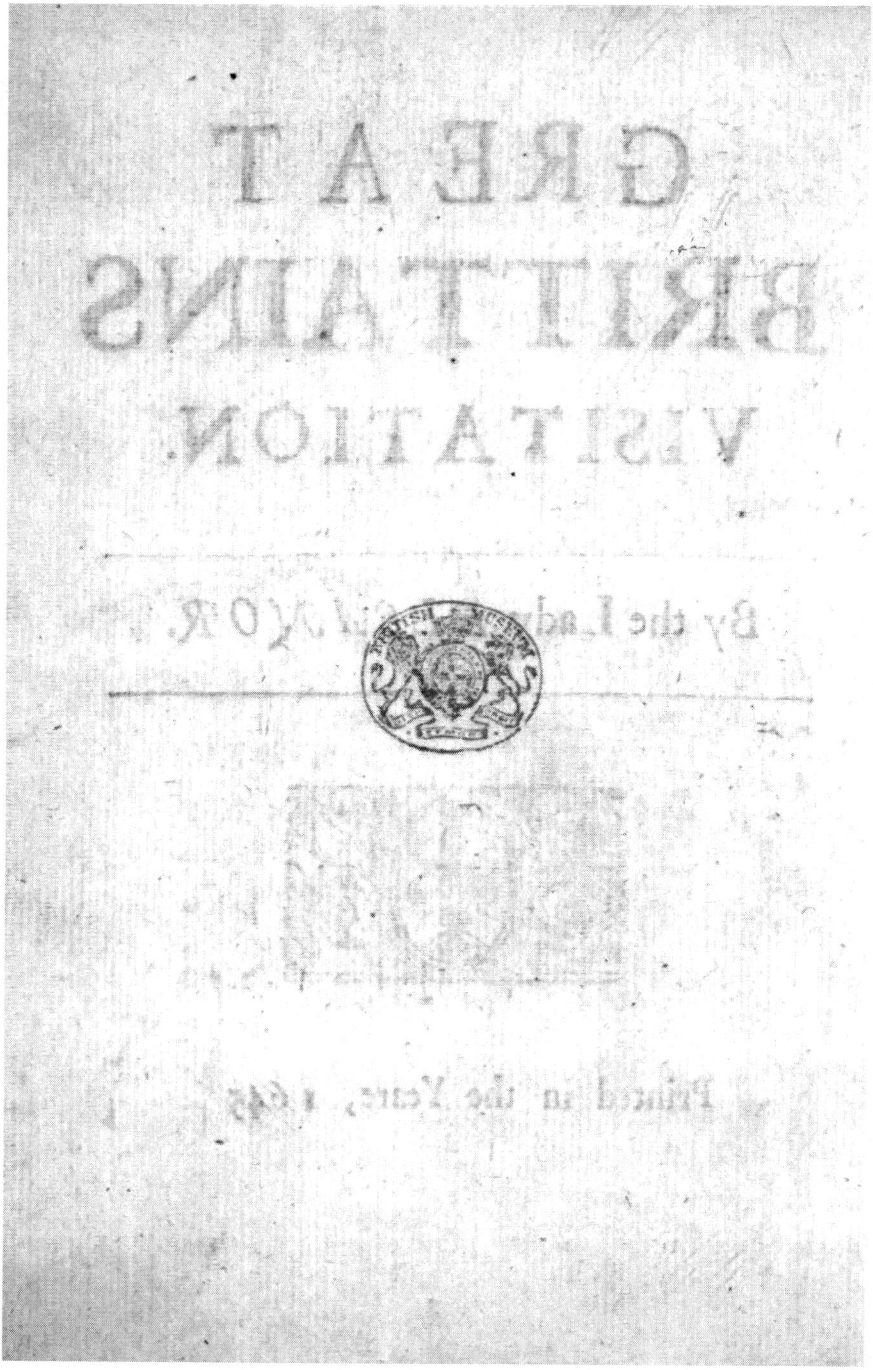
GREAT
BRITTAINS
VISITATION.

By the Lady ELEANOR.

Printed in the Yeare, 1645.

THE APOCALYPS PROLOGVE.

WHerein a revolution or returne, Expreſt, as in thoſe dayes it came to paſſe, when as City and Countrey oppreſt ſo: By ſuch an univerſall impoſd taxx: Inns ſo full that for our only Saviour to be borne in. No place but an open Stable afforded: And thus like the truth

F which

which no Corners or Curtaines requires. The joyfull tydings they in the wide field, First saluted with them: Shepheards that kept watch the glory from the Lord by night which shone round about them.

So lastly at his second comming, or returne also reveald to be afore hand, the watch-full Pastors saluted: ouer Spirituall Flocks from him, saying: I am Alpha and Omega, the morning Starre and evening both: the first and the last. *As this the Lord of Sabbaths Angel whose countinance as the Sun, and at the evening of time come, with the seven Starrs, &c. And Golden Candle-sticks all watch Lights round about him, even so farther for the little Booke of Life, who had its Swadle-Bands (as it were un-loosd: with Seven fold Seales bound so fast up, when wonderfull acclamation such in hea-ven.*

ven & Earth (Revel. 5) as came to passe with the Angel; a multitude of the Heavenly Host suddainly praising God: Luke 2. such Corispondencie ever between the Son of God, and Gods Word which for ever and ever indures. Maugre the Old Serpents malice. And his Angels.

And therefore to say the truth, Though the Bottomlesse pit freely opend, no wonder affording beside evill Spirits their Fellowship, Munition also of all Kinds, And the winds let loose out of their Prisons, And Wrathfull Vialls the last powrd out, Who shall commisserate their Condition? when open house or Court (as it were) kept in Heaven, inviting all, Darkenesse notwithstanding preferd at last shall be before Light: Like those frivolous and light excuses made of marriage its mutability: preferd above the estate of Angels: And before eternall life:

farmes

Farmes their Leases or the like.

Thus no marvel, although with the infernall pit opend, where those Wormes or Locusts swarming out Our Pruining Hookes turnd into Swords, our union into division; And so much for these present vegilent dayes of ours from which nothing conseald is or hidden, even the things in the little golden booke as with no little expedition are presented here.

THE REVELATION OF JESVS CHRIST Interpreted.

SHews how ONE Isle calls unto another, *The Isle of Pathmos*, unto the Iles of *Great Brittaine*. The great day of the Lords comming revealing it: *Whereof let the Isles be glad*, Now or Never.

Of

Of whose Visitation *from him which is, and which was, and which is to come:* what date the time beares, the first witnesse these, *And from the seven Spirits in sight of the Throne or nearest there unto, vers. 4.* Which as it signifies or figures the present Century, *or the last seven hundred years* Also points at the present reigne, when it began, about *Easter,* witnesse these: *And from Jesus Christ the first begotten of the dead,* And the Prince of the Kings of the Earth, *Unto him that loved us, and washed us from our sins in his owne Blood, verse 5.*

Even as two for failing can witnesse

witnesse, *Sonne and Father both*: crown'd or *created Kings*, about the aforesaid *Resurrection feast kept*, concluded thus: *And hath made us Kings and Priests unto God and his father, to him be glory and dominion* for ever and ever Amen. verse 6. *Behold he commeth, &c.* as much to say, the last father and sonne of that kind from the Conquest: since when hath been 24. of them, making up the blessed Prophets and Apostles number.

And so farewell *the blessed yeares of Grace*, and time to be longer as in the yeare 1625. was

reveal'd

revealed *to his Hand-maid*, the *first* yeare of his reigne, *to whom the day of Judgement being at hand declared*: was dedicated in a booke by her: And the generall Resurrection to bee in his dayes as from the Prophet *Daniels* mouth given to understand: concerning the aforesaid time: *And at that time shall the great Prince Michael stand up, which standeth for the children of the people or defender of the Faith*, even Great Brittaines troublesom *time*, pointing thereat with the plagues pursuing one another for mortality as never since a Nation the like: Of whose *Inauguration or standing up*

at

at the aforesaid Resurrection feast thus signified: *Many of them that sleepe in the dust of the Earth shall wake*, some to everlasting life, *&c.Dan.* 12.

And for a faithfull witnesse *So goe thy way Daniel*, as no few in their Mother Earths Bosome dayly take up their lodging of free cost, *till Michael his alarme awakens them*, where also the yeare 1625. (*untill which dayes Daniels visions to waite*) Thus cast up two Hundred & ninety daies and three hundred and five and thirty, 625. (*Dan.* 12.)

But going on with *John whose name*

name to no Nation better known then unto Ours, who ſtiles himſelfe your Brother and companion in tribulation, in the Iſle that is called *Patmos*, where confined *was on the Lords day viſited by the Holy Ghoſts Angel, the* Firſt voice ſaying, *I am Alpha and Omega, and what thou ſeeſt write in a Booke and ſend it, &c.* Wherupon being turned, ſaw that dreadfull appearance, *ONE all looking from head to foot like fire,* that ſtood in the midſt of thoſe candle ſtickes of Gold, and therupon falling dead at his feet by a touch of his Septer, the ſeven Starrs in his right hand, being a-

againe

gaine revived come to himselfe: was againe charged to write the things to come, the mistery of the seven starres which he saw in his hand, the Lord of Sabbath *Even to display times Coate by* CHARLES *Waggon or Wayne,* to wit the seventh present Century, about the midst of it, even to looke for the generall Resurrection time, as present, past, *and future here with times voice testified from him which is, and which was, and is to come.*

Wherefore in the day of Judgements likenesse was presented unto him the Booke of the Old and new

B *Testament*

Testament, that Alpha and Omega: Whose Body as it were clothed and girt. The Bible in gilt paper bound with brasse Clasps which in such a yeare beares date, 1700. *When interpreted the booke of the Revelation* as *whatsoever spoken in darkenesse or in the Eare assur'd to be made cleare as the light. And he* that hath an eare let him heare what the Spirit of prophesie saith, and in time repent and amend, or expect a blow for *his paines, when he stands at the doore and knocks so long, the Comforter sent saying, behold I come quickly. And he shall Sup, and sit with mee that hears my voice opens the doore.*

Cap.

CAP. 4.

THough haſtning with winged time: yet ſome more Evidence requiſit in this a matter of ſuch weight the day of judgement: And ſo ſhewes a doore opened here, as much to ſay, *Nothing conſeald or hidden, as heavens catheder all ſhewed here, the voice ſaying come up heither, I will ſhew thee things to come.* The Reſurrection propheticall alarme verily, like that afore, *I am he that was dead and am alive, &c. and have the Keyes, &c.* Firſt ſaw where the ancient of dayes ſate,

Inthroned under a Canopey, raine bowe like: VVhere all in Prieſtly Veſtments round about *thoſe Elders with reſtleſſe* Thundering voices extolling his name who lives for ever and ever. *And Holy, Holy, Holy, crying out as it were glory be to the Father, &c. Amen.* For whoſe pleaſure all things created. As for the lamps before the Throne, *to wit* the year of God call'd the ſeven Spirits of God, of the ſame influence with the ſeven Stars, requires no farther repetition being both one: Neither theſe in the likenes here of Saints and Angels, in Heaven *whoſe wings ſo full of eyes before*

fore and behind signifying those eye witnesses their watchfullnesse and as personating the blessed *Prophets* and Evangelists: So lastly farther for the *mysterie or morall* of *these crown'd Elders expresly* shews, How many intered Princes in this Isle since the conquest which in the space of seven hundred yeares last past in Alablaster Shrowds clothed, That have cast their Crownes before the Throne or before the great day.

Cap.

CAP. 5.

AND without boaſting or amplifying, theſe the truth in few words: *This bleſſed Booke firſt cryed, He that hath an eare let him heare. And here by a ſtrong Angel proclam'd: Who is worthy to open the booke in the right hand of him ſitting upon the Throne*: No other then the miſterie of times and ſeaſons, in the yeare of the worlds Redemption, 1625. tobe reveald or unſeald. And becauſe this ſo difficult (no man found *worthy &c.*) *John that therfore much wept*, by *that* Elder willed to weep no more

more. *Informed* *E C C E L E O radix David, vicet, to open the booke and loose the sevenfold seales* : being not improper to explain this likewise, as he said, *I am Joseph, so am I David,* This name of mine enterd here: by that Elder even *Daniel*, as much to say, *Goe thy way Iohn, let those words satisfie thee* spoken to *Daniel*: The words are sealed up untill the time of the end, *Thou shalt stand in thy lott,* &c. (*Dan.* 12.) Reservd till a time and times and halfe: Pointing to the present Century so signified in behalfe of it, three periods and a part, &c.

So dignus est agnus, viz. Anno Domini,

Domini, in such a yeare of our Redemption, the first yeare of such a reigne. These Sabbaticall Seales unloosed witnesse, *For thou hast redeemed us and made us Kings and Prophets and we shall reigne.*

Even so let every Creature in the sea, namely the Isles Blesse those right hand yeares, with that Grand Iury, the 24. Elders before the Throne falling down. VVho give up their Verduit, *Davids* Keye hath prevaild honour, glory, and blessing, &c.

Cap.

CAP. 6.

AND the Sonne of Thunder this fourth Evangelist that heard the day of Judgements Sommons, *The noise of thunder as it were, one of the seven Seales being unloosed: One of the foure Beasts saying come and see* : As much to say, *display'd* times and seasons mistery: *In the seventh Century*, And unto what Nation, this new Song of the Lords comming dedicated: as no unnecessary *circumstance time*, a thing observed of old, when the word of the Lord came unto them.

C For

For evidence hereof the Conquerer & *Rufus*, here behold *their ancient* Seales: *Where first saw a White Horse*, and *He that sate on him a Bowe, and a Crowne given unto him*. The English bowe renoun'd farr and neere: (verse 2.) VVhereby cleere as day given to understand *the Sonne of God reveald out of the Scripture to these very Isles. Wherefore listen O Isles.*

And this misterie of time sealed with the yeares foure seasons, their discriptions, *The Sun like a Conquerour: and Gods word like the Sunne which overcomes whatsoever* Dispells all darkenesse, saying: *Hee*

He that hath an eye come and see: The worlds eye, like an expert Horseman upon his Carreer: running his restlesse course about, who first enters the victorious crowned yuory Ramme, the *Wholesome Spring more then Gold to be embraced, the Odoriferous Spring giving to every creature Life.*

The second Rider so furious, he on the Red Horse, giving all one word, Come and see: Not difficult to be discern'd, the *Crabb at all points* armed, *Summers scorching rayes: when red as fire all:* Slaying in Armes as it were with Sythes and such like no short weapon.

C 2 The

The third a Blacke Horſe, he *that ſate on him, a paire of Ballance in his hand, in his proper colours and complexion ſignified not inferior to his fellowes*, *as Automes voice* cleeres it, who theſe Celeſtiall Horſemen, *or Riders* were, a voice heard in the midſt of them, ſaying, *A meaſure of Wheat for a peny, and three meaſures of Barley*. And hurt not *the wine and oyle*], even the Sun in his circuit paſſing by the *Equinoctiall*, weighing equall houres [to day and night: *Thus all the world come and behold alſo the fourth ſeaſons miſterie*, explained in this new Calender or Prognoſtication.

The

The fourth a pale Horſe, he that ſate one him called Death. Or like the laſt day ſo gaſtly and *paile* the grizled Goate with his Beard. *Hoary Winter its wann viſage that ſtarvs with hunger young and old*, ſhaking every Limbe.

And theſe Characters pointing at thoſe foure Beaſts, *Aries*, *Taurus*, *Leo*, *Capricorne*, *Like* as *the foure Evangeliſt*. By winged Beaſts foure, full of eyes. Which Motto, *come and ſee*, may ſerve them to *which reſts not Day nor Night*.

And after foure of the Seales

opend

opened the mistery shewd of the foure seasons, the Suns restlesse course (to say) finish'd. *The next offer'd to considerations veiw, in this Story or Treatise, is the blessed case of those poore Soules intreated a little Season to rest: till their* Fellow *S*ouldiers and Brethren *killed* as they, VVhose Blood for the Testimony they held crying so loud, *How long Lord,* &c. to wit, to the day of vengeance, as behold defferd no longer the day of Iudgement immediatly which followes in its dreadfull likenesse, when as fullfild, white robes given likewise to *the rest of their brethren arrayed,* to (to wit) *in cleane Shrowds.*

Then Time *to his untimely end comes, whose thride of life suddainly cutt off, of whose sable Hearse thus, & what mourners accompanying the corps of time, about* 44. *aged in the midest of his dayes:* First the quaking Earth Mother of all in such a consumption. The Sunn next as blacke as Sack cloth of haire, coverd all over. And the Moone over watched with her red face looking *like blood*, the condoleling *Heavens* shedding their stars in stead of teares as fast, impatient windes as loud: their shrill Throat setting forth, ready to rent

rent all aſſunder with Sighes hollow Grones.

So all departing as they came: the Heavens as it were quartering those Ancient Coates the foure Seasons, which were like Scutchens roled up together like a Scrole: The Islands carried away with the violence of the Seas uproare: Each acting a part, the Kings and Great men ringing out ſuch a Peale, *all* flying away and hyding themſelves for the great day of his wrath to come as who able to ſtand, routed *all*, ſurpriſed in ſuch a moment *darkeneſſe.*

Cap.

CAP. 7.

AND these like *Iacobs* Ladder reaching at last to Heaven Gate: (*Ascendentem abortu solis:*) *Behold saw foure Angels standing on the foure Corners of the Earth holding the foure Winds that they should not blow, &c.* Even gives to understand in what year the Finall blow, saying: *hurt not, &c.* till we have sealed so many, *And there were sealed a hundred forty and foure, &c.* of the servants of God in the fore heads, as much to say, the yeare of God, 1644. when compleat, then the

D dissolution

diſolution comes quickly or is at hand. *And thus like the Covenant of late ſealed, where ſo many names alſo the months of the yeare, ſetting their hands as it were twelve times twelve.* verſe 4.

And as including the yeare compleat or accompliſhed, 44. till when thoſe pernitious winds reſtrayned not to hurt the Earth nor any Tree: *So Aludes to that fruitleſſe tree after the fourth yeare to be for borne*, no longer interceded, for in the Goſpel. Wherefore *Sir*, theſe are to let you know it is ſpoken to your *Majeſtie*, the laſt of thoſe crowned foure and twenty

Elders

Elders, *being full forty foure aged, and reigning since aged 24. saying* Sir *thou knowest who they are, verse* 14.

That Albion Regiment, these Folke in white Robes fleeced and famished as yee see, the very condition of Prisoners taken by you: The Prophet *Isaiah* gives notice of it, They are his words too, *Listen O Isles, &c.* 49. Cap. That thou mayest say *to the Prisoners goe forth, to them that are in darkenesse they shall hunger and thirst no more, neither shall heat nor Sun any more smite them*, for the Lambe in the midest of the Throne having the seven eyes

D 2 which

which are the ſeven ſpirits of God, ſhall wipe away all teares from their eyes.

And more over for theſe words *aforeſaid, as* ſerving for the mideſt of the Century, about the yeare, 44. So points at the very halfe yeare, *about Michael the Arch Angells Feaſt, the aforeſaid Blow,* or laſt Blow, *there about till when thoſe hurtfull winds reſtrained,* Michaelmas riggs ſo called.

As aforeſhewed forbidden to hurt the VVine and the Oyle: all ſpeaking as it were with *Automns* boyſterous *voice,* a greater Blow then great Babylons, when that hand writing appeared, writen

ten by that Angels hand, that Prince affrighting and his numerous Peers, not a little.

CAP. 8.

AND *like as about halfe an houre after the clocke had ſtricken,* ſhews about the ſpace of halfe an houre there was ſilence in Heaven, after the ſeales were opened which imports not only when a vacancie in the Church. *Theſe Angels their ſtanding before God then, preparing themſelves to ſound, but ſhews withall a ſpace of time allotted to repent of their contempts ſtood in, and cruelties before his*

men

men of warre sent forth. But the marriage of the Lambe being ready they unworthy that were bidden: The censure fil'd with Alter Coales is cast downe the curse deser'd no longer, the aforesaid seven Angels so highly preferd, found fire and sword, woe to Land and Sea.

And so the great Ship its being lanchd forth, shewed at large, ver. 12 *likened to* Etnas *burning mountaine with like Sulpharous smoaks smiting of Sunne Moone, and Starrs, the third part: and with such a spacious Lampe like a Starre even well named Wormewood: verily the Arch Bishops Charecter*

recter, His lanching out or advancing both goes together: Bishops and Ships able both to choake all with their smoakes and the like. The very root of bitternesse made of it, and this the meaning of this unluckey Starrs falling burning as a lamp. The contriver of this third kingdoms cumbustion this aforesaid high Officer in the Church, also with the yeare of God 1633. *September accompanied, when he translated as in truth this Prognostication serves from the yeare 1625. untill 44. compleat. The third Angells proclaimes it: Witnesse Woe, woe, woe, treble woes to the Earths Inhabitants*

to

to wit, *England, Scotland and Freland*. And ſo much for theſe Angells alarme imparted concerning the third part of creatures in the Sea diſtroied: and the third part of Ships. And the third part of the lights of Heaven ſmitten, and to ſlay the third part of men, Saying come and ſee or behold great *Brittains Mapp*, *as viſible as the Heavens foure Seaſons ſhewd in the Calender*.

Even *Lucifers* being caſt downe lik lightning in our dayes First the Arch Biſhop in whoſe cuſtodie the Keys of the AByſs power given him to impriſon, Levie Taxes, wage warre at his pleaſure

pleaſure, the looſe Reines laid on his Necke that breake his owne the portion *of that aſpiring Hypocrite full of the miſterie of Iniquitie: And ſo much for the miſterie of that malevolent Starre.*

CAP. 9.

PRoceeding one with theſe calculated for this Kingdom ſhewing, as *Heaven* open'd and thoſe horſemens comming proclaim'd come and ſee. *Alſo open'd the bottomleſſe pit, ecclipſing the Sun and Ayre, ſet open by him the Sonne and Heire of perdition, father of that generation of Vipers:* So Dragons *and Deeps, like the evill ſpirits confeſſe and praiſe God when men faile.* For

E diſco_

discovering whose comming at hand the day of judgements standing at the doore, the very current coine demonstrated of this Kingdome all horsemen, money made their Gold that odored Masse occasion of evills all, *Begetting such unnaturall doings, Warrs, and Imprisonments, desired death where it flees away, of late like Hell throng'd as full every where. Of which flying current halfe crowne peices Currentium in* Bellum, *with Crownes on their heads, what peices of Plate they are no need to aske or goe farre to inquire,* whose Image with deformed haire, Hermophradite Locks, none of that mayden Queens doubtlesse with

Breast-

Breaſt plates all, &c. ſuch tormenting doings and Dolers unknowne in her dayes.

And ſo much for thoſe ſignes with that ſtar of the bottomleſſe pitt in the likeneſſe of *Scorpio and Sagitarious, with faces like men, but as the noſe in the face or the like ſo difficult whoſe to diſcerne, whoſe ſuperſcription or diſcription,* & *with our* old Gold plainly called the Angel of the aforeſaid ABytis (that Diſtroyer) not without a double ſignification like thoſe names, *Abbadon and Apollyon,* giving to underſtand withall as under the Angels feet the Scorpion or Dra-*Anglia* giving the Angells name fatall to the Old Serpent *to receive there his fall.*

E 2 And

And here one woe is past (The sower of debate and division Anatamiz'd) *And two woes more comming after, passing over how farre Civill warre exceeds other. the Navyes preparation comes next, those winged Horses of the Sea with Lyons heads and Serpents tayles.*

The winds withall prepared for an houre, a day, a moneth, and a yeare, which Angels foure commanded to be loosed bound in the East as it were: or Babylons great river *Euphrates*, not only points at that suddain hand writing sent but to the yeare of 1644. past as much to say, then the third woe the day of judgement comes after or quickly, like a theife

Theise. Of which *Horse men even* bound *in the narrow Seas saying. He heard the number of them or list of their names, with fire and smoake and Brimstone issuing out of* their tayles the very firie Lake, to behold with stinging great Gunns or peices chargd as here peices of all kinds numberd, of late since discovered the *Indies*, And so farre for a discoverie of the time also, and these serving to explaine the rest: And the rest of the men that were not killed, &c: (verse 20.) repented not that they should not serve Divels of Gold and Silver, &c. (*Dæmonia*) neither repented they of their murthers

murthers, Fornications, and Theifts. As much to ſay, which had quarter for their lives, being Priſoners, yet ſo beaſtly as it Were come of the breed of bruit beaſt rather then man kind, like theſe monſters between a Horſe and a Foule, ſome GRIFFINS winged or the like, with ſuch renting teeth Ruffins of the pit of Hell halfe Divels: So to them, calling *themſelves Biſhops* but are none theirs the Keye of the kingdome of darkeneſſe.

CAP. 10.

THe Miſterie of God open in the Angels Hand (whoſe Face like the Sun) to give a touch againe of it not amiſſe, as crownd with the dayes of the Flood being 1700. yeares after the creation. So the very yeare 1625. under his hand beares date before this Odoriſerous little Booke to be reveal'd, The

Burthen

Burthen of God Word received from Angelicall hands, The blessed Sacrament or Seale eaten of the Lords comming at hand, & therfore commanded to be publishd even proclaimd beyond Sea also, wherefore to his Lyons voice adds his speaking posture the one of his firie feet setting upon the sea the other on the Earth pointing to Heaven with a high hand, sweares in his wrath the apointed time is come.

By him above who lives for ever and ever, calling withall Heaven and Earth and Sea to witnesse with the things that are therein that time shall be no longer.

As displaied afore by things Celstiall and Terrestriall from the celestiall signes, to peices of coine and ships & great peices &c. And as having shewd this booke his commission no lesse sweet thed Manna to his mouth, how distastfull so ever to others (persecuted by Antichrist,) Most willingly is taken

though

though not unforetold how bitter a pille it would prove: So might be insisted on his writing to a LADIE (willing her) not to salute with God speed them of the faction of Antichrist. But unwilling to be voluminus to intrude too farr on the bounds of patience in distracted times.

FINIS.

13. *For Whitsontyds Last Feast* (1645; Wing D1990) is reprinted, by permission of the Worcester College Library (Oxford University), from the complete copy held at Worcester College (shelfmark AA.1.12[32]). The text block of the original measures 180 × 140 mm. (N.B. the title page has been reduced to fit our text page area.) The handwritten comments in this tract resemble the hand of those that appear in the Folger tracts.

Hard-to-read handwritten annotations and printed words:

Title page	Lecesters Loss: revela. [ ] / The second woe is past. *&c.* [transcription]
9.4	his
9.16	Plagues
12.4	*Languages*
12.5	*loud voice*
12.7	firie tongues of theirs
12.8	suffices for the insuing
12.9	finished
12.10–17	wherefore with the 14 Elders that great Councill or States sitting upon their seats forever with one consent and voice Let great *Brittain likewise* say; *Wee give thee thrice humble thanks O eternal Trinity, which art, and wast, and art to come,* because thou has taken to thee thy great power and hast reigned.
12.21	*held as impossible* a point
13.2–5	*expir'd, ther is a* Release *out of* HELL, *Redemption for all the* DAMNED, *Although granted that sentence Irevocable,* Goe yee Cursed, &c.
13.12–19	*Therefore if* Salt *which* preserves *be good, the fire also necessary like those better to enter maim'd into* Heaven *then otherwise goe into fire* unquenchable *which goes not out, to our dayes without doubt* directed (*Marke the 9.*) *where so often repeated those words concluded,* have peace in your selves.
15.7	*these*
15.8	seald
15.10–11	*Currentium in bellum*
15.18	*Darknesse*
16.1	*deriv'd from hence*
16.6	Tormentors
16.9	…Thou
16.10	So inferr a
16.14	(*let us say*)

FOR WHITSON TYDS LAST *FEAST*:

THE PRESENT, 1645.

Leicesters Loss: revela. xi
The second woe is past. &c

ACTS the first:

The same IESUS *shall come, in like manner as yee have seene him goe, &c.*

Printed in the Yeere, 1645.

THE
LA: ELEA:
HER CREED OR
Confeßion.

VErily *as We all* Beleeve *in* GOD, *the sole* Creator *of all* Things *that were made in the* beginning : *So* according *to His* promise *made also* ; *Concerning the* VVomans *SEED*, *of which the*

A 2 Serpent,

Serpent, on forfiture or *pain of his* head, forewarn'd to beware: *do beleeve in our Lord* IESVS hee the *very* GOD: *alone* Redeemer of the *World*, born *of the VIRGIN*, *which Conceived by the Holy Ghost*, our only Sanctifier.

VVho after he had finished on *the sixt day the* worke of *Our Redemption, and* rested the *seventh, rose* againe. And was by the *space* of *six weekes* seen, *whose last Commandement* was to wait *for his* Fathers promise, of *the Holy Ghosts* comming *in whom We also beleeve*.

Wherfore of beleife not slow: in

those

those Things written by the *Prophets* and *Apostles*, doe for mine own part *Confesse*, how *incredible soever* it seems to *Others*, I farther beleeve the second *Comming* of the *holy Ghost*, imediately before the *day of Judgement* acording to that spoken by the *Prophet Joel*, saying: GOD *saith*, afterward it shall come to passe, I will powre out my Spirit upon all flesh, before the great and terrible Day of the LORD: *Namely, on the Gentiles, their* Sonnes *and* Daughters *likewise*: And I will shew Wonders in the Heavens (*beside a New* Star, *not long* since never) more frequent signes, & in

A 3 the

the Earth *Blood, and Fire, and pillars of Smoake, &c. Witnesse such* warr, throughout *the* Christian world.

Of which last dayes, give M E leave to say, in *Grace* and *Giftes of* LEARNING; how *Rich* so-ever They *esteem* themselves: The *Gentiles* neverthelesse of a *Comforter*, more need had *Never*, how *much* soever *presume upon their Holinesse*: Supposing like the *Jewes* a *Saviour* for them *unnecessary*, which held themselves *so just*: And so *because* Christians already *cleansed*; likewise no more *need to be beholding*: Thus all *concluded under* unbeleif, & *fearfull* blindnes, *unmind-*

full

full of that Charge, to feare by others wofull fall, and not to bee high-minded, Rom. 11. *And so for farther* justifying *this point touching* Prophecie *for ever not extinguished. But as the* Latter raine *no lesse requisit then the former,* though for a time ceas'd: Shall proceed *on with the everlasting* Gospel, *concerning the case of the* Gentiles *cut off,* in case of unbeleife.

As even the two witnesses *comming against them with* firie mouths, *that thinke to* quench *or silence the* Spirit of Prophecie, *well called Spirituall* Sodome *and* Egypt *that Citie. And be the Beast* as Bruitish, *ascended out of the Bottomlesse pit (as it*

were

were) Iudas *ſpirit* conjured up, *or* Herod *that* Fox, *together with the* Nations *or* Gentiles *as outragious as the* Jewes, *becauſe theſe two* Prophets *tormented them, whoſe teſtimony publiſh'd*, the Old and New Teſtament thoſe, *Luke* 21. *There ſhall be ſigns, &c. who* Maugre *their enemies ſtood upon their feet again: the* Spirit of life *entering into them.*

Intruth *as much to ſay, the* Prophet Daniel *ſtiled greatly beloved: and this favourite* Diſciple, *their ſealed* Bookes (*reſerved for the end*) open'd *or to be* interpreted, *like them-ſelves* lying dead and revived: *by the* Angels, *touch or hand. And as thoſe ſent two and two: before the* Lord

Lords face, even so the Messengers of the Resurrection, the two *witnesses* sent to prepare the Iudge of quicke and dead his *comming* Revel. 11. VVhose foes incensed so against them for the same. As the little Booke open in the Angels hand (Revel. 10) declares. Commanded to be eaten, *verily no* other then the Sacrament of the *Lords* returne sworne in his wrath as it were even times finished reigne, or dayes to be shortned.

And for this so distastfull to the world; *therfore* heavie judgements and Plagues and VVarre appointed the day of Iudgements forerunner as worthy of no other, when come to passe on earth such

B distra-

distraction, and the World six thousand years aged too, as in the sixt Century of *Noahs* age the Flood came upon the Earth, but so many dayes of the weeke (as it were,) in the *Lords account*.

And thus *he* one of the *witnesses John* bidden to arise, and measure the *Gospels Progresse* as it were, the Temple, how long until the rising from the Dead, from his dayes bearing date 1700. yeares as the halfe of seven gives it plainly, sealed up in those *Propheticall Characters*, the 42. Moneths given them to prophecie, or a thousand two hundred & sixty dayes, and so a time & times and halfe a-

greea-

greeable to the present division, & *thus* both agreeing in one, stiled by the Prophet *Daniel*, a time and times and the deviding of time, *whose Commission to* continu *so long*: And then *he* whosoever *shall* oppose it *Though* never so great : as here he stiled the *God* of the earth *no* lesse, these two as freely to proclaime open warre so often as they please, to smite the *Earth* or L*and* with *Pestilence and such Judgments*, *as those* Vials *of wrath* directed to the present *Century shew*, so much sufficess: and how they were rewarded, their Sackcloth changed into a glorious cloud, and their Foes so much tormented with their testimony, *how at the same time such an Earthquak the City falling upon them*, except a Remnant

B 2

nant which upon Repentance or peace made, *escaped*.

And all these but speaking one thing in severall *Languages* (to wit) *the Resurrections loud voice*, and that of the Ascention: as *ascendite huc* added to those Propheticall fi ie tongues of theirs or fire proceeding out of their mouths, if any will harme them sufficesfor the insuing feast also, when fully come or finish'd wherefore with the 24 Elders that great Councell or States fitting upon their seats for ever with one consent and voice Let great *Brittain likewise say*; *Wee give thee thrice humble thanks O eternal Trenity, which art, and wast, and art to come*, because thou hast taken to thee thy great power and hast reigned.

And I beleeve *lastly*, though a *Mistery* none of *the lest*, like the *grace of God bestowed upon the* Gentiles, *held as impossible* a point with the

the *Apostles*: *That after the last* Period *expir'd, ther is a* Releale *out of* HELL, *Redemption for all the* DAMNED, *Although granted that* sentence *Irevocable*, Goe yee Cursed, &c.

And the unpardonable sinne, not in this world *nor that to come so given: And the fire* unextinguished, *yet proves their* sufferings *not of like* nature *and condition*: *Notwithstanding in danger*, (were *God* extreame) *of endlesse torment*: *Therefore if* Salt *which* preserves *be good, the fire also necessary like these better to enter maim'd into* Heaven *then otherwise goe into fire* unquenchable *which goes not out, to our dayes without doubt* directed (*Marke the* 9. *where so often repeated these words concluded*, have peace in your selves.

And

And therefore before that Parable *where mentioned the* gulfe *or fixed ſpace, no other then a* prefixed ſpace *of time. (Luke* 15.)*his* Elder *Brother* expoſtulating *reproves like* unnaturallnes *in others, without compaſsion of thoſe undergoing the ſecond death, in the loſt* Son *inſtanc'd the ſecond* brother, *as thoſe words* ſaying: It was meet, &c. For this *thy* Brother was dead, and is alive again, was loſt, and is found.

Approving of that Principle of every thing in the end, goes to its proper place from whence it came to returne. And ſo much for a doore in *heaven* opened; the mouth of Prophesie againe thundering out *Judgements,* (Revela. 4.) together *with thoſe, the* Bottomleſſe pit *opened* alſo, *hels*

hels Epitomie & *their King over them*, where they not having the Seale of God in their foreheads (*some name given as it were*) These not killed seeking death fleeing from them. wher *so many months imprisonment shewd: as prisons never so fild as in these dayes* : Shall not need to add what yeare of God seald with, &c. where such innumerable Horse-men discribed to the life : *Currentium in bellum*, beside current *Coine* Half-Crown-peices, *super capita tanquam corone*, & *habebant capillos sicut capillos mulierum* : Revela. 9. *viz* &c.

And thus having cansel'd Purgatories numberlesse passes *and pardons that take upon them to deliver others, and cannot out of such utter spirituall Darknesse free them.*

themselves, deriv'd from hence: thou *shalt* not come forth thence *untill paid the utmost mite. And hee without commisseration of his fellow*-servant served with the like MEASURE: delivered to the Tormentors, till paid all was due.

All *ye* take to *your* comfort those armes *displayd, as said to the one, this day* Thou *shalt be with* ME, *&c.* So inferr another *like* day for the Other: And therefore, as the Lord lives that shall rayse us from the dust of death *so* the Lord lives (*let us say*) *that brings up out of the Jawes of* HELL *backe to Paradice,* and *increase our Faith.*

FINIS.

14. *The* [*Second*] *Co*[*ming of Our*] *Lo*[*rd*] (1645; Wing D2012) is reprinted, by permission of The British Library, from the incomplete but unique copy held at The British Library (shelfmark 486.f.27. [9]). The text block of the original measures 155 × 84 mm. The text lacks part of the title page, and parts of pp. 7 and 8.

Hard-to-read words:
5.1 *write*
13.3–4 (*as no great misse or losse of it*)

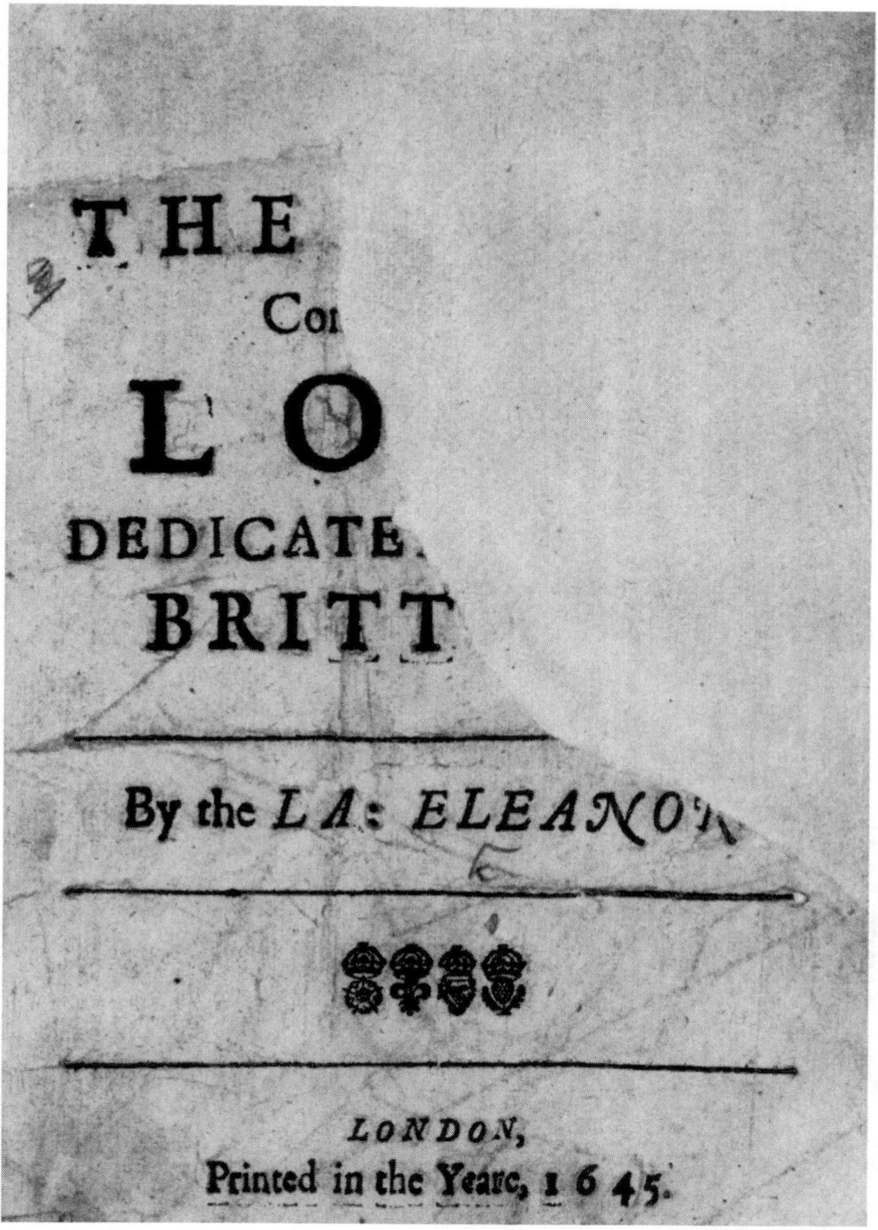
THE

Co

LO

DEDICATE

BRITT

By the *LA: ELEANO*

LONDON,
Printed in the Yeare, 1645.

THE REVEALING OF OVR LORDS ſecond Comming.

Revela. XI.

AND to meaſure or give the *meaning of this place of Scripture*, of age to ſpeake in theſe accompliſhed dayes for it ſelf, a touch whereof ſuffices to be

A 2 given

given: *So touching this Angel which ſtood and made that ſolemne Oath ſwearing by the maker of all things: That* TIME *ſhould no longer bee*; ſaying, *Ariſe* and meaſure the TEMPLE, *and Them that* worſhip *therein, &c.*

Doubtleſſe the ſelfe ſame; beheld by the Prophet DANIEL (12.) *Which ſpeakes to this Evangeliſt, at firſt clothed in Linnon on the waters, and as in his reſurrection raiment then: ſo here in* the Aſcenſions, clothed in a cloud, the Angelicall Robe, giving *by this* to underſtand, when the riſing from the dead to be *reveald, or times reigne finiſhed, ſo com-*

commands him to w ite (as it were) what ſhall come to paſſe, when the Church ſhall be refined before the end or a reformation, leaving and caſting out, *the* Court *O F R O M E* in thoſe dayes returnd to Heatheniſme, that mother of ignorance tyrannizing and treading downe the Church ſtanding out for the truth unto the end, where thoſe *ſacred Witneſſes caſt out for dead, guiltie of the Prophets blood and our Saviours.*

Thus ſhewing, when that Eclips paſt thoſe miſts diſpel'd, and afterward preachd the Goſpel when as farre West as East,

before

before the evening or ſetting of time, for an infalible Fore-runner of the end of the World come, for which all bidden to watch. How then it ſhall come to paſſe, Informes this Diſciple : This bleſsing of Bleſsings how added to the former, even out of the Scriptures, *the Old and New two Bookes to be interpreted, for our Lords comming revealed, and theſe like as in daies of* Old, *with ſignes and tokens evident to all.*

And as here appeares, ſhews then how thoſe new moulded dayes rewarded; oppoſing the Holy Ghoſt, made to waite, They plagued alſo, *fares with them*

the ...
Heavens ...
wher silenced the Spirit of Prophesie.

As came to passe before that deliverance of theirs, out of that Bondage, and before *Bals Preists put down, not one escaping*; great blessings as sometime accompanied with no light corrections: And these the summe of that Angelicall discourse.

So proceeding with the generall Resurrection, and Ascensions

…oſe bo-

…e one taken up, both waiting (40.) dayes in the Mount of God: And that dead Souldier revived by a touch of the Prophets Corps, all prophecying to theſe laſt dayes of ſuch diviſion devided like thoſe waters, ſome-time them.

As here the gift of the Holy Ghoſt like the Cloven tongues in the *ſeventeenth hundred Yeares* under *thoſe Characters* expreſt, (ver. 2.) *And the Holy-Citie ſhall*

ſhall They tread under foote 42. *Moneths*: and ſo again, And I will give *to my two Witneſſes*; and *They ſhall Prophecie a Thouſand two Hundred and ſixty dayes*, *&c.* (to wit) ſeven Times, ſignified by theſe *Three yeares and halfe*, doubled by Moneths and Dayes: including alſo the VVorlds miſtical VVeeke *Cut Off*:

VVhere farther, for makeing plaine of Theſe multiplyed rough obſcure places: Concerning how long the *Churches Warfare, To receive double for all HER* Sinnes: referred unto

B *Times*

TIMES farwell redoubled, as declared also to HIS Servant the Prophets; *Daniel* 12.

And from the Time *that the daily shall be taken away, and the abomination that maketh desolate set up*; There shall bee a Thousand two Hundred and Ninty dayes.

Blessed is hee that waiteth, and commeth to the Thousand three Hundred and Thirty five Dayes, (to wit) as aforeshewd. Seven times even the Number of rest, or so many yeares, under the reigne of *ANTICHRIST*, till which accomplished *Daniel*

niel bidden to be gon, and rest satisfi-ed, or take his long sleepe.

A Thousand seven Hundred yeares (as much to say) from the time of the last Supper given, before HIS *blessed Resurrection day*, (made the *Churches day of REST,)* Vntill the generall rising from the dead: *Like the thrice fourteene Generations:(Mat:1.)* (or three Periods,) *each fulfilling* 500. *yeares.* here in like manner given under the *Angels hand* lifted up, testifying or protesting; *A time, and Times and halfe,* (or part) And thus as five Hundred yeares going to a Period of

B 2 time

TIME, fulfills 1700. yeares, so by taking away a *Thousand, from those Propheticall, two Thousand six Hundred twenty five daies*: Even comes to the *Yeare*, 1625. That unparaleld troublesome Time, where *he* stiled the *great* Prince *MICHAEL, that shall stand up* : going before *the generall Resurrection*, the dead There standing upon their *feet* (*Daniel* 12.) by that *Arch*: Angels dreadfull *Alarme* awakned. And so *Blessed is he that comes (and waits to* 1645. *the end*:) And where every word hath its weight, as points at the last Centurie to be devi-

ded

ded, and the very halfe yeare: So here ſhewes when the *End of time come* ; (*as no great miſſe or loſſe of it*) *Where nothing from head to foot, but* Plagues *and* Vlcers, *the Bottomleſſe-pit opend, Hell* LET LOOSE, *How* it ſhall come to paſſe in thoſe days preferring darkeneſſe before light: Theſe things when as againe Propheſied, to *Nations, People, and Kings*, being come to its *full Time*, even *overcome and Killed by that ſpirit aſcended out of the Bottomleſſe pit*, *Monſter of Mankind*; The aſcenſions *Enemy*, and the *Reſurrections*, not a little inſenced

and

and wyld: whose sentence on Record of old: In this manner. *He must be killed* verse &c. *which offers violence to them from above indued with such power and inspired.* To be plaine, *He* in the yeare 1633. translated to be Arch-BB. And that suffer'd that *Antichrist*; on a *Friday* which made his last Sermon, (witnesse *Revel.* vers. 5.) (where our Lord crucified) VVas the very text (as it were) (*Heb.* 12:) *For the joy set before him who indured the Crosse, &c.*

But proceeding on with these examined witnesses as for fire proceeding out of their mouths

mouths, verſe, &c. as aluding to the Feaſt time, of the firie tongues ſo ſignifies againe, fulfilled that of the Prophet *Joel. That on all fleſh he will powre out his ſpirit* (the Gentils alſo) *and his ſons and Hand-maids ſhall prophecie.*

And ſo againe for interpreting Scripture, by Scriptures for manifeſtation of the aforeſaid meaſured times, accompliſhing the number of ſeven, *here turn'd* to the Prophet *Zechar*. 4. *Who when by the Angel awakend*, as a man out of his ſleepe, *Saw a Candleſticke, all of Gold with ſeven lamps, & ſeven pipes to the ſeven lamps*

lamps, two *Olive thereby*; *empting the Golden Oyle*. Signifying also *before* the Rising from the dead, times mysterie how by the Spirit of prophecie extracted out divine vision (to wit) the Prophets aforesaid or two witnesses whose Bookes that Light so hatefull to men: manifested with a witnesse thus.

Verse 8. *And they shall see their dead bodies three dayes and a halfe lye in the street of the Great City spiritually called Sodome and Egypt*, like *Newes* out of date: Cast about, because *Prophecie* for a time ceas'd: And by the *spirituall calling, made their Pas-*

time

time, as not rare in the laſt dayes ſuch witts or Scoffers, ſo with thoſe tydings of the great day made their ſport And *how* feſtivall times *Eaſter*, *Witſontyde*, and the reſt ſolemnized in City and Countrey with what doings, *in ſtead of workes of charity and Almes deeds, how ſends preſents one to another, Play-houſes viſited and drinking houſes, halfe the Sabbath day, very Sodome, no other poſſeſt with the ſame ſpirit of blindnes.*

And thus here a line and there a line, concerning the Spirit of propheſie to be powr'd out, from yeares diſcending to dayes, (verſe) *And after three dayes and a halfe the Spirit of life from God enterd into them theſe two Prophets, and they ſtood upon their feet, aluding to that, when* they falling dead at the feet of the Angel, the Lord of Sabbaths, *which* were againe raysed, *Daniel* and *John*, those so greatly Beloved, as he *by a touch of the Scepter the seven stars, &c.*

And these *Things* like that *doubled* Dream because the things Established : (*Geneses* 41.) visible in our *Horizon* of the seventeenth Century, wherein held such an *impossibilitie for Prophets againe to arise before the day of Judgement*, yet shall goe on with the meaning also, of *that great voice Come up hether.* And they ascended in a cloud up, beheld by all *Them*, stricken in a moment with no little astonishment. VVhich referred to your judgements, whether

whether or no, ſpeakes not to all you the wonderfull worke of God, Great Brittaines Parliament voice, as before *Whitſontyde* preſented was, unto the houſe this very place of Scripture, *even joyning with the Prophets loud voices* as they *Gods kingdome* proclaime, ſo ſerves for their thankesgiving, and the Cities as come to paſſe ſince the laſt aſcenſions feaſt, after that ſad breakefaſt *blow, beſtowed on their enemies unto which Shall add this for another.*

Verſe 13. *And the ſame houre* (as much to ſay,) at *tenne* in the morning, ſignifying alſo the ſame time when gathered together thoſe ſeverall Nations, (*Acts* 2.) Stranger of *Rome. Jewes* and *Proſelites*: when ſuch a noiſe, wher

C 2 ſhewes

ſhewes moreover within *an houres ſpace*, how many ſlain, and ſo many thouſands taken, *and* a remnant that *tooke the Covenant, or gave glory to God. Alſo the liſt of Names returnd as in the Originall ſignifying,* (*names of men*) *Mens names all*: where alſo thoſe wrathfull *Iriſh Et Iratæ ſunt gentes & advenit ira tua*: as at the day of *Judgement* for them, no *Quarter*; by Their diſpairing of *mercy*, ſetting their *Names too for the riſing of the dead to be revealed before the END* to theſe Kingdomes. And againe, as ſerves for the *houre of the day* (verſ. 13.) ſo beares date in the yeare, *One thouſand ſeven Hundred*; beſide Seven hundred ſlaine expreſt: *ſhewing the ſecond woe paſt is, behold the third WOE comes*

quickly,

quickly, Namely about *Michaels feast* : The ſeventh *Angel or laſt Trumpet* gives warning of it ; So farthermore for thoſe great victorious Voices, where *ſuch Tyranicall power reſigned*, for which the rejoycing *Elders* 24 for evermore ſiting ; Not more extoling GODS power herein, Then the *NATIONS* fil'd with Envy, to ſee the Crown and Honour of the day Conferred on ſuch derided heretofore ſo *much* contemn'd : *As not by might*, (or Army) *nor by power* ; *But by my* Spirit, *ſaith the Lord of hoſts* : And for the Temple opened thoſe heavenly gates, or two Olive trees, to wit (*verſ.*) with the miſtery made knowne of *Time meaſured by his* Reed, or ſharp

Rod

Rod given him to meaſure with: Thus much ſuffices. And for *ſuch* Stormes and Out-cryes, *where* the tree of *Life offered to every one*: Not unlike the tree of *Knowledge*, at firſt pleaſant to Him, afterward all as bitter: Neverthleſſe when the houre paſt, like her Travell the Mother of all *living*, rememberd not at all. And *ſo* farre for the *Cauſe ſet forth of* Canterburys *ſuffering*: *And their dead* Bodies, *not ſuffered to be* B U R Y'D, (expos'd to the veiw) *whoſe ſeven* Yeares *compleat before going into priſon*: The expreſſe EPYTOMIE *of Antichriſts* Kingdome in the 1700. yeare, *alſo deſtroyed to* bee *or Cut off, for Ever.*

Poſtſcript.

Postscript.

SO then what differnce, between them obedient to the Divell, that inquire of evil spirits & others disobedient to the spirit of God, or to whom his command peremtory: Yet like the deafe Adar, stop the Eare, much like the case of thos two Sons in the Gospel, or Brothers, the one where gives such an undutifull answer, the other nothing but faire words: who as though Antiquity were a plea for error, or custome any excuse for any thing, by his Apostles prohibited.

As in that inacted by them, against eating blood (So well Observed,) Acts 15: verse 20. Also, verse 30. Saying; for seemed good to the HOLY GHOST and to us to lay no greater burthen upon you then these necessary things, that ye abstaine from meats offered to Idols, and from blood, and from strangld meat, and from fornication, from which things if yee keep your selves yee shall well, fare yee well.

And againe, cap. 21. verse 25. We have written and concluded, &c. save only that ye keep your selves from things offered to Idols. And from blood and strangld meat and from fornication, Where although disburthened of all the rest, but blood the life of eve-

ry

ry thing. Which like the forbidden tree or the tree of life in the midst of Paradice standing, as this between a branch of the first and second table, afterward notwithstanding ready drest at all essays. The Apostles Ordinances nothing made of it, and not only these freely digested but libels published by authority against holy authority, *too evident some on outsides as that unsufferable fable, stiled a relation of the two Witnesses their coming down from heaven* And *fighting with Antichrist, also for another a late preface with that bold universall, that all spirits which do suffer themselves to be inquired at are evil spirits, and therefore of the Divill as much to say or afirm the Holy Ghost cannot do what he pleases, or that any thing is impossible or too hard for God to do.*

And for their Philosophie as meane & weake as their Theologie behold his produced Booke. De Magia Naturali, *apparent whereby her spirit absent from the body, that for so long might be awakend by no meanes. So to him who is,* Alpha *and* Omega *both: In whom consists all and some, both the only affirmative and negative voice; be all praise.* Amen.

FINIS.

15. *Of Errors Ioynd With Gods Word* (1645; Wing D1999) is reprinted, by permission of The British Library, from the unique copy held at The British Library (shelfmark Tab.603.a.38. [10]). The text block of the original measures 156 × 92 mm.

Hard-to-read words:

4	[page number is slightly obscured]
5.11	end
5.14	thus translated
6	[page number is slightly obscured]

OF ERRORS IOYND VVITH GODS VVORD.

By the Lady *ELEANOR*:

Make straight the Path of our God. Isaiah 41.

Printed in the yeare, 1645.

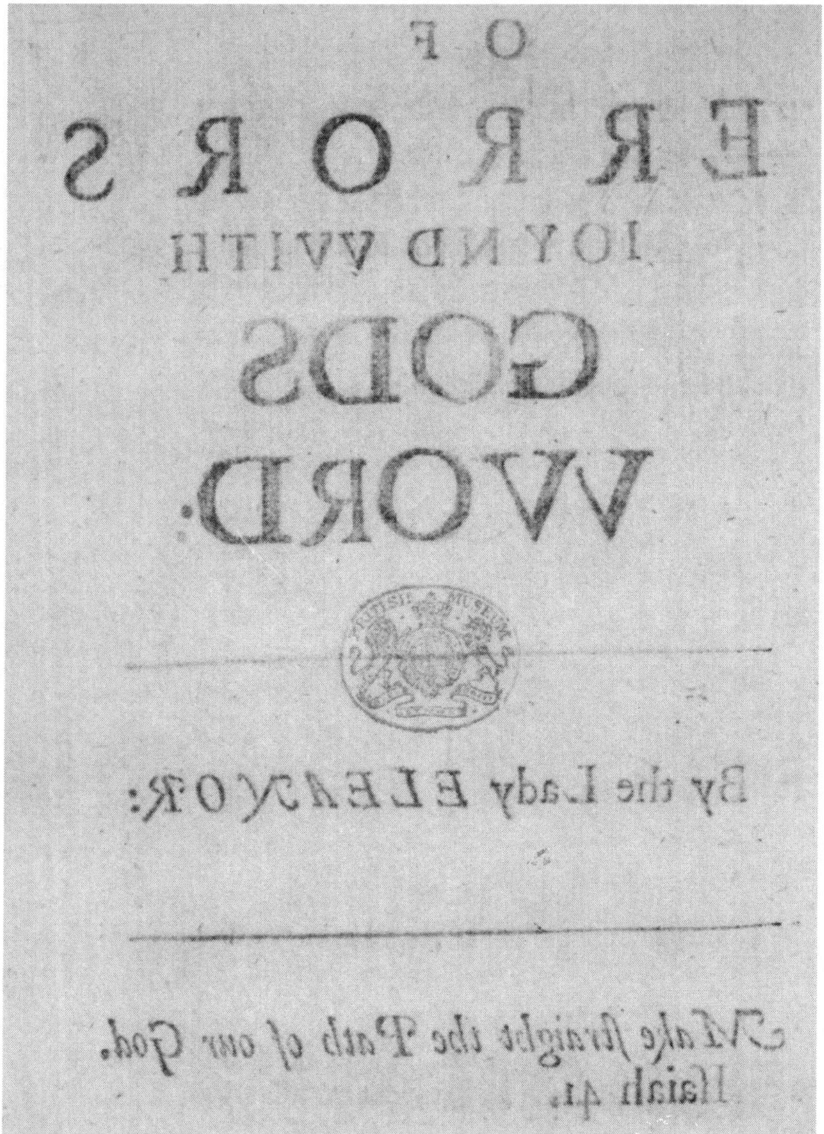

OF

ERRORS

IOYND VVITH

GODS

VVORD:

By the Lady ELEANOR:

Make straight the Path of our God.
Isaiah 41.

Printed in the yeare, 1645.

For the most Honorable the high Court of PARLIAMENT assembled.

From the *Lady Eleanor*.

AS the Blind then foretold of their leading the *Blind*: So verily never more palpable darkenesse: (of that kind) then now: Even such as the very *Legend and Alchoran for a bold fable hardly guilty of the like*: As this witnesse for one published *according to* order intituled: *A divine prophesie of King James a Relation of the two witnesses* their comming down from

A 2 heaven

Heaven, and then fighting with *Anti-christ, &c.*

A thing so contradictory and Repugnant to the truth: *As light and darknesse not more opposite or differing*: they being so farre from any such *declination*: That they ascended up to Heaven in the sight of their enemies, *as witnesse come up hether, the resurrections voice*, being persecuted by that Beast, viz. *such an authority put downe afterward Rev, 12. as even the very beast himselfe as-* scended out of the bottomlesse pitt.

VVhich witnesses signifying in truth *Dan.* & *John*, two Bookes of the Prophets *to be interpreted*, the *Resurrection time* revealing it, & *though accompanied with such signes and tokens at that time*: Yet as in former Prophets dayes likewise persecuted and opposed.

And

And every title of this being so precious that Heaven & Earth cannot passe away till all come to passe, *shewed & manifested to the world, shal shew of some other places as barbarously corrupted also*: *Kings* 2. For whereas the Holy Ghost saith, *there shall be none left to burie of Jezabels body*. They have made it; there shall be no body left to burie her, and *Daniel* the 11. Cap. thus: VVhere shewed at the end of yeares, *The Kings daughter of the South pointing at Austria, shall be delivered* namely of a child, is by our Doctors thus translated: (But she shall be delivered up to death) whereof even the true meaning is. *To shew at the time of the end such a remarkable thing of one so long time childlesse*, Neverthelesse to be delivered or brought a bed of a child: to wit the marriage of *France* with *Spaine*, &c.

And

And so for another mistake a word of no small difference namely the word *Sacrifice* added in so many places; whereas the Holy Ghost renders it thus.

And an Host was given against the daily:(Dan:) our daily bread given in the *Lords Supper*, as much to say, by them translated as it were the host offer'd up, or Transubstantiation, and such like *linsie wolsie woven together by them, because they receive not the truth*, is just with God, to leave them to the spirit of Error. And though there is a certain place faultie: 2 *Chron.* 22. shewing *Ahaziah* to be two yeares elder then his father *Jehoram*: yet being reconciled else where in holy writ, as in 2 *Kings* Cap. 8. verse 26. is not to be plac'd placed amongſt the aforeſaid errors : As in truth *Ahaziah* 22. yeares old when he began to reigne. And not 42 though ſo accounted there. 2 *Chron.* 22. Cap. 2. verſ.

And ſo much for a ſcourg of ſmall cords made, or ſome *Correction* as *here* requiſit : where *Gods word which paſſes not away*, is chang'd into ſtuffe, paſſing for current.

FINIS.

16. *A Prayer or Petition For Peace* (1645; Wing D2002) is a reissue of a 1644 tract that is no longer extant. It is reprinted, by permission of The British Library, from the unique copy held at The British Library (shelfmark Tab.603.a.38. [5]). The text block of the original measures 157 × 88 mm.

A
Prayer or Petition
FOR
PEACE.

November 22. 1645.

R. Eleanor L. Douglas

Behold, your houſe is left unto you deſolate; And verily, ye ſhall not ſee me, till ye ſay, Bleſſed is he that cometh in the Name of the Lord.

Printed in the Year, 1645.

A
PRAYER & PETITION FOR *PEACE.*

By the Lady *Eleanor.*

O Lord, the great and dreadful God, as we have ſinned deeply and offended, guilty of no leſs then open Rebellion, by excluding thee, fleeing from thy preſence, with one voyce (as it were) *We will not have this man to reign over us* (or) *He defers his coming*, as others; Even departed from thy Precepts and Judgements ſet before us: ſo here proſtrate before the foot-ſtool of thy

A 2 Throne,

Throne, implore neverthelefs pardon and forgivenefs.

For this no ftoln or fecret tranfgrefsion committed, but with a high hand; and fo much the rather prefuming on this accefs, becaufe hitherto the vulgar (the burthen and heat of the day though theirs) thofe fheep yet not guilty or acceffary to this trefpafs or capital Crime, of depofing thee, or oppofing thy return, as manifeft in hearkning not to the loud voyces of the Prophets accomplifhed thy Meffengers: But to our Kings, Princes, Heads and Rulers, which appertains, fo ftraitly commanded, faying, *What I fay unto you, I fay unto all*, the Gentiles watchword alfo charged in readinefs to be; and figns of the Time they

not

not diſcerning them , ſuch and ſuch expreſs evident Signs and Tokens, wherefore haſt watch over them, as ſince this a Nation, or under the whole Heaven the like unknown, witneſs ſuch a VVinter flight, and Sabbath journey, &c. thoſe bloody peſtilent Vials, ſo violently poured out (without doubt) not ſince the Flood as in this preſent Century.

Thus neither taking warning (by Foraign Nations) our Neighbors houſes ſet on fire firſt, like his ſetting in the front the handmaids and their children, as it were; that great maſſy Image firſt ſmitten in the feet, like it; before broken in pieces, others before hand for our uſe, as lighted Beacons to awaken us; but ſo lightly weighed, nothing at all accounted, till ſud-

denly

denly at laſt, like *Sampſons* ſevenfold new Cords and green VVyths, all pluckt aſunder, when linked ſo faſt and knit, *France* with *Great Britain*, *Spain* with *France*, *Germany* with *Spain*; together with theſe late married Iſles or United Kingdoms, now in widows forlorn woful eſtate, or worſe, as divorced; ſometime that as had it been a new world, with ſuch *Creations* flouriſhing, and Titles all new *Names*, even walking like days of old, alſo become as thoſe, when God repented he made *Man*, brought to a like Ebbe or fall, as thoſe inſaciable Gyants, Great *Britains Babel* towering thoughts confounded.

And now behold, O Lord, through a high and heavy hand abaſed and ſo ſo low brought, humbled to aſhes and ſackcloth, from the higheſt to the loweſt; then tread not on a worm, break not the bruiſed reed, the wounded ſmite them not; but hear us out of the deep, O thou our Anchor, hope and preſent help, ready to be conſumed utterly and ſwallowed up, if thou calm not and aſſwage theſe working tempeſtuous Seas, through unruly raging winds let looſe, wrought and contrived; And ſo with him praying in his poſture, *Elijah*, when as without *Rain* ſo long, forty two Moneths (that prophetical Number inſiſted on ſo much, of Three years and a half) he bowing himſelf double, or kneeling on his head; alſo behold ſuch our eſtate turned up ſide down, ſince the

the year 1642. defer us not these miserable Isles and Kingdoms of ours, whose Store-houses exhausted, like those Rivers dryed up, and like the dead Trees, burnt up our Nation and Habitation.

To conclude (O thou of unspeakable Mercy) cause thy face to shine upon us, for the Lords sake, our alone Savior: let thy voyce be heard, forsake us not, that spakest sometime to the Fish, the Fig-tree, the Deaf, the Dead, and very Devils subjects: And at whose motion the Sun and Moon moved not, heard him; and turnest the hard Rock into standing waters, &c. Also the waters of this City, heal them; say the word and it is done, that henceforth let there be no more DEATH, no more

Killing

Killing and Slaying, I beseech thee, like unto those unhappy forty two Infants torn by two she-Bears; Stay thy hand, let it not be deferred.

For an Absolution, or a general Pardon, October 1647.

AND, O Lord of Sabbath, our King, the God of Hosts, sitting between *the winged Cherubims*, inclosing thy glorious Throne; that without delay vouchsafest to hear this the humble address of thy Handmaid: And the waters healed accordingly of this our Spiritual *Jericho*, the very next Moneth, witness *December*, dated the 5. sent from the other side, such a conjuring Letter unto us, for Arms to be laid aside,

B when

when as about three Moneths after, they waxt at thy consuming presence, like melting wax, the Enemy put to flight, as known to the whole world, he how vanished and gone to his own Nation disguised in that fashion, amazing all that knew him, signed with the years of thy right hand, 1645. complete.

And the Sword of VVar sheathed thus, whereat the VVoods and Fields rejoycing: Neverthelesse, Iustice her sword thusdrawn, as that *the Epilogue or end worse :hen the beginning*, amended like his taking unto him *Seven Spirits worse then himself, which entred in; he after returned to his house, swept and garnished so within and without*; as without respect of any now King, Princes, Heads

and

and Rulers going to wrack; and which miſrule and diſtraction, by the Eccleſiaſtical or Spiritual calling occaſioned as afore inſtanced in that reſtles man(*Luke* 11.)things amended ſo by others come in their room. Then here crooching at thy feet, O Heavenly Bounty, Royal Mercy, greater then *Solomons*, exceeding Fames report, let not the Heathen triumph, ſuffices we have been and are an open Example; thy Iuſtice hath not been wanting.

Confeſsing withal our treſpaſs, juſtly charged with no petty Treaſon, even thine own Citizens conſpiring againſt thee, hated of them; O our Savior, acknowledging moreover afflictions, inabling offenders to know themſelves, for reſtoring

ſtoring eye-ſight, or to humble us with the onely Spittle and Clay, Oyntment: So, behold us with the eye of Commiſeration forgive our ignorance, who through default of others, thus by their ſubtilty inſnared, have brought upon us theſe Iudgements; as truth Lord, *our houſe behold, left unto us deſolate*, the great Trees felled down for company, as well as coppes wood not ſpared.

And whether this the prophetical and true meaning be not of this place likewiſe (*Mat*.24.) and fit for any mean capacity or knowledge, the queſtion referred to themſelves, ſpeaking even to theſe worſt of Times, the hour of Darkneſs, *That if the good man of the houſe had known at what hour the Thief would have come,*

come, had not suffered his house, &c. Also, *Every Kingdom divided against it self, is desolate*: And, *one house doth fall upon another*; and other like Oiconomical caveats all in vain: yet as some crums begd in others behalf, of compassion, so for their sight a drop somewhat; Lord, magnified most of all in thy Mercy, for *these blinde leaders of the blinde*, or *false teachers* to convert them, seeking base and false delights, mask'd for true, in stead of thy Kingdom sought; upon whom come well to pass the true Proverb, *Men serving God and the World*; those two, as they sitting between two seats dismounted, by those gone before them, that took no better heed; with whom, as the Spirit of Prophesie out of request, de-

despiſed, likewiſe grown out of faſhion the VVedding garment, better ſeen in eye-ſervice, that thus will not ſee, *Thy Kingdom come upon them*: And ſo, King of Glory, pardon too this ſtoln touch again of thy Sacred Robe, *Of vertue gone from thee*.

Prov. 31. *She openeth her mouth in Wiſdom; and the Doctrine of Mercy is under her tongue.*

F I N I S.

17. *Prophesie Of The Last Day* (1645; Wing D2004) is the English translation of *Prophetia de die* (1644; Wing D2005), a Latin text by Lady Eleanor that is not included in this volume. *Prophesie* is reprinted, by permission of The British Library, from the incomplete but unique copy held at The British Library (shelfmark 486.f.27. [7]). The text block of the original measures 156 × 87 mm.

Hard-to-read words:

7	[page number is slightly obscured]
8	[page number is not visible]
8.2	*And the Nati*

PROPHESIE
OF THE
LAST DAY

to be Revealed in the

LAST TIMES;

And then of the cutting off the Church, and of the Redemption out of

HELL.

THE VVORD OF GOD

by the Lady ELEANOR, &c.

I am Alpha and Omega, the beginning and the end.

MATT. 17. 11.

Elias truly ſhall firſt come and reſtore all things.

London, Printed in the yeare. 1645.

PROPHESIE

OF THE

LAST DAY

to be Revealed in the

LAST TYMES;

And then of the casting off the Church,

and of the Redemption out of

HELL

THE VVORD OF GOD

by the Lady ELEANOR, &c.

I am Alpha and Omega, the beginning and the end.

MATT. 17. 11.

Elias truly shall first come and restore all things.

London, Printed in the yeare 1645.

I am the first, and the last, the beginning and the ending:

FROM THE LADY *ELEANOR*, The word of *GOD*.

AS shewed in the Scriptures, *There is nothing so secret, That shall not bee discovered*: And the Cleareneſſe now of theſe *future Things*, being come to paſſe, with the reſt ſhortly

A 2 to

to be accomplished; Begets or creats this *Boldnesse* in *MEE*, to disolve or breake this precious *Yuvory-Box* of *Times and Seasons* Mistery: shewing of the Last day at hand, the happie time *of* the *End*.

Three *Articles* or *Arguments* which contains:

The first, That notwithstanding *These words for the present to satisfie Them* as best able to expresse his meaning: Saying, *Of that day and houre knowes no man*: Not the Sonne, *but the Father*, &c. *Mat.* 24. 42. vers. 50. *Mat.* 25. 18. Neverthelesse forbids not the month or the yeare to be foreknowne: And *therewith* refers them to the *Prophet Daniel*: VVhere sealed up untill the time

time of the end. *The Mistery of time*, as let them that reads *Daniel* understand, &c.

Being much like the answer given them afore. *Yee aske yee know not what, it is not mine to give or grant.* First, *Follow me*, as much to say, *yee aske the day of judgement*, or at least joyned to be in commission with *John Baptist*, he first which did *drinke of my cup*, *a Prophet, and greater then a Prophet.* Not a greater borne of VVoman, And so no lesse then to be the Messenger of the great day to come: As here is shewed such then asked an impossible thing, the distance between *his right hand and his left hand*, prepared for such: *shewing at hand his comming.*

And so to come againe to the

A 2 matter

matter *of the revelation of Jesus Christs* comming, which God gave unto him, &c. ſhewed out of the Old and New Teſtament, *The Prophet Daniel, and his Deſciple John*, their teſtimonie, where notwithſtanding his longing: Bidden *Goe thy way Daniel for the words are ſhut up till the end*, (to wit) times and ſeaſons miſtery, whoſe *Charactar* not to be underſtood till then reſerved for a *time and times and the deviding of time*. Dan. 12.

The halfe of ſeven untill which *Sabaticall Number* fullfilled, *be bidden to reſt*, &c. viz. the 1700. yeare.

And therefore St. *John weeping much becauſe no man was found worthy* ſo *so much as to looke thereon*: which more would have wept, in thesedayes, to see such unbeleise in men: having their wits and understanding in that manner shut up, *notwithstanding all fullfilled and come to passe which was foretold* in the Scriptures.

Though witnesse as (for these very dayes) The 11. and 12. of the *Apoccalyps*. *Where* like him possessed beseeching not so soon to torment them &c. & *they* who besought him to depart their City, &c. *So* here *this City styled* spiritual *Sodome, where those two persecuted witnesses said to torment them that dwel on the Earth*, that alway would here dwel, *Shewing how wellcome* and what entertainment amongst the *Gentiles* his comming should find, even *how hateful the Tree*

of

of life to them as exprest here. (Cap. 11.) *Revela. And the Nations were angry the time of the dead was come, and that they should be judged.* (Ergo) the time made knowne.

And *Satan* because he knew his time was short raging & roaring in *such* wise: *Shewing in truth the madnesse of the World,* when the day of judgement shall be prophecied unto *them* and their reward, as followes.

VVitnesse out of their mouthes fire proceeding, *the two witnesses of the Lords comming:* Like the Baptist his going in the Spirit and Power of *Elias*, before him such power likewise given them : *Shutting the Heavens, and turning waters into blood.*

where

18. *For The blessed Feast Of Easter* (1646; Wing D1989) is reprinted, by permission of The British Library, from the clear copy held at The British Library (shelfmark 1104.b.2. [6]). The text block of the original measures 163 × 98 mm. The handwritten comments in this text resemble the hand of those that appear in the Folger tracts.

Hard-to-read handwritten annotations and printed words:

3	[bottom] ye revelation [transcription]
4	[page number is obscured]
4.10	shews
6.1	that prevailed to open the seven
6.18	un [transcription]
7.1–2	Sealed
7.7–8	*number, so he saw of all Nations standing*
14.22	forebeare [transcription]
19.4	Late [transcription]

FOR
The bleſſed Feaſt
OF
EASTER.

Writs, By the La. ELEANOR.

Let the Heavens reioyce, and let the Earth bee glad:
Let the Field be ioyfull, and all that is therein, before the Lord, for he commeth, for he commeth to iudge the earth: he ſhall iudge the world with righteouſneſſe, and the People with his truth.

Printed in the yeare, 1646.

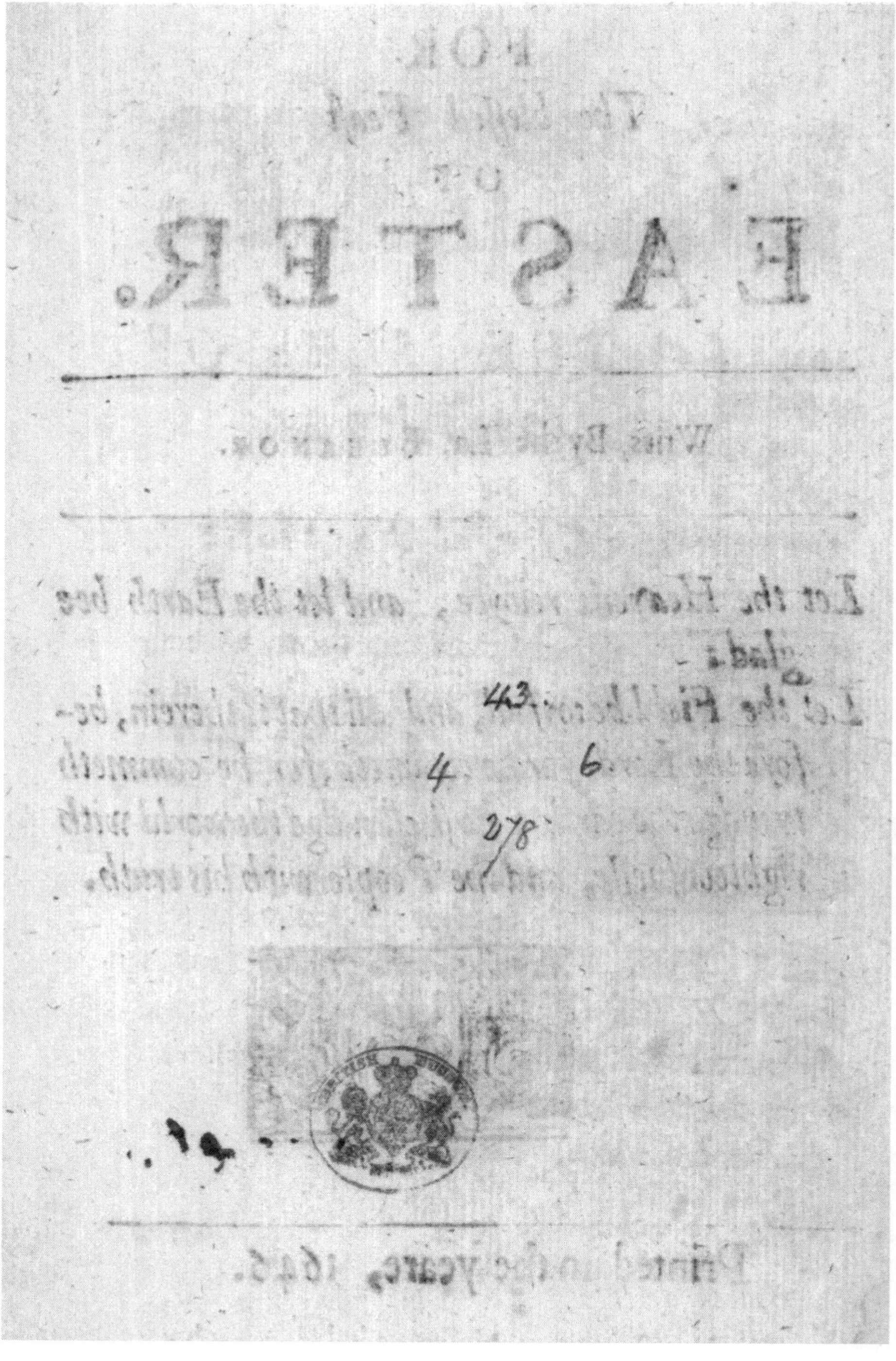
EASTER.
Printed in the yeare, 1645.

TO THE ISLES OF Great *BRITTAIN* these;

From *PATMOS* ILE:

BEcause the time short, as here shewed, in the *NAME* OF GOD, Amen: shall name the Child, Namely *the blessed LAMBE* extold so, *and* magnified in the *Apocalyps* : Even the weeke of EASTER, (as much to say) *when the generall RESURECTION time* : And this is the interpretation thereof ; of which aforesaid Feast covered under NO few figures, Metaphors and the like; Thus, ye revelation

Given with ſuch a ſpeciall charge, *to keepe the things written therein* ; *verſe* 3 (to wit) *containes Infalible fore-runners and ſignes* , *when the End of time at hand for the* Churches Preparation *to ſtand on their* gaurd, *leſt ſurpriſed unawares.*

And as here *Times* and *Seaſons* miſtery proclaim'd with *Times* treble voices : *grace and peace from him which IS, and which WAS, and which IS to COME* : *And from the ſeven ſpirits before* (or in ſight of) *the THRONE*, ſo ſhews withall His day of comming a GREATER then his proclaimed *BY* great *BRITTAIN*, whoſe feaſt ſolemnized about the Reſurrections feaſt, *March* 27. : Thoſe *firſt and laſt Princes, or Kings* ; Of which laſt time the Prophet *Daniel* Thus in his laſt ; *And at that time ſhall* Michael *ſtand up the great* Prince *&c.* who ſeales it *with* theſe, *Dan.* 12. *And many that ſleep in the duſt, ſhall awak, &c.* including thoſe obſerved Feaſts aforeſhewed, for an expreſſe token of the generall *Reſurrection* in their Reigne, and at that very time and ſeaſon.

Touching which turning again to the *Revelation*

And with the Signe of the LAMB, *proceeding lation,* bearing the same date, *verſ.* 5. *And from Jeſus CHRIST the faitfull* Witneſſe, *the firſt begotten of the dead,* PRINCE *of the* KINGS *of the Earth: That loved* VS, *and waſhed* VS *from our ſins in his own blood*, concluded With theſe, *and hath made us* Kings *and* Prieſts, *&c.* To HIM *be glory and dominion, for ever and ever*, Amen.

Behold HEE *commeth, &c.* Saying, *I am* ALPHA *and* OMEGA: Even ſo upon the LORDS day ſhewed unto that happie man: The Diſciple whom he Lord above the reſt entruſted, The likeneſſe of the dreadfull day of *JUDGMENT* ſtanding in the middeſt of *Watch-lights*, ſaying; feare NOT, *I am the firſt and the laſt* King; *I have the* Keyes of HELL and DEATH: *Write the things which Thou haſt ſeen, &c.* And he that hath an *Eare* let him heare the *Spirit of Prophecie, and repent.* Behold, I ſtand at the doore and knock, *to Supp with him who holds the ſeaven* Starres in his *Hand*, The evening of *TIMES* Enſigne.

And

briefly beyond hope, that prevailed to open the seVen Sealed Booke of Times Mystery; *after his much weeping, because no man was found worthy to read, or look thereon : No not the Prophet* Daniel, *who more then once was bidden go thy way,* (Dan. 12.) *for the words are referred for the end of time.*

Thou shalt rest, &c.

Even so, Glory, Honor, *and* Peace, *be ascribed to the* Lamb, (Easter our Rest) *before whose face* (Rev. 6.) *Kings of the Earth, Mighty men, Great men, Rich men, and chiefe Captains, then taking their flight, as who able to stand in such a Storm of confusion, then commeth the great day of the wrath of the Lamb.*

Revel. Chap. 7.

As here the yeare of Grace 1644. *followes, when accomplished* (Or Seal'd) *those pernitious* Windes *till then not let loose.*

And the Scales *being sealed or oppened, thus proceeds.*

And after these things, I saw foure Angels standing at the foure corners of the *Earth*, holding the fower *Winds*, that the *wind* should not blow: Saying hurt not the *Earth*, nor the *Sea*, till *Wee* have sealed the Servants of God in the Foreheads.

And

And I heard the number of them that were Sealed, and there Was seald a hundred and forty &c. twelve times twelve, *serving both for the months and yeare, and the equall houres divided between day and and night, when those unrestrained windes.*

And as he heard the number of the one: Thenafter that (or the following yeare) which no man could number, so he saw of all Nations standing before the Throne, and before the Lamb, saying salvation to our God that sitteth upon the Throne, and unto the Lamb, *the yeare of our salvation (to wit in the month of* March) *renown through the world beginning about* Easter. *And as by sitting on the throne expresses the* Rest or Sabboth day *when it began also, observ'd by Christians so long, likewise every one by those Palmes in their hands Ensignes of* Victory *and* Peace, *even proclaiming the Ioyfull yeare* 1645. *this victorious time of such thanksgivings, wherein* Babylon *is blown up, and thus the last yeare, and the* New Model *signified hand in hand who have washed their Robes in the bloud of the Lamb, and made them so fayre.*

Wherefore there needs no further question to be made of that *Albion Army*, who they are that serve him day and night, since not unknowne the condition

condition of souldiers, companions of restles time, of whose service hard to indge between the state of prisoners, where desired, death flees away, and such liberty as they enioy, which to be preferred or desired, (as the Prophets *Esay* 49) shewes or bindes them together here. That thou mayest say to the prisoners go forth, and them that sit in darkenesse, shew your selves. *They shall hunger no more, neither shall the heat of the Sun smite them : The* Lamb *is their leader,* asmuch as to say *Easter* shall bid them welcom to the *Lords* table, and thus from their eyes teares wiped away by the *Lamb* in the midst of the throne, when peace and the day of iudgement together going.

Revel. Chap 14.

AND following the *Lamb* whether he goeth, and his *Albion Troups* in their Virgin spring aray, his fathers name having in their foreheads, such a year of God, of the interpretation whereof as followes. *And loe a* Lamb *stood on mount* Sion, *and with him a hundred forty and foure &c.* where again the foresaid yeare of our redemption, witnes these words.

These

These are redeemed from among men, being the first fruits unto God and the Lamb, And these whereas *singing a new song before the Throne, which song no man could learn but such a certain number a hundred forty foure which were redeemed from the earth, no other then some watch word given (as it were) shewing* When such a New time come to passe of Reformation, That then our Redemption drawes neere ; As hereby shewed the houre come of his iudgement, This for another signe *Babylons fall*, first her Nnmerous *Idols* cast downe its faln, its faln ; The time exprest in that overflowing Wine presse of hers, a thousand six hundred bearing date.

Wherefore no marvell though *Syon* tun's up her Harps, so long out of tune, for such a blessed day where rhe Cup or Chalice of his indignation, not in a corner or in privat administred, but powred out in the Presence of the holy Angels, and in the Presence of the *Lamb* : Even N O more of their reall P R E S E N C E and the like, to wit, who have no Rest day nor Night, with sulphorous Smokes suffocated, in their own kind rewarded for the blessed Sabboth dayes violation, That solemne rest prophand.

B *Even*

Even so again on the other side *write*, *Blessed are the dead which dye in the Lord henceforth, that they may rest from their labours, and their workes follow them.* Shewing also for them with such Vallour and Courrage that have followed the Cause, these their everlasting Epitaph.

And so much for the NEW *Time*, and for *Babylons* judgement, the day of judgements forerunner, Her grapes being cryed full ripe, the houre unexpected Come, the Wine-presse trodden without the Citie up to the Horse-bridles, the horses too drinke their fill of blood without measure, the sixteen hundred yeares being fulfilled, serving for the measured compasse of this Island, 1600 myles also, Those furlongs. And this the contents of the *Apocalyps* 14 Chap. where Like the fruitlesse tree after the fourth yeare cut downe, sufferd to stand no longer.

And proceeding on, *Revela.* Chap. 19.

FOr the great dayes Preparation, as here : a greater priveledge then those *Writs* of Parliament to bee cal'd hether, to partake of The *Lambs*

Lambes marriage Supper ; A blessing to bee desired mnch more Then the *beauty of Lillyes*, to beare H E R Company, granted she *should be arrayed in fine Lynnon, cleane and white* : As cleare by such *voices* and *Acclamation* : Of which marriage *Writs* to be published ; briefly as followes : Requiring rather a quire of paper, Then circumscribed within the Narrow limmits of a sheet or two.

For such a meeting so long waited for : Represented (as it were) by the *ghests invited Now to the Lords table the* Easter-weeke : when as that Deciple about to fall down and *worship, Charg'd* ; *See thou do it NOT* : not the first caveat entred to to flee *Idolatry*.

But going on with the *Season and Time*, a thing of such Consequence, as here the *Virgins day in Lent, after which, when Marriage licences so frequent*, accompanied with the *victorious Bridgrom, clothed in his Easter robes* : *a Vesture dipt in blood, proclaimed King of kings, and Lord of lords, that in righteousnesse makes war* : his Coronation feast then, as crownd with so many Crowns, followed with his Saints, mounted or white Horses every one ; a greater shew then St. *Georges* his coming at hand, or any other. B 2 Whose

whose Name called the *Word of G O D*, that unknowne Name in another language (as it were) written, Not unlike those words: *Rex* : *Parliament*: *Peers &c. ver.* Where shewd lastly the fowls feasted on flesh, *the Storke and Crane &c.* Not ignorant of their time of comming, in the Spring time; *as the Horse* (Chap. 14.) *swimming in blood up to the neck, which know their owner*; called unto the supper of the great God, to *assemble and muster* themselves *to eate the flesh of Kings, the flesh of Captains, the flesh of mightie men*, even Licenced by the *Lamb, all the fowls to bee filled*: All but so many *tokens, or Ensignes* displayed proclaiming when the houre of his *Judgement*, Come.

Revela. Chap. 21.

AND as cald to witnesse here, a Reformation set forth before the *End*; a new Modell, a new *Heaven and a new Earth*, new *Jerusalem prepared as a Bride to meete her Husband; where no more paine, teares, and the like*, but like the Peaceable Spring; when painfull Winter past, to such infirmities subject, as that heavenly voice making known; *Behold I make all things new, former things are past away, saying, it is done*: *I am* Alpha *and* Omega; seales it with that *unsearchable Name*, the quintessence of *Mistery* and *Mercy*. And

And (in the second Moneth the Flood) of the dayes of *Noah*, returned in that *Angelicall name* inclusive Thus shewing *and, there came one of the seven Angels unto me, which had the seven vials full of the seven last plagues, saying, Come hether, I will shew the Bride the* Lambs *wife* ; The seventeenth Century having its Vials, as from the Creation to the flood so many, being Baptismes figure, in the Fish preserved alive, those Creatures.

: When the shining Bride at that time, preparing her person, *whereunto Solomon in all his* Lusture, Odors, *and* Ornaments *not comparable*, as insues; no, Not the *Jndies* and *Virginæ* like the Churches glory before the End : accompanied then *with* the Spirit of Prophecie, to bee powred forth that odoriferous *Oyntment*, ever murmured at and envyed though.

: And walking thus about *SION*, counting her Towers, also of that golden measure : Measured *a hundred forty and foure Cubits*, by the measure the Angel (*Winged time*) whose Viall or last glasse running : The meaning whereof having shewed afore, to be the accomplished yeare of grace 1644. So long before peace and truth to meet : shall passe by this point ; where her Virgin reigne too of 44· years pointed at : together

with

with those daies between *Ashwednesday* & *Easter*, as preparatives both, unmeet to be drowned in oblivion in this *divine* Calender.

Where the foure times three gates of that foure square City, even the foure seasons, each three Moneths allotted, and every gate, one pearle (or Margarit) there one and thirty daies (to wit) *So* the moneths every one, with the Apostles names written in them, in this new Ierusalem, this no newes to shew it further, nor difficult to discerne by Sions impregnable Towers: the Tower of London its description: But then finished in St. Iohns daies: when old Ierusalem at that time demolished, of which great store-house, with all its priviledges, let this suffice: These golden transparent streets being not unknown, letticed like glasse on both sides the mint: onely unlike in this, Those heavenly gates not shut at all: where no night there, no other then (as much to say) *This Booke to bee unsealed of the Revelation*; *And faithfully interpreted, whether* or No approved; Whether They heare or feare. beare.

Revela.

ANd as afore : By ſuch a lightſome Citty expreſt, how clearly the *Truth to be revealed at Laſt* : SO againe, ſeverall Demonſtrations not wanting, and Similituds by a *Chriſtall ſpring proceeding out of the* Throne *of God and the Lamb, that pure river of Life*; ſhewes the Reſurrection *Time not unrevealed*, in that cleere Mirror ſhall ſee His face, as it were.

And ſo for this place, another Paradiſe, or Celeſtiall ſpring-garden ſet forth, let this ſuffice. A *Garden and a Cittie both*, where like the precious ſpring Times priviledge, no more *Curſſ*, there needs no Candle, there ſhall be No tedious *Night* verſ. 2. *As by the tree of life, on either ſide the river* : *And in the midſt of the ſtreet*, &c. Being this New Paradice its deſcripiton. The preſent times face.

Where like the Communion, and Faſt-dayes; yeelding her fruite every moneth, alſo *Thoſe golden* Leaves *for the healing of the Nations* in *ſuch* endleſſe *diſtreſſe and diſtraction* on every ſide, were it not for the Angels, ſaying, *I Come quickly* : Who takes his Leave as He began : *I am Alpha and Omega* : *Bleſſed is he that keeps the ſaying of this Booke*, even *the laſt Will and Teſtament of our Saviour given to his Diſciple, who tooke and eate it up ; that rree of life*, had the favour

favour again to kisse his Masters hand that way, *with such a charg to read & hear the same, commended by him to the Churches*; only adding these, *because he comes so quickly*, now too late to repent or amend, *he that is unjust, and unholy, let him be so still; sleep on, and take their rest*, as it were, *the houre is come, when these Things come to passe* : *fulfilled* such a time.

And again, *John* so taken with these things, *seen and heard*, who could not forbeare or refrain; *but fell at the Angels feete*, again forbidden, *see Thou do it NOT*, worship God, concluding with that blessed time Thus. *And the Spirit and the Bride say come, and he that heareth These, let him say come* : Bearing date the blessed Virgins day, 1646. *And him that is a thirst come; and whosoever will, let him take the water of life freely*; And thus as invited to this Temple, forty six yeares which was a building, the *Resurrections banquet to partake thereof*. So these to be understood, together with the Sacraments divorce : (*the separation of the Cup from the Bread*) That he that shal take away also from the time prefixt of the Lords *blessed* comming, inclosed in this Booke, *shall not enter into, or be admitted his* Rest. Whose reward is with him, about *Easter*, to give them their wages every one.

The grace of our LORD, *&c. Amen.*

FINIS.

19. *The Day Of Ivdgements Modell* (1646; Wing D1983) is reprinted, by permission of The British Library, from the clear copy held in the Thomason Tracts Collection (shelfmark Tab.603.a.38. [11]). The text block of the original measures 170 × 96 mm.

Hard-to-read words:

11.3	*hand*
11.6	*he goes*
12.2	or Six times 24.
13.2	*sand*
14.20–21	When as *Augustus He deceased*

THE
DAY
OF
IVDGEMENTS
Modell.

By the LADY ELEANOR DOUGLAS.

REVELATION, Chap. 7.
To day if yee shall heare his voice.

Printed in the Yeare, 1646.

FROM THE

La: ELEANOR DOUGLAS.

Upon the 7. Chapter of the

REVELATION.

THe Time come to remove, the *Covering* having NO short space been shutt up in the *ARKE*, our *present* state *also* have *presented an Olive-Leafe plucked from the* Tree *of* LIFE, *of the* VVaters *abate dryed up*, as it were, *those* Teares *from the face of the Earth*, as appeares finish'd a tedious *Vale of Vanity* : for *soules* imprisoned without *re-*

lease and restlesse, till *Times* utmost minnit run out, or *Expired.*

So of the *DOVES-LAST return findes rest for the* Sole *of her foote,* as followes : Revealed even the most *holy and reserved of* Time *and* Seasons *conseald Mistery* ; Except that of the unknown DAY and Houre imparted NOT to *Angels* : Namely, *NOT Yeares* ; But forty *dayes,* The day of *Judgements* Last *Warning-peice* ; AS the number of *forty* no stranger to the present either : which here bears date from *Easter-weeke* 1646. to the *ASSENSION* thereabout, for appearance before the *Judge of quick and dead* ; His great *Tribunall* extracted out of that *sealed* Number, *a Hundred forty foure &c.* Saying, *he heard the Number of Them* Revelati. 7. Chap. Wherefor the Keeper of the great Seal, and the Cryers voice, Thus (*verse 2.*)

Where

VVhere farther contains These, belonging to Our *Clymate* or *Jland* described for a *Tryall before a Thron of Judicature*, NOT *heard till such an appointed* Time : witnessed by those restrained *Winds foure*, withall points at *Easter* Terme in *May*, the first Terme; VVinesse the fresh Boughes in their hands, (*all in white Robes*) *Where the innocent Lambe*, as it were, *araignd before Them* : And by Them also evident, where the *Jury* called by Name *Judah*, the *Fore-man* of those Twelve *godfathers* or *Elders sealed in the Foreheads*, or *sworn-men*; And such innumerable attendants as though the great day *Come* : *Such* Legions of *ANGELS standing about the Throne, and about the Jury*, where *face to face the foure* VVITNESSES *all* Thronging *to heare their* Testimony, *Namely the foure Beasts*, what they pro-

 duce,

duce, These makes it plaine enough : About this *Prisoner*, his holding up the hand at the *BARRE*, the very *MODEL* of a Court, representing it : where shewes withall in the Peerlesse Lambs Livory and posture ; This his humble Servant, (*by the* Lambe *represented*) presents his Person before the *Throne*, together with the woefull state of so many Prisoners at this Time, being accompanied there-with :

But proceeding with this, the day of *Judgements Usher* ; doubtlesse where made by Them, such Lowe *Obeysance* to **HIM** *sitting on the Throne, subscribing* & submitting to his Pleasure, saying, *Amen*, &c. (verse)

And so the *Jury* also, those *Elders* No ordinary MEN : declares this Prisoner one of their owne degree : NO com-

Common ONE, pleading Not guilty, neither deserving *death* or *imprisonment*: The L*amb acquits HIM here, though* Condemn'd. Neverthelesse; *The white Robes* suffers, where so many hands (as it were) held up; AS goes the *VERDICT*: SO the sentence *LORD have mercy on Them*; *And so theirs the* KINGDOM *of* Heaven, as declared; *The* Lambe *hath Compassion on them*; *HIM-*SELFE *shall* L*ead Them to* Living-Springs *and* Fountains: *Cœlestiall FOUNTAINS* and *SPRINGS*, *which never fayle, or shall be taken away*, intayld so sure.

And in which portion of Scripture, as inclusive *Whitsontydes* mistery: Shadowed too under the *White* R*obe*, (as much to say) *The great and dreadfull day* in the Moneth of *MAY*: NO more

more *Whitsontides*, as by the Suns not *Lightning on them*, *&c.*

And so much for *Easter* and *Penticost*, a *feast* observ'd by *Jew* & *Christian*, cleerly exprest *by that sealed Number*, *and by the* others *without* Number *of so Many severall* Nations, *whereas* Noting withall ; *Baptisme*, and the LORDS *Supper* adminstred (only) at those two Feast-times , as heretofore an Old custome : (*vers*) *So they shall* Thirst *no more*, NOR *hunger* either *in that Kind*, an unlawfull restraint, without doubt points at the Present. VVhere *Virgins* excluded from *living Waters those*.

Herewith, one Thing more : Making known, touching That question By one of the Grand-jury-Elders, saying,

ing (*verse*) *What are These which are Arrayed in white, and whence come They?* Answered *H & M*, Sir, *Thou knowest*; (as much to say,) The present *Reigns character* or Colours : Serves both for the Yeare 1644. to bee accomplished before the Church her Triumphs or rejoycing shew : And his *Crownation* solemnized in *March* 1624. compleat about *EASTER*: HE, the foure and twentieth since the *Conquest*, of those *Elders In-Thrond*: As Not unknown, both Father and Sonne about the aforesaid RESVRRECTION *Feast* Crown'd. VVho needs Then inquire what *STRANGERS* These ? Much like as in the *Glasse*, one knew not *his owne FACE* : Or these in the SPRING, as it were, going a PRECESSION, *with those Palms in* Their *hands*, extended from the

B yeare,

yeare, 1625. to the yeare, 1645. That deliverance *Time*: Hetherto forborn, (as it were, *the Winds restraind*) as since *Yeare*, 1605 so long since that *Powder-Blowe* intended.

Revelation, CHAP. XIIII.

AND thus, abrupt for Expedition sake; Farthermore a touch *of This the finall blowe, for the sake of his Chosen: As* the *Time* shortn'd in consideration *of which*, the hastened *END*, So shewes how the VVORLDS *mistical Weeke abated*, how much; *Before the houre COME* of HIS *Judgement*: By that great ARMEY *a hundred forty & foure Thousand, singing both one song*, with the former sealed Number, as *Chap.* the 7. informes: Extoling such a Yeare accomplished of our SALVATION, with these harping *The same* Note, *The yeare of our* Redemption, 1644. to bee accom-

accomplished, *Accompanying the Day of JUDGEMENTS houre, immediately which followes, Who before hand tune the* MARRIAGE-SONG, *so all following the* LAMB *whethersoever he goes.* Also which Number includes the 4000. *yeare* of the *world*, his Incarnation Then. *Chap.* 21

And so much for *the Brid*, prepared the *LAMBS Wife*: *Compared to such a uniform CITIE*; where *a Hundred forty foure Cubits* the measured *wall*; (called *Salvation, Isaiah* 60.) Namely, the aforesaid Yeare of GOD, and serves for Dayes and Houres too, with the 4000 yeares (afore-shewed of the *World*, our Saviours being born of the *Virgin*.

As for the MISTICALL VVEEKE *of six* Thousand *Yeares* current, Thus exprest in the Number of the *Lambs followers*: The *Hundred forty and foure, &c. standing on the* Mount: Even the *Houres* fulfilling of SIX

B 2 Dayes,

DAYES, amounting to a *hundred forty foure Houres*; or Six times 24. (or 12 times 12.) As the equall Houres distributed to *DAY* and *NIGHT* about EASTER: *And six dayes, and six thousand yeares, all one with* HIM *Eternity*, so much suffices.

VVhere also *forty odd* DAYES, (*Chap.* 14.) between *Easter* and *Whitsontyd*: By his sitting on the *WHITE CLOUD proclaimed, One like the Son of MAN crown'd*; (to wit) *Whitsontyds figure or expression*:

As this for another, *Cast in the same mould*, (Chap. 19. *&* 20.) *seal'd with Him that satt on the White* HORSE, *with his* Albion-trayn. And again, *Hee, who satt on the great white* Throne: from whose dreadfull face, *EARTH* and *HEAVEN fled away*; And *hell,*

hell and death delivering up their Prisoners, *as the sand of the* SEA : as the VVorld *Then* to receive *Condigne reward*, NO better which have improved their *precious Talent* of *TIME*, sixteen compleat *Centuries* since *OUR blessed* Saviours *INCARNATION*, proved by Scripture account.

VVitnesse that *Universall* imposed *Taxe*, in the Yeare ONE *and* FORTY of *Cæsar August-reigne* : which OF the present heavie dayes since (1641) *comes short* : Of whose difficult Number *666*. so obscure ; The *truth of it*, even so many Moneths as stiled the Number of a MAN. And the Moneths of *WOMAN* her *Reckning too*; So Fullfils HIS 55. Yeares Reigne and a halfe. VVherein the *peace-maker, the Lamb of* GOD, *came in-*

B 3 *to*

to the World: confirm'd *by* the 42 *moneths* (or yeares 3. and a halfe) of the cruell Beast, *bearing seven heads and tenne horns*, (*Chap*. 13.) That who needs then to be unresolv'd, *who the* Man *of sin*; *Or* what *date* that writing bears (*mistery Babylon*) Or whom it Concerns (*Chap*. 17.) No lesse then the day of *Judgements* expresse *Character*, by those *Sabbaticall heads*, *and sinfull horns ten*: when *as the Man of sin*, the ROMAN *Beast* aged 17. *Centuries*. *And the servants of the Lamb as sealed in the foreheads with His Fathers* Name: Likewise the *Beast with his marke*, shews what *Communion* his Factors (*papists*) have, with *Sathan* their *Father*.

And thus in the 15. Yeare of *Tiberius* Reigne, (as Saint *Luke* beares witnesse) Our *Saviour* about 30 Yeares of age *Then*, That Was about the age of Yeares 15, When as *Augustus HE deceased*, since when the Moneth of *August*,

gust Continues in the Name of the *BEAST* ever since ; So then the aforesaid Monethes his Numbred reigne. Who that Other, with *two Horns like a Lambe, That exerciseth all the Power there, where NO Man buys or sels, &c.* No more but referred to themselves.

So prayse him the ancient of dayes, for ever more Day and Night, his ancient servants, Hee that hath begining None or ending.

Lastly, for which premises concerning *Prisoners* araignd, *These keyes of darknes*, excluds Not these, of expressing the Churches power *of* binding & loosing: As here The Model or patterne Therof: What Discipline Agreeable with the APOSTLES, Rules Included: where The PEOPLES approbation and Consent : As it were shadowed under That Multitudes Holding up their HANDS, with Those Sealed ELDERS Verdict or Iudgement, joyning Their Voyces, saying; AMEN, &c. As directed to *Eastern and Western Churches* both, (Verse 2) By that *Angels ascending from the East.*

And thus concluding with the Number of *his* rageing Reigne, the *Antichristian Beast* : Even since that *Sea-Monster* 88. With *that Admirable* Victory, *Just* 666. *monethes*, or 55. Yeares and a halfe; *So just and true are Thy wayes : Thou King of Saints. &c.*

FINIS.

20. *The Lady Eleanor Her Appeal* (1646; Wing D1972) is reprinted, by permission of the Bodleian Library, from the copy held at the Bodleian (shelfmark C 14. 11[14] Linc). The handwritten comments in this text resemble the hand of those that appear in the Folger tracts. The text block of the original measures 150 × 90 mm.

Hard-to-read words:

4.19	a
17.4	Vnion
18.1	safety
18	shewing she should haue a sonn [transcription]
18.19	My Gentleman
19	Coming before Her time [transcription]
20.1–3	not to passe, to abjure such my predictions, wimzees, as he termd it, that sold the blessing was disappointed.
20.9	because it
21.1–4	from him, *and know what I had to do with his affairs*; *and if I desisted not, he would take another course*. To which my answer was, I would take my course
21.9–14	In the conclusion Mr. Kirk said, *He was not carried with the vulgar*; *but prayed me to tell him whether the King should have a Son, or no*: unwilling to send him empty away, assured him a Son, and a strong Childe; which he
23.1	as
23.19	at the
23.20	Dean *Young*
24.1–5	him, saying, *I had turnd him now into his long Coats indeed*: And which aforesaid Divine was drownd, soon after the Boat cast away, that then lose his jest, would sooner lose his friend.
24.10	*Iames*
24.10–11	*lex talionis*
24.19	Brothers Text, Thus
24.20	*to us*, *Deut*. with
25	scripsi, scripsi [transcription]
26.6	my
29.17	harken to me, for 49 was his
29.18	suddenly to
29.18	Jubile [transcription]
29.19	Year [transcription] deceased on his Birth
29.20	Earl of *Pembroke*
40.14	*on the*
40.16	that
40.17	*thank*
40.18	*then*
40.19	*but to*
40.20	*secret*

THE

LADY *ELEANOR* Davi[es]

HER

APPEAL

Present this to Mr. *Mace* the Prophet of the most High, his Messenger.

2 PETER 3. 3.

Knowing this first, that there shall come in the last days Scoffers, saying, Where is the promise of his coming?

JUDE 18.

Remember yee that they told you, there should be Mockers in the last time, having not the Spirit.

Printed in the Year, 1646.

From the Lady *Eleanor* the Handmaid of the Holy Spirit,

TO

Our beloved Brother Mr *Mace*, the Anointed of our Lord.

HAving in the burthen of his precious VVord been my ſelf a partaker, made a publique Example, no mean one, concerning the way before the Lords coming to be prepared, Have thought it not unneceſſary by what means it came to paſſe, to impart and publiſh the ſame unto your ſelf, in making known ſome paſſages, the truth of which unknown not unto the whole world, almoſt ever ſince the Year 1625.

Shewing withall about a few dayes before the former Kings departure this life, how firſt of all there came a Scotiſh Lad to this City, about the age of Thirteen, one *George Carr* by Name, otherwiſe cald the dumb Boy or Fortuneteller, ſo termd, that ſpake not for ſome ſpace of time, with whom it was my hap, upon a viſit, to meet where ſome of them would needs ſend for this Boy, although few more jealous of ſuch acquaintance or ſparing, yet able to diſcern between ſuch a one and Impoſtures, making bold before my departure thence, to direct him the way to my houſe, where care ſhould be taken of him, not the leſſe becauſe a Stranger; accordingly who there abode,

abode, where no simple people, but expert and learnd as any, try'd no few conclusions; some instanced as here:

Sometimes who would take the Bible or a Chronicle, and open it, and close it again, then cause the aforesaid Youth to shew by signs and such like dumb demonstrations, what was containd therein; which things he so to the life exprest and acted, as were it a Psalm or Verse then feignd to sing, though saw not a letter of the Book; and sometime that suddenly behinde him would blow a Horn, whereat never so much as changed his look, seemd so hard of hearing. And again thus, to sound him farther, one must stop his ears fast, and then what two whisperd at the other

end

end of the Gallery, he muſt declare what they ſpake in the ear, as often as they pleaſed ſeveral times.

Having by that time gotten a whiſtling voice, as plain as any can ſpeak, like a Bird; before that had uſed ſigns for the ſpace of three Moneths, then no longer dumb or deaf.

To conclude, whatſoever it were he able to manifeſt it, whether containd in Letters encloſed in Cabinets, or by numbring how many pence or pepper corns in a Bag or Box before it was opened, or any thing of that kind fit for the vulgar capacity too; or when he was brought into any place amongſt Strangers, one ſhould write in ſeveral papers every ones Name, and he muſt give them accordingly to to each his own Name, at firſt making as though he were in ſome doubt which way to beſtow himſelf, where the chief Divines of the City preſent, ſome of them beſtowing a ſhilling on him, without farther conſideration thought it ſufficient, &c. whileſt others of that calling as liberal of their ſlanderous tongues; that no longer might be harbored in our houſe, likened to Friar *Ruſh*, Servants had ſo incenſed their Maſters, ſetting all on fire, with Iuſtices of Peace and Church-men, giving out he was a Vagrant, a Counterfeit, or a VVitch. Immediately upon which the Spirit of Propheſie falling likewiſe upon me, then were all vext worſe then ever, ready to turn the houſe upſide down, laying this to his charge too: when

when laying aside Houshold cares all, and no conversation with any but the VVord of God, first by conference with the Prophet *Daniel, cap.* 8. *ver.* 13. I found out this place, *Then I heard ONE Saint speaking unto another Saint, said unto that certain Saint which SPAKE* (in the Orinal (to wit) *The Numberer of Secrets, or the wonderful Numberer* (Hebr. *Palmoni*) *How long the Vision concerning the daily, and the Transgression making desolate, to give the Hoste, &c. And he said unto me, Unto Two thousand three hundred days, then shall the Sanctuary be cleansed.*

The sum of it this, as much to say, Inquired of such a one that spake not at first, How long from the Vision before this Prophesie shall be reveald, or or whether I ſhould be able, &c. as now about Two thouſand two hundred years complete ſince the Captivity, as here anſwered, *O Son of Man, for at the time of the end it ſhall be: Behold, I will make thee know in the laſt end of the indignation, for at the time appointed ſhall be the end, Daniel, cap.* 8.

And thus not only providing for that aforeſaid admired Gueſt, but adored him almoſt; how it afterward came to paſs, like that leaſt of all ſeeds, how it ſprang up, as follows: Here following the Prophets their order in theſe circumſtances, Time, Perſons, and Place, obſerved: Shewing,

In the aforeſaid Year, 1625. the firſt of his Reign, the firſt of his Name, in the Moneth of *July*, ſo

B called

called after the first Roman Emperor, in *Berks*, the first of Shires, my self whose Father the prime Peer, or first Baron, being at my House in *Englesfield*, then heard early in the Morning a Voice from Heaven, speaking as through a Trumpet these words;

There is Nineteen years and an half to the Judgement day, and be you as the meek Virgin.

VVhen occasioned through the plague, that heavy hand, like the VVise mens coming from the East, the Term came down to *Reading* our next Market town; and that first Parliament following it posting down to *Oxford*, not far off either: And somtime as in *Augustus* days, so in this

of

of great Britains ſecond Monarch, taxed likewiſe with no ordinary taxes levied; when this morning Star, this ſecond Babe born, ruling the Nations with an iron Rod, no light Iudgements foreſhewing at hand: which words in a Manuſcript annex'd to an Interpretation of the Prophet *Daniels* Viſions, A few days finiſhed afore, was then immediately for to be publiſhed, carried to *Oxfords* Parliament, that ancient'ſt of Univerſities, this golden Number heard, extending to the Year 1644. *January*.

VVhich Book perfected about the firſt of Auguſt, was with mine own hand delivered and preſented to *Abbots* Archbiſhop, where the Babe ſigned in the preſence of no few witneſſes, with this token, That the great

B 2 Plague

Plague ſhould preſently ceaſe; that Curſe ſo furiouſly pourd out on the deſolate City, where graſſe grew in her chief ſtreets ſhould be inhabited.

At which time the weekly Bill amounted to Five thouſand; but becauſe the next week it increaſed Six hundred, this Token of ſuch deliverance was utterly caſt out of remembrance: Howbeit before the end of Auguſt, ſcarce Five hundred of the Plague deceaſed; in ſuch an inſtant vaniſhed, which ſomtime was grown up to that height as the Age of the VVorld, Five thouſand ſix hundred.

Concerning which aforeſaid judgment or blow, foreſhewed no other then the day of Iudgements expreſſe forerunner, the worlds final blow at hand; upon farther conſult with

with the Scriptures, the Book of the *Revelation*, underſtood how with the 7. Chapter it accorded, ſaying, *And I ſaw four Angels ſtanding at the four corners of the Earth, holding the four Winds that they ſhould not blow*, until expired ſuch a time, ſuch a year.

VVhere that new prognoſtication beginning with the loud Moneth of *March*, ſhews till 1644. thoſe pernicious winds reſtrained under the ſeald Number of One hundred forty and four, &c. the conſeald time in thoſe Characters incloſed: So again Chapter 14. where thoſe muſtered Troops on Mount *Zion*, ſeald in the forehead with the ſame Number, *One hundred forty and four thouſand*, encluding the fourth thouſand year of our Redemption, when he born

of

of a Virgin not only, but the year of Grace, 1644. when *Babylon* falls; *Shee's faln, shee's faln*: together with the Kalender for that year, beginning with the blessed Virgins feast (vers.) saying, *They are Virgins, &c. Redeemed from amongst men the first fruits.*

And so much for the new Song, which none besides could learn, too difficult for former Ages, too high a noat to reach.

To which the 21. Chapter answers, where she that virgin Cities walls measured, *One hundred forty four Cubits*, the Churches preparation then, or Reformation before the end.

And since prophesies Thundring Reign began, what judgments since the

the year 1625 *July*, ſhal give you a liſt of ſome of them; beginning at home firſt, where this Book of mine was ſacrificed by my firſt Husbands hand, thrown into the fire, whoſe Doom I gave him in letters of his own Name (*John Daves*, Ioves Hand) within three years to expect the mortal blow; ſo put on my mourning garment from that time: when about three days before his ſudden deceaſe, before all his Servants and Friends at the Table, gave him paſſe to take his long ſleep, by him thus put off, *I pray weep not while I am alive, and I will give you leave to laugh when I am dead.*

Accordingly which too ſoon came to paſs, for contrary to a ſolemn Vow within three Moneths married to another Husband, who eſcaped not ſcotfree:

ſcotfree: he likewiſe burning my Book, another Manuſcript, a remembrance to the King for beware great Britains blow at hand, ſhewd him thus, *Dan.* 12. *And at that time ſhall Michael the great Prince ſtand up, and there ſhall be a time of trouble, ſuch as never was ſince a Nation*, with the Reſurrection in his time to be propheſied: & for a token of the time, *At that time the people ſhall be delivered*, their oppreſſors put to flight; where very Parliament-Stars ſhining for ever, as by ſuch a ſolemn Oath taken there ſworn, &c. the contents of that laſt chap. verily concluding with the firſt year of the preſent Reign, 1625. ſignified in thoſe no obſcure characters, *Bleſſed is he that waits*: And comes to Three hundred thirty five; which being

being added unto the former reckoning of Two hundred and ninety, amounts to 1625. to wit, when this sealed Vision before the end shall be revealed, witnesse the troublesome time.

And of *Daniel* signifying Iudgement too: Thus about two years after the Marriage, I waiting on the Queen as shee came from Masse or Evening Service, All-Saints day, to know what service shee pleased to command me; The first question was, *When she should be with Childe*: I answered, *Oportet habere tempus*, Interpreted by the Earl of *Carlisle*: and the next, *What successe the Duke would have, who* (the queen said) *was intrenching, and much forwardnesse in*: Answered again, As for his honor, of that he would not bring home much, but

C his

his person should return in safety with no little speed; which to neither side gave content, satisfied not his Friends, much lesse such as look'd after his death.

Besides, I told the queen, for a time she should be happy; *But how long said she?* I told her, Sixteen years, that was long enough. But by the Kings coming in our discourse interrupted, saying, *He heard how I foretold my former Husband of his Death some three days before it:* Said I, I told him of a certain Servant of your Majesties, one extraordinary proper, &c. that forthwith was to come upon earnest businesse to me; and that he ask'd me the next day before his Death, when I expected my Gentleman: To which his Majesty replied, *That was the*

shewing she should have a sonn.

the next way to break his heart, who was pleaſed ſo much to commend my choyce without excepting any.

And ſo that time Twelve Months the queen conceived of a Son, and although had forgotten me, yet ſome about her I informed, that her Son ſhould go to Chriſtning and Burying in a day. Comig before Her time

And the Duke accordingly too miſcarrying, arrived ſafely the week after I had been there; of whoſe moneth of *Auguſt* to continue till then, not miſinformed of it by perſons of quality, told him from me; whereat Sir *Archibald* my Husband ſo much vext, ventured (at my motion) to lay the Breeches, before Mrs *Murray* for one, and Mrs *Maxfield*, if I would be bound when it came not to passe, to abjure such my predictions, wimzees, as he termd it, that sold the blessing was disappointed.

VVhereupon seconded by his Uncle the Dean of *Winchester*, who wrote up to him to put me in minde *September* was at hand, *and that secret things belongs to God*, &c, but shortly after craved me pardon, because it seemd I had added, *The Duke should never see a day in September*; one bewaild on all sides, as though I would throw the houses out at windows, VVorshipped so much before; But still pressing Great *Britains* blow, for which purpose to be neer the Court, taking a house at Saint *James*, where the King not pleased with such Alarms, commanded one of his Bed-chamber, Mr. *Kirk*, to go

from

from him, *and know what I had to do with his affairs; and if I desisted not, he would take another course.* To which my answer was; I would take my course against him, namely, Sir *Archibald Dowglas* that had burnt my papers to purchase his favor, and that he and all should know shortly.

In the conclusion Mr. *Kirk* said; *He was not carried with the vulgar, but prayed me to tell him whether the King should have a Son, or no:* unwilling to send him empty away, I assured him a Son, and a strong Childe; which he not sparing to impart, accordingly solemnized was with Bonefires, &c. within a Moneth.

At which time, the first day of *June*, his Servant Sir *Archibald Dowglas* in *Martins* Church at the Com-

munion,

munion, was ſtrooken bereft of his ſences, in ſtead of ſpeech made a noice like a Brute creature, doubtleſſe his heart changed into a Beaſts too, for ſo would put his head into a diſh of Broth, of Lettice or Herbs, and drink Oyl and Vinegar, and ſometimes Beer all together, inſatiable that way, knew no body but only my ſelf, though it was not my hap to be at *London* then, nor when my former husband as ſuddenly dyed, but in *Berkſhire*, through Gods providence the day before that ſaw them both.

Some three months before in the preſence of the Lady *Berkſhire* & the Lady *Carliſle*, who imputed it to want affection, that needs would have reconciled tne buſineſſe, declared ſentence,

tence upon him, *Not so happy to be as to dye, nay worse then death should befal him*; and so before all his Friends, who witnessed it with their Hands, the writing was drawn up, bearing Date in *March* 1630, &c. *That if in the Moneth of June next some such wonderful judgement from God came not upon him, then in a Sheet I would walk to Pauls barefoot*; whilest he boasting, *How with a Greyhound he could run up a hill in the Snow*, and the like. VVhere a witty Divine, one of the witnesses, saying, *Sir, give my Lady* Youly *for it*: And so though until the Moneth of *Youly* given, yet accomplished the first day of *June* on a Sunday at *London*, going up to give his Attendance at the Princes Birth; his Uncle Dean Young when he saw

him,

him, ſaying, *I had turnd him now into his long Coats indeed*: And which aforeſaid Divine was drownd, ſoon after the Boat caſt away; that then loſe his jeſt, would ſooner loſe his friend; And as *Eliſha* ſaid to *Elijah*, *Hee would not leave him*; ſo paſsing on with what became of the houſe where thoſe papers of mine at Saint *James* received Martyrdom, *Extationes*, immediately was burnt down, with no few of his Majeſties choyce Books, re-edified ſince; And firſt of all as ſince in *Ireland* in a houſe of ours burnt eighty, all Scots; which unhappy houſe (left by me) Mr. *Patrick Yong* the Deans Brother would needs take it, turnd to a Library, and he following his Brothers Text, *The reveald things belongs to us*, Deut. with

his

his hand in Hebrew, Greek and La-tine, written on a piece of the Book, having to the fire, like an old Sot for his pains, ſacrificed the reſt.

And not thus reſting, ſhall give you a paſſage or two more ; ſhewing the holy Spirit beſides ſpeaking with other Tongues,able to ſpeak without a Tongue ſometime, as by the Prophet *Ezekiel* to that rebellious Age, growing downward, by his portraying and the like : Shewing a few days before my deſerting the aforeſaid houſe, coming home, having been forth, and meeting with one ſeeming dumb, that came along with me, Soldier like, with a long garment or ruſſet Coat, a red Croſſe on the ſleeve, by ſigns uttering his minde ; where leaving him at door, without

D other

other notice, cold welcom, that had watched about the houſe all day, as they told me, calling to minde what trouble by ſuch a one befel: preſently after comes in Sir *Archibald Dowglas* my Husband from *Whitehall*, followed with a Chaplain and ſome ſix Servants, affrighted all, proteſted he had met with an Angel, whoſe cuſtom always to give ſomething to the poor, ſaying, He was come with him, a yong man very handſom, about his age, praying me to come forth; the Servants vowing he came out of Heaven, otherwiſe might (in the open fields) ſeen him afore ſuddenly who caught their Maſter by the arm.

VVhich man applying himſelf wholy to Sir *Archibald Dowglas* by ſuch diſcourſing ſigns, of his late

mar-

marriage, and former courſe of his life; would not a look vouchſafe me, till at laſt by locking, as it were, and unlocking a door, which I interpreting to preſage priſon, he aſſented unto this token beſtowd on me; and Sir *Archibalds* back turned, then ſtept within the door as none ſhould ſee him but my ſelf, by pointing at him, and bending the fiſt, looking up as it were to Heaven, as though ſome heavy hand toward: About a Moneth after that loſt both Reaſon and Speech, by like ſigns feign to learn his meaning, as he able to impart his minde, formerly ſhewd.

VVhen this Meſſenger departing, as though had far to go, as ſwift as an arrow, having taken a ſhilling in good part, though promi-

D 2 ſed

ſed as many pounds would he come again, by ſpreading the hands which he ſeemed to underſtand; where like conference to have, many of the Court ſending after him, ſtanding at St. *James's* gate to ſtaid him; but no more of him heard, amongſt the poor though inquired, whether knew any ſuch. Moreover ſhewing us a Verdict ſhould paſſe on our ſide for *Englefield*, pointing weſtward; about a-fortnight after coming to paſſe in *Eaſter* Term: whereof all our neighbors at Berkſhire houſe, and Maſter *Gwin* and the reſt till it came in much expectation, the only Tryal that gave us our right.

And ſince faln on this chronological Diſcourſe, a paſſage or two more that would fill almoſt a Library, were all

written

written as that Diſciple wrote, the world would not contain the Books: Upon day viſiting the Counteſſe of *Berks*, where the Earl of *Holland* preſent and others, and the Counteſs of *Carliſle*, who as I was informed by Lord *Andevere*, made no ſecret of it; And ſome Relating of the Lord *Stewards* ſending about caſting his Nativity to one at *Clarkenwel*; the wiſeman had told he ſhould live to the Age of Fifty nine: But my judgement otherwiſe I told them, for being born when the great Earth-quake was, by the ſame token his mother ſaying, *He would prove a Coward*, wiſht him to harken to me, for 49 was his Jubile time appointed, who ſuddenly a day and Year deceaſed on his Birth-day 49. *William* Earl of *Pembroke* by some Citizens there weighing plate, on fames wing was mounted.

As this for another then blazed, being invited by the Lady of *Berkshire* to her Childes Christning, sent word I might not, nor would not come; howbeit a fortnight after went, being Neighbors, finding there the Lord *Goring* and the Lady *Carlisle*, the Lady *Berks* aspect somwhat sad, relating my denial to her, saying, *She knew it boded something to her child*: The Lady *Carlisle* saying, *He is well, is he not? Yes, I praise God said she, as any of the rest*: Then quoth the Lord *Goring*, *I pray let us know what thundering thumping thing it is about my Lady* Berkshires *Son*: To which only thus before I went, enquired of her the Name of the other born before this

this laſt, as I take it ſheſaid was *Philip*, then he muſt be again the yongeſt I again replied, as after a few hours the ſame night the Childe ſuddenly was gone and died, &c.

And though theſe things not done in corner or remote place, reſtraind neither city nor court from ſuch violent doings, vain laughter, like the crack of thorns, as the wiſeman, *cap. &c.* ſhews to be regarded as much, of whoſe high preſumption on record, ſuch a blaſt from *Whitehall*, bearing Date *October*, 1633, *&c.*

From the Court of *Whitehall, &c.*

His *Majeſty doth expreſly Command the Lord Archbiſhops Grace and his Commiſsioners, for cauſes Eccleſiaſtical,*

cleſiaſtical, That the Petitioner be forthwith called before them for preſuming to imprint the ſaid Books, and for preferring this deteſtable Petition.

Sidney Montague.

VVhich blaſphemous accurſed reference thus occaſioned was; upon their taking away of my Books printed at *Amſterdam* : But preſsing to have them reſtored paſſages taken out of the Scripture concerning great *Babylons* blow, *Dan.5. And the Beaſt aſcended out of the Bottomleſſe pit, Revel.* 11. Applied to Great Britain, with the Hand-writing (*cap.* 5.) *Thou art found wanting, &c.* extended from that Marriage feaſt, ever ſince 1625. into the year 1645.

or

or from the abomination, &c. *Dan.* 12.

And of the aforesaid reference, thus; save Reverence his Grace the foreman of the Iury, 1633. *Octob.* 23. commanding first a Candle, he that would not be warnd; but said *No more of that*; burnt the Book, saying, *My Lords, I have made you a smoother of Dooms-day, to be in such a year about Candlemas, till then she takes time enough: What shall we do next?* when with one voice, *Let her be fined Three thousand pounds, Excommunicated, no Bible alowed her, or Pen and Ink, or woman Servant; carry her away,* as by a VVarrant under twelve Hands, confined to the Gatehouse for ever, where kept a close prisoner for two years, the Lords day unknown from another, the rest for brevity and

E mo-

modeſty ſake diſmiſſed.

To this day which ſentence and remains of the ſmoked Book remain extant in the Office, Trophees of his Triumph, buried by this *Achan*, this golden wedge or tongue, he ſirnamed the *Beaſt*, from *Oxford* deriving his Name, ſmothered as other things.

And *Irelands* Maſſacre, was it not *October* 23? and *Edgehil* fight the 23? Then *Octobers* VVine-preſſe trodden; even ſhewing you a Myſtery withal, *Rev.* 17. *The Beaſt that was, and is not, even he is the eighth, and is of the ſeven, and goeth into Perdition.* Even Kings and the Beaſt both put together; as from *H.*8. *H.*7.&c. with his 7. years complete, and 8. current, the Archbiſhops lawleſs term before his going into priſon, that Son of Perdition,

dition, tranſlated to which place 1633. *September*, his aſcending then, &c.

And twelve Biſhops at once, were not ſo many ſent to the Tower? hee likewiſe in the year 1644. *January* on a Friday put to death or killed, according to the tenor of that Petition, ſtiled in ſuch a probrious maner; compoſed as follows:

Moſt humbly ſhews to Your Majeſty,

THat *the Word of God the first year of Your happy Reign ſpoken to the Petitioner, upon Friday laſt did ſuffer early in the morning, the B. Beaſt aſcended out of the Bottomleſs Pit, ſeven Heads having ſignified ſeven years his making War, hath overcome and killed them Books ſealed with the Prophets Teſtimony, &c.*

ELEANOR. 1633, &c.

For unfolding the myſtery of which referring unto *Rev* 11.

E 2 And

And ſo much teſtified in this Compenduary for this crucifi'd Book, containing the year of God 1644. for the treading down then his foes, ſuffering between Sir *Archibald Dowglas* on the one hand, and the Archbiſhop on the other; as both in one year, Sir *Archibald Dowglas* departing this life 1644. *July* 28. on Sunday the Lords Reſurrection, interred in *Pancras* that Mother of Churches, Aged 44. the other on a Friday, the day our Lord deſcended, &c.

And with *Job* that good man with evil things, not unmindeful of the good, ſo of this mans double portion, living the flower of his days ſuch a Monaſtical life, not admitting his own Brothers to ſee his face, ſent from his parents out of *Scotland*, with ſuch violence

lence ſet upon the Kingdom of Heaven, wreſtling like *Jacob*, his Candle till three in the morning not put out, he ſubſcribing *Eliſha*, calling the Clergy no other then *Baals* Chaplains from pregnant Scripture proofs; and at his death admitting none, ſaying, *His place without them was prepared*, with *Moſes* injoying a view of *Canaan*: as in truth ſuch deſpiſers of Propheſie could not conclude them other then ſuch, even forbidden to bid them *God ſpeed*, it being ſtiled the teſtimony of Ieſus, *Rev.* 19. and by ſhewing them of their ſaltleſſe Collects out of ſeaſon, praying as it were, Hear us for thy Servant St. *Andrews* ſake, St. *Thomas*, St. *Bartholomew*, &c. without a word or mention how *Peter* ſerved him, and St. *Thomas*; the

ten

ten like *Josephs* Brethren, so envying the other twain, all because they would be greatest as about the Keys, now at such strife: Turnd to the keys of the Gatehouse prison and Bedlem, those in their custody without question of such marvel may boast.

So lastly shewing of that writ served on the Kings house, *Dan.* 5. this also *Zech.* 5. serves for our meridian; *The flying rowl twenty Cubits in length, visiting the house of the false swearer, the thief*; appointed for plundring perjured witnesses and Jurors, their whole Estate of it, robbing no few: And with the Coat of the present, displayed too, directed to the sign of the Flying Stork, not unlike the French vertugal like sails, the wind in their wings, mounted in the Air, that

that fugitive Mother (Sorcerers wickednefs) and her Daughter, erecting Caftles, old *Babels*, decaid Towers, (befides their *Sedans*) where the leaden weight bids beware the fheet of lead, *Zech.* as by her fitting in the midft of the Ephah carried, &c. So no farther of their cariage, his weighd in the Ballance, as hers meafured by the Bufhel.

And to like purpofe, witneffe our Parliament LIKE-VVISE daily vifited, though fhewd our God a Revealer of fecrets, *Daniel* 2. *Sets up Kings, puts down, changes Times and Seafons*, by the great maffy Image, as that for ONE piece armed at all points (great Britains figure) points withal to Idolatries downfal for ever; And this although declared unto them

them aforehand, the *Whitsontide* before the Irish Rebellion brake forth, that the brittle iron feet of the fearful Image broken in pieces, served for the Kingdom of *Irelands* Sad Climat, the first blow to be given there; but so taken up, like the *Athenians*, every one hearing and telling News, passages coming forth every day cry'd, spending their times in nothing else but such Commentaries.

This the sentence of our aforesaid Wise-men, ***What will this Babler say?***

That it might be fulfild, shewd & assur'd also by our Savior, *There is nothing so secret and hid which shall be unreveald or not preacht on the house top*, from that below, even to that High, High Court of House, yet asleep all, like that sleeper *Ionah*, or those bidden *sleep on*: So *thank thee, O Father, that hast hidden from them these these things* (of thy councel not made) *but to us reveald them*. Dan. 2.19. *Then was the secret reveald to* Daniel, *Ver.* 21. & 28. & 47.

Anagr. { *Reveale O Daniel.*
Eleanor Audeley.

FINIS.

21. *Je Le Tien: The general Restitvtion* (1646; Wing D1996aA) is reprinted, by permission of the Folger Shakespeare Library, from the unique copy held at the Folger (shelfmark D1996.5 bd. w. D2010). The text block of the original measures 140 × 92mm.

Hard-to-read handwritten annotations and printed words:

Title page	According to Esther Cope (199), the lengthy annotations read as follows: [Top]: "'Gates of Heeven & Hell as if a palace [ ] a prison'; [beneath the words 'Je Le Tien']: 'such as we hear ye hell this age'; [beneath the word 'Restitution']: 'as ye numerous [ ] the sunn mone & stars Cor. 15 Father forgive them. Though they did good service in it" [Above the imprint]: 'requisit'; [Bottom of page]: 'Sinister suspition they have murdered the [ ].' [The bottom of the page is cut off.]
4.12	By [transcription]
8.14	not *Isaac*
10.17	*everlasting fire*
10.18	*of dayes*
19.5–9	According to Cope (206): "a reformd meaning His Hower not yet come" [transcription]
21.10	do not understand which way God is
22.10	An Age [transcription]
31.4	Like Jonah angrye to the death [transcription]
33.7	tricate
34.16	which be
38.3	Poets
38.9	piece
38.11–20	of those reverend Masters, how close stools, those seats sir-reverence lined clean through with the Bible, from Genesis to the Revelation, those precious leaves for the healing of the Nations, polluted in that most base unmanerly manner, worse far then if burnt by the hangman: More sacred then Sauls Garment, when he coverd his Feet, (the modest Scripture
39.2	David,
39.7–20	*Josuah* likewise: How comes it to pass no scruple made, by these Scorners, who fleeing Superstition, run upon gross contempt such prophanation: questionles then priviledge of Parliament being subverted, or infringed more material these which indure for ever, purchased with his Blood, any thing destructive thereto: a liberty far from that preacht by our Savior, in observing his severe stile, who stiles himself *The Preacher*, (*Eccles.*) that well blesses the day of death before the day of ones birth and mourning.
40.1–2	So where a rash word and a look awry extended to Murther & Adul-
40:5–8	in such contempt ever held, even blesses such and no other, who chuses the foolish things, and the weak, the Base, to confound and confute the Mighty.
40.10	matter
40.11	these men
40.12	beheld
40.14	the *Affirmative*

FE I, E TIEN:

The general

RESTITVTION.

Who then is a faithful and wise Servant, whom his Lord hath made Ruler over his houshold to give them their meat in due season.

Printed in the yeer, 1646.

Of the general Restitution.

AS no few deceiving themselves, because of the day and hour no man knows, not Angels of the very day of judgement: conclnde or conceive therefore the time unknown of the Lords coming not possible to be reveal'd to any, in regard of a watch-word given out, to keep such on their guard: otherwise, which would fail; or like the unwise Virgins, should let their lamps go out, &c. So this other mistake, upon parables or proverbs unnecessary now to be continued any longer, such sowre sawce out of season: The sayings of old time (name-

A 2 ly)

ly) That *out of Hell is no redemption*: Of which heavie ſentence here revok'd, the deadly pottage heal'd as follows; this ſtone (the evening come of Time) from the well of Life its mouth rolled away, held not unuſeful heretofore; but like the back parts, beheld in compariſon of his reſerv'd countenance, ſo full of grace and glory, firſt making known only, *I will be gracious to whom I will, &c.* And ſuch paſſages by or ſtraits, ſetting forth his prerogative, as with the potters power over the clay compares his: Though in another place thus, As wide as Eaſt is from the VVeſt, ſo far ſets our ſins from us; and not ours only, but the ſins of the whole world; knows whereof wee bee made, remembers wee bee but Duſt. And

And where Mercy and Goodnes so immeasurable, and we but a grashopper, a shadow, &c. how stands it with so much equity, to make such bare near measure, even world without end, without compassion, out of remembrance to cast the world, the workmanship of his hands.

As by this attainder of *Adams* house suppos'd irrevocable, O far be it from him, after such deep protestations of old, and Heaven and Earth promis'd to bee renew'd; so to forget him, Man, for whom they were made, to have dominion over them, for the first offence of our first parents deceiv'd, no better knowing good from evil in their minority.

Through a sleight of the evil angel, by his subtilty beguil'd, not of dust

dust made, as man, whose doom to eat dust, yet beleev'd they forsaken, who without number, like as the sand of the Sea, so many millions of Legions, because over-reacht in state of Innocency, not only utterly cast out of sight, but left to exquisite torments, such as no pen able to express them, or tongue to utter, much lesse to number or measure, the bounds of that so far beyond all Ages and Times."

Even this proverb yet continu'd, *The childrens teeth set on edge for the fathers default*, so expresly prohibited; as suppos'd impossible for God to change or alter it, as it were the Decree of the Medes and Persians, whereas the Lyons mouths stopt, and the sevenfold heated furnace its furious

rious flames of no force qualified.

And in that maner alſo fore-warn'd, how incredible ſoever in the ſight of men, as for a Camels going through a needles eye: that very point no more difficult vvith God in his appointed time, then for them to thrid a pack-needle, or to caſt a wedge of Iron into the fire, taken forth again, and the like, all things with him as eaſie.

VVhereas intolerable ſinful *Sodom*, for ſo few their ſakes had been ſpar'd, preſt, *Shall not the Judge of all the Earth do right?*

As by ſuch a qualification admitted, which may be merciful as hee pleaſes, rather then unjuſt in the leaſt.

And pardon'd *Ninivehs* great

city,

City, where like Hell out of the belly of that great fish, he was heard and deliver'd: Also in tender consideration because of so many, the right hand not knowing from the left, for the childrens cause the fathers preserv'd, lucky Babes, the state of Innocency, such respect had thereunto.

And here spreading his bleeding hands and arms, extended from paradice to hell, a greater then *Isaac* or *Abraham* either, saying, *Before Abraham was I am*: His onely begotten offering up himself, so did not *Isaac*, saying, *Here's the fire and wood, but where's the Lamb?*

And to be so well pleased in him, and so exceedingly displeased with them, The world, for whom he here prays; not for those given him out of the

the world, ſaying, *Father, forgive them, they know not what they do:* But all them in ſtate of Ignorance, they who do they know not what. And therefore between them crucified, as it were, thoſe two Thieves in paradiſe, which robd the garden of God, even forgave all the world at his death; that before knowing the power given him over all fleſh, made that ſolemn prayer to his father, and thankſgiving for them which believ'd, &c. whoſe prayer *Steven* borrow'd, *Lord, lay not their ſin to their charge, and fell aſleep.*

VVho them told afore, *If I be lifted up, I ſhall draw all men to me;* ſo to the one as ſaying, *This day thou be in paradiſe with me;* another day infers for the other: Howſoever,

B the

the contrary passes for currant, like that mistake touching that Disciple; that *He should not dye*: from some reserv'd meaning of our Saviors, misunderstood by the standers by.

As from this doubtfully given out, likewise of no inferior quality or consequence, concerning the fire not extinguished; where it follows not, their pains of like nature to be endlesse: the punishment, though granted inevitable, not avoided to be, yet the perpetuity thereof in suspence, uncertain how long to continue: as indeed the word *For ever* signifies but during pleasure, & so *Go ye cursed into everlasting fire*, in the original, to wit, *length of dayes*, or *a long time*.

VVhich mysterie of their restitution

ution, The worlds general pardon, inferior not to their being made fellow-heirs the Gentiles, these Sacred Olive boughs (sayings of the Prophets and Apostles) make bold to go over them again; for the going forward with it, how impossible held soever, any such gleanings or multiply'd Fragments belongs to them, because long lay hidden; as taken here from the Tree of Life.

Proclaim'd, *Behold the Lamb of God that taketh away the sins of the world*; also the Angels first salute, *Behold, tidings of great joy to all people*: and of like healing nature, that *He the propitiation of our sins not only, but of the whole worlds*: and thus as at the first, *Behold the world made whole*; as, *God saw every thing, and*

B 2 *behold*

behold it was very good that he made: so returns to their former or first estate; as, *Dust thou art, and to dust thou shalt return*: confirm'd by the Apostle *Paul*, *If the first fruits and root holy, also the lump and branches*.

And again, *Who gave himself a ransom for all, to be testified in due time*: of which time *Peter* not unmindful gives command, *Therefore gird up the loins of your mindes, and hope to the end for the grace to bee brought unto you, at the revelation of Jesus Christ*; in whose Sermon, *Act*.3. *Whom the Heavens must receive at the restitution of all things*. And concerning which grace of general Redemption, and the Lords second coming to be reveal'd, as expresly shewed from good witnesse, to

be

be waited for, and to prepare for it; moreover our Saviors charge, *Therefore be yee ready alſo, for in ſuch a time as yee think not the ſon of man cometh*, (*Matthew* 24. *Mark* 13.) And as to the dayes of the unexpected flood, points to the ſame time, three periods and a half, a time and times and half, ſworn in *Daniel* and the *Revelation*, as it were with him but evening, midnight, cock-crowing and morning, for his coming, then to expect it, ſaying, *Truly Eliah the Prophet firſt ſhall come and reſtore all things, before the great and dreadful day of the Lord, in whoſe ſight a thouſand years as yeſterday.*

According to *Malachi, Behold I will ſend you Eliah*, &c. And in another place bears date thus, *Behold*

hold your house is left unto you desolate: and ye shall not see me till ye say, Blessed is he that comes in the Name of the Lord, namely *Eliah* so cald, one after his spirit; for convincing them of their hard sayings and opinions; *Who shall render them meat in due season, Mat.* 24. and by the same token how then it fares with them, even the priesthood, *And in the day that I shall do this, saith the Lord of Hosts, I shall leave them neither root nor branch* (to wit) the *Gentiles* Church also cut off departed from the Faith, except a remnant that have not bow'd the knee, or have declin'd their Antichristian Tenents, as this for one, That the gift of Prophesie is extinguished; and that for another, the root of Heresies, That there is no restoration from the second death,

death, which begat the popish purgatory, which begat the *Manichees* error which begat *Arrianism, Pelagianism.*

Besides the abominable eating of blood authorised, against that so solemnly inacted by the apostles, *Acts* 15 after such deliberation, & a thing observ'd for a long time after, verily procreating that inhumane opinion of Transubstantiation of the very Blood communicated in the Sacrament; otherwise which never had bin broach'd such an Abomination, standing on the Lords Table adored: So *Rev.* 16. *Worthily ye drink of the bloody Vials your fill, poured out now if ever.*

Now unto the aforesaid, what more may be said or added, then this, *If I be lifted up, I will draw all men to me*; Though our Doctors prophecying

ing out of their own Envious Spirit, would have it, as if the number of them to be heald, ſtung by the old Serpent, in compariſon of the reſt: But as thoſe in the laſt age which taſte not Death, ſuch a handful to the dead ſince the world began, or as ſome Eight perſons as it were ſaved by Faith: Or like her houſhold ſpar'd alive, deſtroyed not with the accurſed City; yet *Jericho built again, its foundation laid, and gates ſet up that lay waſte.*

Though granted ſhadows forth, how few the number of the faithful to others going the broad way, whoſe Antichriſtian plots proſper not, ſhall not be able to ſtand in the Iudgement that hold, Notwithſtanding the root our firſt Parents franckly forgiven,

Luke,

Luke, yet for their offence their poſterity cut off; the branches ſuffered never to grow again, againſt Law and Iuſtice, whereas recorded of that King concerning the murtherers of his Father, the children not put to death, 2 *Kings* 14. and *Deuteronomy*, &c.

He then which much more pardons, leaves not ſo much as a hoof in *Egypt*, the very Beaſt the old Serpent ſets him at liberty: Satan in proceſs of time unbound, reſerved until the laſt day in chains of deſpair, though ſuppoſed Sodoms captivity and her ſiſters never returns from endleſſe exile, much leſſe thoſe infernal ſpirits.

Becauſe before the Tree of life taſted of, their future happineſſe made

C known,

known, gives them a touch of the tree of knowledge, the Law.

Lets them know what he is able to do, as the Apoſtle *Paul* ſhews, *What if God willing to ſhew his wrath, and make his power known* &c. So after *Joſephs* way, before making himſelf known, ſaying *I am Ioſeph* to his unnatural Brethren: who notwithſtanding foreſhew'd how they ſhould all bow before him: yet poſſeſs'd with ſuch ſpirit of misbelief, whom they ſold into *Egypt* knew him not.

Leſt preſumption, which knows no meaſure, take advantage of unlimited mercy, a main point, for a long time permits them to wander in like ignorance, *Having ſworn in his wrath*, firſt ſuffers fieryſerpents to vex them.

Much like the miſt caſt before their

eyes,

eyes, becauſe their task increas'd who mutin'd (*Exodus*) anſwerable but to that in the Goſpel, by his Diſciple being deſired to ſend her away, anſwered, *I am not ſent but to the loſt ſheep of the houſe of Iſrael.* VVhere ſhe cald dog, the *Canaan* woman, which would not take it for an anſwer, but after him ſtill cries out, partakes of the childrens bread, afterward the devil caſt out of her daughter; The Gentiles forerunner and figure not onely, but thoſe gone into perdition.

And this his Kingdom, like *Davids*, reduced by degrees, made wait for his promiſes; and that every one may come to the knowledge of the Truth. VVhich Army a refuge for the diſtreſſed and diſcontented, as *Solomons* kingdom a patern, after Iudgment ex-

 ecuted

excuted according to his fathers command, of our expected reſt. The peaceable new Heavens and Earth, who though commanded a ſword to be brought him, thought not to take the Infants life; the ſtanders by put in a doubt notwithſtanding,and the mother of it much more.

But leaving him, that knew what he had to do with *Joab* and *Shimei*, who excuſed not his own Brother *Adoniah* in ſuch a nice point, for the firſt fault, which was winked at by the Father.

For proſecuting of this nicety of the word *For Ever* and *Everlaſting*, ſuch a ſtumbling block to them ſo blockiſh, that make us believe, beyond theſe pillars or periods there is no paſsing or going farther, not as

much

much as a poſsibility of it will allow for this new VVine to drop down, or to be drawn forth, reſerved till the laſt, *Joel* the third and 18. v. ſuch a gift in miſconſtruing of Myſteries, have attain'd unto, with the Iews, ſo ſtumbled about their aboliſh'd Ceremonies and Ordinances, becauſe ſaid they, *Stand faſt for ever* (*Pſalms* &c) do not un[redacted] way God is able to diſavow or diſanul them for the better: for example, becauſe Circumciſion cald an everlaſting Covenant, *Gen.* together with the promis'd Land paſs'd or given unto his ſeed for an everlaſting poſſeſsion: And yet ſo long kept out of poſſeſsion, ſtrangers there: no more ſtrange then that for another, where ſuch an expreſs Deed canceld (ſaying) *I ſaid indeed, Thou*

and

and thy Father's house should walk before me for ever, but now far be it from me.

So farther now for the aforesaid, in the Original signifying but for *Ages*, and likewise for *Ever and Ever*, for *Ages* and *FARTHER*, or *Et cetera*, as it were (to wit) with God during pleasure: The burthen of that gracious Psalm, *For his mercy endures* [redacted]

And yet this burthen continued, supposed out of Hell there is no Redemption or Restauration, which also signifies *The Grave* (*Psalm* 16) one word expressing both.

Though elsewhere, as the Holy Ghost where he pleases able more abundantly to express it: In our Saviors being parareld with *Melchisedeck, Heb*. 7. mentions an endles life;

22 in

in the Original (to wit) indissolvable; And again, *But this man because he continueth ever, hath an unchangeable Priesthood* (or) *which passes not away to another*; And to that end such passages.

So concerning the ability of our Savior, inferior not to *Adam*, with whom he is paraleld too; with *Adam* the first man, *Rom.5. As sin entred into the world by him, and death by sin, which passed upon all men, for that all have sinned.*

And by one mans obedience much more came upon all, *Justification to life*, so much prest by the Apostle.

And if ye will receive it, *Rev.14.* resolves it, ordered by a voice from Heaven to be written, where shews as there smoke ascends *For Ever and Ever,*

Ever, that day and night that have no rest: so they that dye in the Lord from *Henceforth* rest from their labors or pains: The which besides useful for demolishing the aspiring walls of Purgatory, for any Saints ever coming there, to be partakers of such sulpherous smokes.

This Text of the Angels commanded to be preacht upon, farther informs, stiled *The Everlasting Gospel*, that the true meaning of it, even *For Ever and Ever*, it signifies but *From Henceforth*, a time determinable, and not infinite or unlimited, if credit may be given to the holy Spirit (*Revelations* the fourteenth, saying, *Yea* or *Content saith the Spirit*; so what spirits soever resists it, or sayes *No*, touching those disobedient Spirits cast out of of his preſence, as if for thoſe priſoners, ringleaders of rebellion, remains no hope or mercy; whereas Lucifer not excepted, confined though to extreme darknes, of whom *Jude* ſhews, *The Archangel Michael* DURST NOT *bring railing accuſation againſt him*, being againſt the Law of priſoners to revile them, as indeed Hell no other then a priſon, implying a Releaſe thence, like as death cald ſleep in reſpect of the Reſurrection, to which end is ſhewed by *Peter* (3.) *He went and Preacht to the Spirits there impriſoned*; and therefore ſaying, *If I go down to Hell thou art there alſo*, Pſalm, &c.

That each in his order; The firſt fruits redeemed from among men, for ſo *The everlaſting Goſpel* informs us:

D Then

Then the latter Fruits or Harveſt which follows, reſerved for the hour of his Iudgement, even 1600. bearing date, paced forth by time; howſoever expreſt by the ſpace of ſo many Furlongs for Centuries (*Revel.* 14.)

As hereof (*Luke* 16.) teſtifies where that diſtance between them termed a ſpace fixt (or a Gulf) ſo much by our Adverſaries inſiſted on; whereas the verity of it, a ſpace of time prefixt, becauſe otherwiſe (ſince time moves not) but an improper or unneceſſary Speech; with that of *Abrahams* Boſom concurs, or like thoſe Corn Ears interpreted ſo many years to come: Likewiſe his own Dream of *The Sheafs of Corn doing obeyſance*, and the like.

VVhere touching his pedigree the

the *RICH* (man) *SON*, ſtiled by *Abraham*, ſome *PARSONS SON*, as is probable by that Reply, *They have Moſes and the Prophets*; ſo without contradiction bids beware of lying, by his ſcorchd tongue inflamed, teſtified *Pſalm* 120. *Thou falſe tongue, &c.* So again a material point from *Abrahams* calling him *SON*, even points or refersus to her Story, after the Bottle ſpent, who had her eyes opened, ſaw a well of water, bidden *Fear not*, called unto from Heaven, *lift up the Lad* Iſhmael, named ſo of the Angel, namely, *God ſhall hear*, when ſhe again, *Thou God ſeeſt me.*

VVhere farther of what profeſsion or Fraternity, he *lifting up his eyes ſaw afar off Lazarus in his Boſom*: whom

D 2 he

he again calls, *Father*, whoſe laſt motion, that *Lazarus* then might be ſent to his Fathers houſe to teſtifie and and forewarn them (*Leſt his Brethren, &c.* (to wit) Beſides Arch.B. other Biſhops, 25. in number, how they come there to have a care, as here in their formalities, that Brotherhood not alone, but thoſe of the Lew, their Coat diſplays herewith a chief Iudge, who call Brothers too: This Stone or Bone caſt amongſt them, ſaying, *They have the Law and the Prophets , let them hear them.*

So then no ordinary Beggar taken up into Heaven, but one of the Prophetical order granted, who was to perſwade them, coming in the Spirit of *Eliah* the *Tisbet*, DOUBTLES, whom they did not or would

not

not know: And ſince he in Hell received no abſolute denial, who knows but that it was obtained (to wit) a line of mercy from his finger top, as it were never ſo little of the water of life.

And herewith the Prophetical Date ſhall proceed, which belongs to the preceding Parable to unfold, containing his diſcharge, ſhewed, he might be no longer Steward, accordingly whoſe Stewardſhip was reſigned; where the meaſures of Oyl annointing him, for no common Steward eitner, but how it ſhall come to paſs in ſome waſtful unjuſt reign, for his paſs given him ſerves.

And ſo much for the teſtified preſent evil time, with the quaif-degree, and thoſe of the Lawn ſleeves, their

read

fine Linnen, without doubt visited, holding it enough to have *Moses read and the Prophets*, though understand them not at all, so all watching thus with one consent, stopping their ears as their forefathers.

And thus it fares with this *Lazarus* whose ulcers Allegorical, those evil things received in his life time, *viz.* Imprisonments, Excommunications, and such like entertainment, by some forlorn suiters only licked or visited, of whom well the blessed Virgin prophecying, shews how it shall fare with them in those rebellious days, *He hath shewed strength with his Arm, and he hath put down the mighty from their seat*; with whom the Apostle accords, *Corinthians* 15. *Puts all his foes under his feet before his coming*: And as this

no

no news to him that hath ears, so this opinion as strange, for which serves the parable of that envious elder Brother + that would not be perswaded either to see his lost Brother, or enter the house; of like evil nature bids others beware, lest like that Servant that obtaind mercy himself, yet so unmerciful shew'd none at all to his fellow Servant, they be also rewarded with him (till the debt discharged, every farthing accompted for.) And for the same purpose as *Peter* forbidden such remission by measure, *Not to pardon until seven times, but until Seventy times seven*, ; likewise in *Luke* 17. *Seven times a day to forgive*; where the Apostles replying, *Lord increase our Faith*, being by our Theologers termd a certainty for an uncertainty,

+ like Jonah angrye to the death:

tainty, what they pleaſe, yet not only points to very Eaſter, thoſe weeks be-before it, when ſent forth that firſt pardon, *The Meſsiah offered*, pro-claimd Lord of Sabbaths, but as gives notice of this laſt pardon for the ſpace of 1700. years hidden, ſo ſhews by the 70. times ſeven which amounts to the ſum of Four hundred and ninety, the ſet time between the Prophet *Daniels* Viſions and our Lord the Son of God his taſting death for every one, *The Lamb ſlain, &c.* without exception praying for all, a greater then *Daniel* praying then.

VVhich Four hundred and ninety years, ſeventy weeks, of years that fulfil, by ſeven years alotted to a week, after *Daniels* computation a-greeing with *Jacobs*, ſaid to accom-

pliſh

plish her week too, (*Gen.*) in his seven years service for her.

And so the sum of the matter since by Scripture confuted this erroneous opinion, by breaking open Hel gates, or opening the meaning of such an intricate case, beyond any case in Law ever reported, consisting of such niceties, where since proved to be but prison, follows their remaining there no longer, but till the Debt satisfied, according to all Law and Iustice imposed: As to him belongs only the mysterie of Times and Seasons, reserv'd in the power of the Father, reveal'd to whom he pleases, (*Acts* 1.) Therefore what hee appoints determinable, let none extend it to be without limitation, since *Rev.* 14. declares it, where the everlasting Gospel clears

E Gospel

the miſtake of the word *Everlaſting*, *viz*. ſo long as day and night laſts.

And now moreover of the Book of the *Revelation* too, a word or two more, ſuch an eye-ſoar to the Clergy; where too manifeſt what rottennes & Antichriſtian Abuſes of late crept in, requiſite to be purged out; as firſt, in our Bibles, where like *Jeroboams* policy, who made *Iſrael* to ſin, in this ſinful Age have under colour of diſburthening the congregation, teſtified and ordered by like Authority, That the New Teſtament ſhall bee read over every year once, with this proviſo, Except certain Books which be leaſt edifying, and may beſt be ſpared, and therefore left unread, as the *Revelation*.

And if he that ſhall think little of any

any jot or tittle of the Law, was to be least in the Kingdom of Heaven, what shall they be worthy of that have cast such a flood of Iniquity out of their mouth, as the dayes of *Noah* not guilty of the like.

Having excluded that blessed book directed to the Churches, with *Blessed is he which reads, and they which hear the words of it, and as thus opened,* so closed with these, *For the time is at hand, Behold I come quickly.* Doubtles the days of the flood pointing unto, by the seven Vials poured out, filled with the seven last Plagues, in the seventeenth Century, so long after the creation, when as the world drown'd.

And so seven times cryed, *He that hath an ear, let him hear what the Spirit saith!* And last of all, *He that shall take*

E 2 *away*

away from the words of that Book, God shall take away his part out of the Book of Life. Alſo, he that ſhall adde (as much to ſay) ſhall ſay in his heart, The Lord delays his coming, not remembring the Flood time, God ſhall adde to him the plagues of *Egypt*, the waters turned into blood, &c. (*Revel.* 11.) And yet this Book by name caſt out of the Church, under colour of being obſcure, though aſſured nothing ſo covered or hidden which ſhal not be proclaimed or preached on houſe tops: And thus his promiſes waited for, the Holy Ghoſt knocking at the door, made to wait and ſtand without: which Antichriſtian Scoffers (in our dayes) without doubt *peter* teſtifies comes not ſhort of them, 2 *Pet.*3. in their proper colours

of

of unbelief dissplayd, saying, *Where is the promise of his coming*, &c.

Even of the breed of the lawlesse seven-headed Beast with the Ten horns (to wit) in his head or Frontispiece, *Anno Dom.* 1700. who have annexed such open Blasphemy to the Bible. Nor this done in a corner, for a second of these unsufferable doings against the third Commandment, although all Heathenism Repetition forbidden, Notwithstanding by a noise of Boys, that name rent in so many pieces in Churches where the Schools kept, indeed better much deserving to be whipt out then those defiling but the Temple, where that dreadful name taken in vain so, babbling at every word, *I pray God*, and *God grant*, and *Would to God we* *love*,

love, &c. or have this or that, &c, upon any lascivious Lines of Heathen Poets, their amorous Poems, when those children unlucky ones, not held guiltless; so lesson'd for their mocking of him, by unshorn Bears torn so many of them in pieces.

And moreover for a third course or piece of unsavory service; witnesse *Pauls* Churchyard, under the Noses of those reverend Masters, how close stools, those seats sir-reverence lined clean through with the Bible, from *Genesis* to the *Revelation*, those precious leaves for the healing of the Nations, polluted in that most base unmanerly manner, worse far then if burnt by the hangman; More sacred then *Sauls* Garment, when he coverd his Feet, (the modest Scripture phrase

phrase also worthy the observing) and was but cut off by *David*, that man after *Gods* own heart, if his heart smote him for so doing: And *Moses* bidden to put off his shoes, because the very ground was sacred: And *Joshuah* likewise: How comes it to pass no scruple made, by these Scorners, who fleeing Superstition, run upon gross contempt such prophanation; questionless then privilege of Parliament being subverted, or infringed more material these which endure for ever, purchased with his Blood, any thing destructive thereto: a liberty far from that preacht by our Savior, in observing his severe stile, who stiles himself *The Preacher*, (*Eccles.*) that well blesses the day of death before the day of ones birth and mourning.

So

So where a rash word and a look awry extended to Murther & Adultery: referring us to the blessed Prophets before us *Antipodes* to the world in such contempt ever held, even blesses such and no other, who chuses the foolish things, and the weak, the Base, to confound and confute the Mighty.

But returning now to the former matter of his abundant love to all; by these men, how much so ever envied, beheld with such an evil eye this light extraordinary: So then for proving the *Affirmative*, (to wit) there is redemption for the *Damned*; confirmed though sufficiently by the Apostles Spirit, *Rom.* 2 *Cor*. 15. shewing as all dead in *Adam*, so all made alive again, &c. yet this for an addition, *Rev*. 20. touching those that lived not again,

being

being not unbound until ſuch a ſpace fulfilled of time, as known times bounds ſet alſo; where they that lived and raigned with Chriſt, whoſe part in the firſt Reſurrection, as with them Antichriſtians no partakers; but of the ſecond Death, implying a ſecond Reſurrection for thoſe Children of Perdition; ſo ſhews like the loſt Son, ſtiled ſo but in reſpect of being found.

Laſtly notwithſtanding the dreadful word for *Ever and Everlaſtiug*, as mentioned by *Jacob* at his death, *Unto the utmoſt bound of the everlaſting Hills, &c.* (*Gen.*) and *Jonas* in that danger, crying, *The Earth with her bars was about me for ever*; So for the doubling of it for ever and ever, howſoever may ſerve ſometimes to

F ſhew

shew the thing established, as *Pharoahs* Dreams, or where he in stead of smiting five or six times, because came short, was shewd lost his pains by the coming shortly again of the Enemy.

Yet the truth of it, but like a Key that opens and shuts, serves also to give warning of some remarkable passage appertaining to the future for the most part, by him having *the keys of Death and Hell*, in due time made known: And hereof being ignorant unobserved, because of the unknown day and hour only mentioned, hold themselves not bound to wait for that time to be revealed.

Like as in the days of *Noah*, observe neither signs nor forerunners of it. As not without some mystery included (*Rev.* 20.) where se-

ſeveral times a Thouſand years fufil-led, repeated no leſſe then ſix times; like that of the inextinguiſhable fire (*Mark* 9.) tranſlated, Shall never be quenched, with the worm, &c. only (as much to ſay) Better there to indure any pain a long ſpace, then to have had no being at all; where compared to ſome gangren'd member, *Better cut off then the body periſh*: Inſtanced though in the caſe of the Kingdom of Heaven, & as explained that place here for the ſin againſt the Holy Ghoſt, puniſhed here and hereafter, where a poſsibility of eſcape, as the word Danger imports, *He ſhall be in danger, &c.* ſo concludes even *Judas*, though good had he been unborn, yet extends not to annihilate him.

Otherwiſe no ſuch abounding

F 2 bleſſing

bleſſing added to *Abraham*, without number to have a Seed or Generation as the Stars above, and the Sand of the Sea, if his mercy exceeded not much his Iuſtice, *Merciful unto Thouſands*; whereas but to a few, the third Degree, or fourth Generation, ſhewing hatred.

And as this relation thus concluded of the whole creation, accompanying the preſent Age, in the ſufferings of late, groaning for ſo many Ages under the burthen of the word ſignifying but for *Ages*, or from *Henceforth*; ſo let this *Amoveas manus* ſerve: This Olive leaf for ſiniſter conſtructions, ſuch illegal extent of unwarrantable words to make them accurſed and void.

Foraſmuch as ſhould it repent God

God he had made man, &c. yet that ever he ſhould reverſe his own Iudgment, God forbid, which no ordinary Iudge can or will do, without a *Writ of Error* brought, ſince nothing but confuſion brings; which *Writ* either upon any terms not feiſible now as the ſtate ſtands, a thing obſervable; ſo having pronounced every thing created and made was very good; then he which is the VVord, not to make good his word, far be it from the Iudge of all the Earth, the God of all Gods, and let every one ſay to this confeſsion, *Amen*; yea ſaith the Spirit, by reaſon of the *Law and ſeveral Statutes*, ſince the world hath faln in *DANGER* of ſuch penalties and forfeitures: The King of Kings, the grand Creditor, ſends forth

forth his Pardon, yea to the whole Creation.

Je Elen: Ti:

I hold it.

FINIS.

---

22. *The Revelation Interpreted* (1646; Wing D2009) is reprinted, by permission of the Folger Shakespeare Library, from the clear copy held at the Folger (shelfmark D2009 bd. w. D2010). The text block of the original measures 150 × 104 mm. The following pages are misnumbered (and the correct number is shown in square brackets): 7 [10], 3 [11].

Hard-to-read words:
Title page 6–8: *Let no man deceive you, by any meanes for that day shall not come, except there come a falling away first*

3.16	gives to
4.1	so
[10].4	directly
12.10	out
12.16	Or of the meaning of that *Head so wounded*:
12.18–19	*the* Last day at *hand*
12.20–21	ahealing of any soare
13.3	Name
13.8–9	Hee translated, or That was NOT: *whose Successor Eternity*, *like Methuselah*,
13.11–13	His reigning fifty five yeares and a half shewes it too: Even 666. moneths his Number.
13.14–22	And againe, as *Eternity* preceding *Time*, so K: *James* his 60 yeares reign, before his NOW aged 46; bearing *Times marke or Seal* 1646. Time to bee Longer: HIS *power* put downe too: And so NO farther of the *Dragons* old quarrell to Saint *George*, in advancing One of That *Name*, or Seating in the *Saddle*

THE REVELATION INTERPRETED;

By the La. ELEANOR.

2 THESSAL. 2. 3.

Let no man deceive you, by any meanes for the day shall not come, except there come a falling away first, &c.

Printed in the yeare, 1646.

THE REVELATION INTERPRETED:

By the LADY *ELEANOR*.

Chap. XIII.

PAſsing by *Cæſars* adored Image: with the Time amounting to about 1700. yeares paſt, ſince their upriſing, as hereby appeares giving *the ſeaven Heads and ten Horns*: untill its ſetting, that *Monarchies period,* RATHER proceeding with theſe, to ſhew the *Truth*, who the *Founder of great BRITTAINS unhappie faction*, as the Holy Ghoſt here gives to underſtand so plainly, *That none needs to aske*, whose description This, *of this Sea-monster no other* then the *Admyrals-Office*: where the waters having the priority, Thus shewes:

Verse, I.

And I stood upon the Sand of the SEA, *and saw a* Beast *rise up out of the* Sea, *having seven heads, and ten horns, and upon his horns ten* Crownes, *and upon his heads the Names of* BLASPHEMY: *The Dragon giving him his power and great authority*: namely, *George Viliers*, created Duke of *Buckingham*.

VVhere follows the Names given to Ships, one cald the *Leopard*, another the *Beare*, and the *Lyon*, and the like, as not unknowne. *vers*.

And so of his deadly wound given at *Porchmouth*, that addored *Minnion*, for two seven yeares who was so followed of every one, and admired: Of *whose* Large gifts *Thus* farther:

Verse

Verse. I I I.

And I saw one of his heads (as it were) *wounded to death, and all the* VVorld *admired the* B E A S T : *And his deadly Wound was healed. And there was given him a* Mouth *speaking great* Things, *and Blasphemie: And power was given him to continue* 42. *moneths; and he opened his mouth in* Blasphemy, *&c.*

VVhere shewes here, besides *the healing* of *that foule* Soare *the* Kings-*Evill*, *Porch-mouths* BLOVV, by a Butchers knife given, how *Cured*. also what an insaciable *Mouth* by him opened; daily *fed with such Gifes, Offices, and Titles of* Honor *not a few*; wanting NO kindred to bee supplyed. This aspiering man *Buckingham*, from the *Beast* deriving *his* Name, so much bound to the *Dragon* his Patron, rather then to Saint *George*. This supporter of the *Spanish* FACTION, colour'd or clok'd under *Arminisme*: That beyond expectation

A 3 after

ter ten years, his Fathers *VNLUKYE Favourite who* continned his too, from 1625. *March*, untill 1628. *August*, two and forty Monthes, or three Yeares and halfe before his Pay receiv'd, not behind with it Then. Being as not unknown fore-warnd OF that very Moneth, *Cæsar*, as he foretold of the *Ides* of *March*.

VVhere serving for both *Meridians* shews. The *french* K: for his Blasphemous *Tongue* also how Rewarded, who gives the ten *HORNS* Crown'd. *That in the* Yeare, 1610. Likewise *was* slaine, whose *Faction* revived again or continu'd too. As by the Power of the *KEYES*, Conjured up such SPIRITS *or Factions set a foote*, begeting in *KINGDOMS* such desperate VVARRES and doings; where The one NOT more suddenly in that *Manner taken away*, Then the Other

Other remaining in *Prison* so long: waiting His appointed Time, as extant upon *RECORD*, sometime made known to him: *But no more of that NOW. But of his Sorceries and Witchcrafts as revealed here, or miracles.*

VVhere farthermore, for the Treasurers-Office thus, usurp'd by the *Clergie*, (*verse* 11.) And *I beheld* another *beast comming out of the Earth, with two* Horns *like a Lamb, spake like the* Dragon, *and exerciseth all the* Power *of the* first *Beast, &c.*

And so no farther, of This *Canonized* expert DOCTOR or Saint, inspired by the Red *Dragon*, (with such a gift in healing,) by whom this *deadly Wound healed*, worse then when *Buckingham* was living. The Number of whose Name, even (*VIS-COVNT VVILERS*) as count the Number of the *BRITTISH*-

Beast.

Beast, Namely *666.* These numerall Letters *H J S* : VIC *LVVVI, viscount vvilers* : Together with the weight of *Solomons* gold Yearly *666. Talents,* (*Chron. 9.* Chap.) Included in those *Characters.* Of a truth directly pointed at great *Brittains* Revenue and Customes rather ; amounting to about six Hundred Thousaud pounds *per annum* : Put on this Account, &c.

And so much for this peice finished in such hast: The last dayes story. Dedicated to *HIM that hath Understanding and Eares,* to weigh it too : The vanity setting forth, and instabillity of WORLDLY Things, or perferment in this Admirable *BEAST* : *his rising, and falling,* Whose power To the wonder of all Continuing from the Yeare, 1625. *March* (first of this present Reigne :) untill *August,* 1628. As afore-shewed, even the Dukes due 42. *MONETHS* : And concerning the TREASVRERS-Office ingrossed by the CLERGY, our *HIGH-*

Priest

Priest, horned like *the Lamb*, (to wit) *The* two Arch-bishop-pricks, *voyced like the old* Red *Dragon*. *That wonder in* Heaven *whose place found no more there*: Sceleing *Themselves* like *the Arch-angell*, no lesse.

Aud thus passing on: from That *SEA-Wonder*, to this VVonder *coming out of the Earth*; faining (as it were) Himself to bee *Elias*: *When* Bals *Priests slaine*, and to say the Truth in this comes not short; He the occasion of their Ruine, the *Bishops* their Downfall: And for such, *Fire descending from Heaven*, witnesse *the Wrath of* GOD; *as fire and sword*, who can gaine-say it, *but* HEE *the* Author *thereof doubtlesse*, *And the day of* Judgement *too*: hastend it, not far off.

SO farther, as here Noted or Signified for the Time of *Easter* Thus, or the *RESURRECTION-Feast*: VVhen

B such

ſuch a Bloody reigne beganne, Namely; VVherein that *abomination* (the cauſe of theſe *Judgements*) Idolatry again ſet up; directly in theſe expreſſed : *And all whoſe Names are* Not *written in the Booke of* Life, *of the* Lambe *ſlaine from the begining of the* VVORLD ; *ſhall worſhip or obey* HIM : As againe, this for another witnes of the aforeſaid Feaſt ; Touching *Peters cutting Off that Mans* Eares, *againe healed*: Even pointed at, as cryed here. *IF ANY MAN HAVE* AN EARE, *Let him heare*: Verſe, *He that* Leads *into Captivity, ſhall goe into Captivity ; and hee that killeth, ſhall be killed*. (as much to ſay) As ſome want their Eares, So others their *Underſtanding* more, That diſcerne Not Theſe.

VVhere ſhewes, unto ſuch Cruelty, and Blood-thirſtyneſſe, how this man added *Blaſphemies-madneſſe*: As theſe giving

ving to underſtand, ſaying; *That hee hath Power to give* LIFE, BREATH, *and* SPEECH, *&c.* verſe. (as it were) Becauſe *the Keys of the Bottumleſſe pit His,* where gold ſo current: Therefore *in Him all Live and Move, &c.* fearefull to bee Named or Spoken.

And theſe are The *IMAGES* thoſe Angels adored alſo: And as for *the Beaſt that had the deadly* VVound *with the Sword and did Live,* (or was healed) beſides the *Faction* continued, points withall at the great Plague, *When the* Angels *Sword ſo ſuddenly ſheathed*, 1625. with worſe Plagues accompanied; The advancers of *Idolatry* and *Tyrranny*:

As here farther more aludes to great *BABYLONS* Proclamations *of The golden IMAGE*; *He that would not*

B 2 *fall*

fall downe before it, to be killed: (as much, to *say*) ALTARS *served, and bowed unto, &c.* And at last, *what Measure they meted to* Others, *served with the same* Themselves: Sometime that were *so Observ'd*, Feared and Flattered; This Sea-god: And god of the *Windes like, Dragon-like* by Sea and Land roaring, *setting* KINGDOMES together by the *Eares*: Breathing and Thundering out *LYING* and *BLASPHEMIE*, as They please, without Controule: And so Hee, VVho *hath Understanding*; needs NO farther to wonder or bee informed, what These revealed LAST *Monsters* are; Or of the meaning of that *Head so wounded*: (to wit) *DUX*, &c. His cheife title Then.

The Signes infalible of the Last *day at hand*: VVhere besides *Cæsars* golden Image, *adored*; *gold made their god*: a healing of any soare, aluding to the That; *for the*

KINGS-

KINGS-EVILL so dangerous to bee *LOST* or VVanting. And as *the* moneths continu'd after their Name, *July* and *August*, signified *vers 5*. So *deified* *Cæsar*, of his translating of the *Yeare*, points thereat: *Those* 365 dayes in these *Characters* 666. Like *Enoch* dayes also 365 Hee translated, or That was NOT: *whose Successor Eternity*, *like Methuselah*, likewise *Cæsar Augustus*, who out-reigned the rest and succeeded; His reigning fifty five yeares and a half shewes it too: Even 666. moneths his Number.

And againe, as *Eternity* preceding *Time*, so K: *James* his 60 yeares reign, before this NOVV aged 46; bearing *Times marke* or *Seal* 1646. Time to bee Longer? HIS *power* put downe too: And so NO farther of the *Dragons* old quarrell to Saint *George*, in advancing One of That *Name*, or Seating in the

B 3 *Saddle*

Saddle ſuch a graceleſſe ONE: breaking his owne *Neck*: And ruine of the KINGDOME. This *New* adored Saint, (as no doubt *Canonized*) Saint *George* the ſecond, ſaluted with ſevenfold *Blaſphemous ſuperſcriptions* dayly ſuch, and the Like made upon His *NAME* (His grace): *Whereas* thrice SIX *666*. The reſtleſſe Number thereof. Here unto the *VULgare* not referred or directed: *But he which Underſtands* Miſteryes of State to Him:

Proverbs XVI.

How much better it is to get wiſdome *Then* gold: *And to get* underſtanding *rather to choſen then* Silver.

And

And thus wild as the *Dragon*: Hee with Sathans *Marke in the head, of* the *old Serpents cut*, (Geneses. 3.) By some MERMAYDE, as this Blaspheme-MER: spewd up doubtlesse; so from Them his inchanting *Noats* had, of Menacing such, reaching from *Earth* to *Heaven*.

FINIS. FINIS.

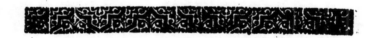